Decolonising the University

Decolonising the University

Edited by
Gurminder K. Bhambra,
Dalia Gebrial and Kerem Nişancıoğlu

First published 2018 by Pluto Press
345 Archway Road, London N6 5AA

www.plutobooks.com

British Library Cataloguing in Publication Data
A catalogue record for this book is available from the British Library

ISBN   978 0 7453 3821 7   Hardback
ISBN   978 0 7453 3820 0   Paperback
ISBN   978 1 7868 0315 3   PDF eBook
ISBN   978 1 7868 0317 7   Kindle eBook
ISBN   978 1 7868 0316 0   EPUB eBook

This book is printed on paper suitable for recycling and made from fully
managed and sustained forest sources. Logging, pulping and manufacturing
processes are expected to conform to the environmental standards of the
country of origin.

Typeset by Stanford DTP Services, Northampton, England

Simultaneously printed in the United Kingdom and United States of America

Contents

PART III   DECOLONIAL REFLECTIONS

1

Introduction:
Decolonising the University?

*Gurminder K. Bhambra, Dalia Gebrial
and Kerem Nişancıoğlu*

The call to decolonise universities across the global North has gained particular traction in recent years, from Rhodes Must Fall Oxford's (RMFO) campaign for a public reckoning with its colonial legacies, to recent attempts by Georgetown University, Washington DC, to atone for its past ties with slavery.[1] The UK's National Union of Students (NUS) has been running 'Why is My Curriculum White?' and #LiberateMyDegree as two of their flagship campaigns since 2015. Both campaigns seek to challenge 'Eurocentric domination and lack of diversity' in curricula across UK universities.[2] These dissenting interventions take their inspiration from and build on similar campaigns in other parts of the world – for example, the Rhodes Must Fall movement in South Africa and the campaigns against caste prejudice occurring in some Indian universities. They also build on earlier movements and protests organised under notions of social justice and addressing inequality. These include campaigns such as those led by the Black and Asian Studies Association concerning the representation of Black history within the UK National Curriculum and those in defence of the 'public university' organised by the Campaign for the Public University and Remaking the University, among others.[3] These movements, collectively, sought to transform the terms upon which the university (and education more broadly) exists, the purpose of the knowledge it imparts and produces, and its pedagogical operations. This collection aims to critically examine the recent calls to 'decolonise the university' within this wider context, giving a platform to otherwise silenced 'decolonial' work and offering a resource for students and academics looking to challenge and undo forms of coloniality in their classrooms, curricula and campuses.

I

Given the prominence of decolonisation as a framework in student- and teacher-led movements today, it is incumbent upon us to think more carefully about what this means – as both a theory, and a praxis. How is it distinct from other forms of anti-racist organising in institutions such as the university, and why has it gained particular purchase in the contemporary higher education context? What does it mean to apply a term that emerged from a specific historical, political and geographic context, to today's world? And what are the possibilities and dangers that come with calls to decolonise the university?

'Decolonising' involves a multitude of definitions, interpretations, aims and strategies. To broadly situate its political and methodological coordinates, 'decolonising' has two key referents. First, it is a way of thinking about the world which takes colonialism, empire and racism as its empirical and discursive objects of study; it re-situates these phenomena as key shaping forces of the contemporary world, in a context where their role has been systematically effaced from view.[4] Second, it purports to offer alternative ways of thinking about the world and alternative forms of political praxis.[5] And yet, within these broad contours, 'decolonising' remains a contested term, consisting of a heterogeneity of viewpoints, approaches, political projects and normative concerns. This multiplicity of perspectives should not be surprising given the various historical and political sites of decolonisation that span both the globe and 500 years of history.

There are also important methodological and epistemological reasons to emphasise contestation over definitions of 'decolonising'. Indeed, one of the key challenges that decolonising approaches have presented to Eurocentric forms of knowledge is an insistence on positionality and plurality and, perhaps more importantly, the impact that taking 'difference' seriously would make to standard understandings.[6] The emphasis on reflexivity reminds us that representations and knowledge of the world we live in are situated historically and geographically. The point is not simply to deconstruct such understandings, but to transform them. As such, some decolonising approaches seek a plurality of perspectives, worldviews, ontologies, epistemologies and methodologies in which scholarly enquiry and political praxis might take place.[7] And yet there also remain approaches situated squarely within the anti-colonial tradition that seek to eschew the particularity of Eurocentrism through the construction of a new universality.[8] The contested and multiple character of 'decolonising' is reflected in the contributions to this volume.

This volume is written from the position and experience of academics and students working in universities primarily in the global North (although many contributors would perhaps insist they are 'of' neither). It seeks to question the epistemological authority assigned uniquely to the Western university as the privileged site of knowledge production and to contribute to the broader project of decolonising through a discussion of strategies and interventions emanating from within the imperial metropoles. In this way, we hope it complements the work of scholars and activists elsewhere who have similarly engaged with such issues from across the global South and North.[9] In doing so, we hope, collectively, to contribute to practices which provincialise forms of European knowledge production from the centre.[10]

For example, there are rich and increasingly visible histories of how anti-racist and anti-colonial resistance in the imperial metropole were central to building connections across anti-colonial movements in the global South.[11] At the same time, numerous national liberation struggles in the colonies refracted back into struggles around racism and citizenship conducted in the imperial centre.[12] In some instances, anti-racist and anti-colonial struggles were articulated in, through, and against Western universities. Campus mobilisations, the formation of student societies, and the publication of student papers knitted higher education and anti-colonialism into a rich tapestry of radical activism in the colonial metropole.[13] Taken together, such histories of anti-racist struggle have always included concerns for research and education, in the form of alternative community schooling projects, political education in organisations or campaigns to reform existing educational institutions and policies.[14]

In short, the turn to decolonising as rubric for political organising in the global North is not rooted in a particular identity; rather, it emerges from shared historical trajectories of forms of colonialism. We hope that a discussion of decolonising from the imperial centre – of which this volume is only one part – might help to reveal something about the machinations of empire in general and the deeply understudied relationship between coloniality and pedagogy. In doing so, it also has the potential to open spaces for dialogue, alliances and solidarity with colonised and formerly colonised peoples, contributing to the making of 'a global infrastructure of anti-colonial connectivity'.[15]

II

Why decolonise *the university* specifically? Should decolonising projects even be concerned with the university as an institution? In an important article, Eve Tuck and K. Wayne Yang remind us that 'decolonization is not a metaphor'.[16] They argue that the language of decolonising has been adopted in ways which empty it of its specific political aims; namely the repatriation of dispossessed indigenous land. Such emptying might include educational practices that seek to move away from Eurocentric frames of reference or using the language of decolonisation while pursuing a politics distinct from indigenous struggles over land. They argue:

> The easy absorption, adoption, and transposing of decolonization is yet another form of settler appropriation. When we write about decolonization, we are not offering it as a metaphor; it is not an approximation of other experiences of oppression. Decolonization is not a swappable term for other things we want to do to improve our societies and schools. Decolonization doesn't have a synonym.[17]

Such acts, Tuck and Yang argue, generate various settler 'moves to innocence', which attempt to contain or reconcile settler guilt and complicity. Using 'decolonization as a metaphor' thus 'recentres whiteness, it resettles theory, it extends innocence to the settler, it entertains a settler future'.[18] In contrast, Tuck and Yang insist on decolonisation as a struggle over dispossession, the repatriation of indigenous land and the seizing of imperial wealth. Such a project is less about seeking reconciliation with settler pasts, presents and futures, but about pursuing what is 'irreconcilable within settler colonial relations and incommensurable between decolonising projects and other social justice projects'.[19] These are serious warnings which should give us all pause for reflection, not least because we have observed discourses around 'decolonising the university' which fall prey to precisely these problems. This volume is an attempt to go beyond such limitations, but will, necessarily, have its own such limitations. We think there is value in complicating the substantive claim made by Tuck and Yang (that decolonisation is exclusively about the repatriation of land to indigenous peoples) in order to extend and deepen their political warning (that decolonisation is not a metaphor).

We hope that the contributions to this volume demonstrate that colonialism (and hence decolonising) cannot be reduced to a historically specific and geographically particular articulation of the colonial project, namely settler-colonialism in the Americas. Nor can struggles against colonialism exclusively target a particular articulation of that project: the dispossession of land. To do so, would be to set aside colonial relations that did not rest on settler projects (such as, for example, commercial imperialism conducted across the Indian Ocean littoral, the mandate system in West Asia, the European trade in human beings, or financialised neo-colonialism today) or to turn away from discursive projects associated with these practices (such as liberalism and Orientalism). It would not only remove from our view these differentiated moments of a global project of colonialism, but also interactions and connections of these global but differentiated moments with settler-colonialism itself. Put differently, whereas dispossession might be the 'truth' of colonialism, it is not its entirety.

Taking colonialism as a global project as the starting point, it becomes difficult to turn away from the Western university as a key site through which colonialism – and colonial knowledge in particular – is produced, consecrated, institutionalised and naturalised.[20] It was in the university that colonial intellectuals developed theories of racism, popularised discourses that bolstered support for colonial endeavours and provided ethical and intellectual grounds for the dispossession, oppression and domination of colonised subjects.[21] In the colonial metropolis, universities provided would-be colonial administrators with knowledge of the peoples they would rule over, as well as lessons in techniques of domination and exploitation. The foundation of European higher education institutions in colonised territories itself became an infrastructure of empire, an institution and actor through which the totalising logic of domination could be extended; European forms of knowledge were spread, local indigenous knowledge suppressed, and native informants trained.[22] In both colony and metropole, universities were founded and financed through the spoils of colonial plunder, enslavement and dispossession.[23]

The fall of formal empires did little to change the logic of Western universities. Calls around 'decolonising the curriculum' have shown how the content of university knowledge remains principally governed by the West for the West.[24] Disciplinary divisions, theoretical models and Eurocentric histories continue to provide intellectual materials that reproduce and justify colonial hierarchies.[25] Subjects of Western scholarship are enduringly pale, male (and often stale); where people of colour do appear, they are all too often tokenistically represented,[26] spoken on behalf of,[27] or reduced to objects of scholarship. Products of university research are still strategically deployed in the pursuit of imperial projects conducted by Western states and firms in former colonies.[28] These imperial projects – past and new – remain central to the financing of higher education in the West.[29] Postcolonial scholars and anti-racist activists have made significant strides in bringing these issues to the fore. However, as numerous activists as well as contributions in this volume argue, the foundations of universities remain unshakably colonial; there is, as ever, more work to be done.

III

The volume is organised in three parts, covering contexts, initiatives and reflections respectively. The first part 'Contexts: Historical and Disciplinary' situates contemporary calls to decolonise the university in contexts of institutional change, pedagogical reform and student activism.

The opening chapter by Dalia Gebrial, 'Rhodes Must Fall: Oxford and Movements for Change', charts the emergence of calls among students to decolonise the University of Oxford under the banner 'Rhodes Must Fall in Oxford' (RMFO). Sketching a history of RMFO's emergence in the context of the anti-racist movement in the UK, Gebrial assesses its mistakes and successes, and evaluates what it means to bring the call to decolonisation back to the heart of empire. Gebrial sets and explores a series of questions that recur throughout this volume: What is decolonisation, and how does it differ from diversity work? How is the demand to decolonise the university related to the struggle for a public university? What are the challenges faced by those wishing to do decolonial work in the university and beyond?

John Holmwood's chapter, 'Race and the Neoliberal University: Lessons from the Public University', locates its concerns in the context of changes in US and English higher education policies that have seen the 'privatisation' of higher education and a shift from it being regarded as a social right to something that is seen as the personal responsibility of individuals. In this context, he argues, the call to decolonise the university can be seen as paradoxical to the extent that the neoliberal university claims to be race-blind and only interested in the differences between individuals and not those between groups. However, this does not take into account the fact that universities in the UK and US 'were embedded in social structures that derive from histories of colonialism and empire' and, as such, the call to decolonise the university is a call for social justice more broadly. While social rights (and access to higher education) were racialised, the answer is not the market, but the deeper democratisation of the university and society more broadly.

In the chapter 'Black / Academia', Robbie Shilliam traces the genealogy of racism in higher education through the racialisation of public culture from the nineteenth century onward. This involved an institutionalisation of who can be said to be a competent 'knower' and who can only ever be considered incompetent to know – the 'known'. Shilliam argues that this racialisation of public culture has been 'institutionalised' in the hidden curriculum, the set of administrative and pedagogical practices that reproduce expectations about the competencies of the 'traditional' student. For Shilliam, it is not the institution of higher learning per se, but public culture, that is problematically racist. Therefore, to strike at this racism in the name of higher learning is to insist upon a cross-sectoral struggle against inequality, disenfranchisement and oppression.

The final chapter in this section is a multi-authored account of the 'decolonial' turn in philosophy. The chapter, 'Decolonising Philosophy', by Nelson Maldonado-Torres, Rafael Vizcaíno, Jasmine Wallace and Jeong Eun Annabel We, starts from the fact that the discipline – in terms of its curricular design, content, and faculty and student demographic profile – remains 'a bastion of Eurocentrism' and whiteness more generally. They locate this situation as a consequence of the histories of imperialism, enslavement and colonisation that provided the context for its configuration. As such, they argue, simply diversifying the field is not sufficient, it requires a more thoroughgoing decolonisation of 'structural problems and deep-seated habits' across the 'various aspects of philosophy as a field and as a practice' – this is something that is manifestly visible in their co-authored and intergenerational practice in the writing of this chapter.

In the second part of this volume – 'Institutional Initiatives' – contributors offer experiences and suggestions for concrete practices they have undertaken. These include specific initiatives, movements and interventions, as well as predictions, strategies and frameworks for future action.

Kolar Aparna and Olivier Kramsch's chapter, 'Asylum University: Re-situating Knowledge-exchange along Cross-border Positionalities', reflects on recent student struggles in Germany and the Netherlands which explored the intersection of university financialisation, managerialism and the demands of equal rights for and by newly arriving asylum-seekers. Developing what they call an 'asylum university lens' they argue that asylum serves as a symbolic and powerful metaphor for speaking from a space of refuge. From this lens, the university serves as a space of solidarity for knowledge-exchange, the everyday interactions of classroom debates and academic writing, both on campus and beyond. For Aparna and Kramsch, such a lens calls to our attention the instability and uncertainty of borders while acting and situating knowledge production from embodied relationalities that are nevertheless sensitive to differential privileges and conflicting ambitions.

Rosalba Icaza and Rolando Vázquez's 'Diversity or Decolonisation? Researching Diversity at the University of Amsterdam', recounts the experience of the University of Amsterdam's 'Diversity Commission', which was established following demands by students of colour to decolonise the university. The Commission examined the knowledge being produced and how it is being taught by developing a research framework that would transform the epistemic practices of teaching and learning within the university. This chapter details these challenges and uses the theoretical frameworks of Black feminist intersectionality and decoloniality to think through the processes of decolonising the university. This has three core elements: the pedagogies of positionality, the pedagogies of participation and the pedagogies of transition. Icaza and Vázquez argue that this helps to disclose the decolonial deficit of the university and to understand how epistemic practices can be decolonised.

In 'The Challenge for Black Studies in the Neoliberal University', Kehinde Andrews recounts the experience of creating the Black Studies undergraduate programme at Birmingham City University – the first of its kind in Europe. Andrews examines the impact of student and academic struggles against the institutional racism of the university and how these have informed the pedagogical intervention of the Black Studies programme. Andrews argues that the contributions, experiences and perspectives of Africa and the African Diaspora are central to the wider struggle to decolonise the university.

Pat Lockley's chapter, 'Open initiatives for Decolonising the Curriculum', critically examines the potential of MOOCs (Massive Open Online Courses) to improve access to higher education for students in the global South. Lockley argues that a pedagogical emphasis on 'open' also includes, and is not limited to, many things – the Open University, Wikipedia, Open Educational Resources and creative commons licensing. For Lockley, each of these broadens, diversifies and obfuscates what 'open' could mean, and how openness as a concept can facilitate or hinder decolonising the university.

The final section of the volume, 'Decolonial Reflections', situates these specific examples in the broader theoretical question of what it means to decolonise in institutions in the global North.

In 'Meschachakanis, a Coyote Narrative: Decolonising Higher Education', Shauneen Pete explores the decolonisation of higher education through the practice of storytelling: a decolonising strategy. Pete argues that story as research methodology is a decolonising approach because it encourages a reclamation of (ab)original ways of transferring knowledges and troubles hegemonic systems of education. The chapter invites the reader to join with Coyote (a trickster figure) and the author as they engage in a reflexive conversation that explores ways of undertaking decolonising practices in higher education. The chapter begins with a critical view of how colonial institutions of higher education are; and how these colonial structures are experienced by the author. Then, the chapter explores some of the ways in which the author has led university reform towards decolonisation.

Through a personal account of positioning and positionality, Azumah Dennis's chapter, 'Decolonising Education: A Pedagogic Intervention', explores what it might mean to decolonise education. By problematising 'the space of the unmarked scholar' Dennis proposes a decolonised educational project that places counter-hegemonic curricula and pedagogy at its core, by recognising different forms of understanding, knowing, experiencing and explaining the world. Through an Ubuntu pedagogy, Dennis offers an alternative way of thinking about and being in the world, which challenges 'the hegemony and universality of capitalism and a Western civilisatory logic'.

Angela Last's chapter explores some of the dangers of institutional co-option and marketisation of radical demands. In 'Internationalisation and Interdisciplinarity: Sharing across Boundaries?', Last identifies two types of 'internationalisation' that have taken hold in British universities. The first relates to the sort of diversification of the curriculum that has been called for by students as part of attempts to decolonise the university. The second refers to attempts by universities to expand their market towards overseas and minority ethnic students and improve their competitiveness in the global market. Last brings these two types of internationalisation into critical conversation by exploring their implications in practices of scholarly editing, teaching and curriculum design, collaborating with academics in the global South, and interdisciplinary research.

William Jamal Richardson's chapter, 'Understanding Eurocentrism as a Structural Problem of Undone Science', closes the volume by exploring the effects of Eurocentrism in the discipline of sociology and implications of this for both scholarship and university institutions more broadly. Richardson argues that, in disciplinary terms, Eurocentrism has largely rendered invisible the sociological perspectives and work of both scholars of colour and the societies they come from. In addition, Eurocentrism in the discipline also allows for intrinsically racist and colonial theory and findings to be developed and disseminated within academe and among the public. Richardson argues that the sum total of these processes is that in many spaces sociology, like the social sciences more generally, perpetuates systems of inequality and the social logics that justify them.

IV

The contributions to this volume contextualise and set out what is at stake in calls to decolonise the university. We hope it might also provoke further debates, provide strategic and tactical prompts, inform policy and clarify praxis. Decolonising the university is part of the broader projects of decolonisation and cannot be understood as separate from those projects for social and economic justice. Offering alternative ways of thinking, researching and teaching is necessary, but not exhaustive.

Bibliography

Ahmed, Sara (2012) *On Being Included: Racism and Diversity in Institutional Life*. Durham, NC: Duke University Press.

Allen, Amy (2016) *The End of Progress: Decolonizing the Normative Foundations of Critical Theory*. New York: Columbia University Press.

Andrews, Kehinde (2013) *Resisting Racism: Race, Inequality, and the Black Supplementary School Movement*. London: Trentham Books.

Anzaldúa, Gloria (1987) *Borderlands: The New Mestiza = La Frontera*. San Francisco: Aunt Lute Books.

Bhabha, Homi K. (1993) *Location of Culture*. London: Routledge.

Bhambra, Gurminder K. (2007) *Rethinking Modernity: Postcolonialism and the Sociological Imagination*. Basingstoke: Palgrave Macmillan.

—— (2014) *Connected Sociologies*. London: Bloomsbury Academic.

—— (2017) 'Locating Brexit in the Pragmatics of Race, Citizenship and Empire', in William Outhwaite (ed.) *Brexit: Sociological Responses*. London: Anthem Press.

Boyce-Davies, Carole (1995) *Moving Beyond Boundaries*. New York: New York University Press.

Centre for Contemporary Cultural Studies (1982) *The Empire Strikes Back: Race and Racism in 70s Britain*. London: Hutchinson.

Césaire, Aimé (2000) *Discourse on Colonialism*, trans. Joan Pinkham and with an Introduction by Robin D.G. Kelley. New York: New York University Press.

Chakrabarty, Dipesh (2000) *Provincializing Europe: Postcolonial Thought and Historical Difference*. Princeton, NJ: Princeton University Press.

Deloria Jr, Vine (1991) 'Research, Redskins, and Reality', *American Indian Quarterly* 15(4): 457–68.

Fanon, Frantz (1963) *The Wretched of the Earth*. New York: Grove Press.

Gebrial, Dalia and Shi, Chi Chi (2015) 'The Violence of Liberalspeak: Eulogizing Cecil Rhodes, the "Businessman" and "Munificent Benefactor"', *Discover Society*, available at: https://discoversociety.org/2015/12/01/the-violence-of-liberalspeak-eulogizing-cecil-rhodes-the-businessman-and-munificent-benefactor/

Gilroy, Paul (1992) *There Ain't No Black in the Union Jack*, 2nd edn. London: Routledge.

—— (2006) *Postcolonial Melancholia*. New York: Columbia University Press.

Hargreaves, John D. (1973) 'The Idea of a Colonial University', *African Affairs* 72(286): 26–36.

Holmwood, John (2011) 'The Idea of the Public University', in John Holmwood (ed.) *A Manifesto for the Public University*. London: Bloomsbury Academic.

hooks, bell (1994) *Teaching to Transgress: Education as Practice of Freedom*. New York: Routledge.

Kelley, Robin D.G. (2016) 'Black Study, Black Struggle', *Boston Review*, 24 October, available at: http://bostonreview.net/forum/robin-d-g-kelley-black-study-black-struggle

Lorde, Audre (2007 [1984]) 'The Master's Tools Will Never Dismantle the Master's House', in *Sister Outsider: Essays and Speeches*. Berkeley, CA: Crossing Press, pp. 110–14.

Matera, Marc (2015) *Black London: The Imperial Metropolis and Decolonization in the 20th Century*. Oakland, CA: University of California Press.

Mohanty, Chandra T. (2003) *Feminism without Borders: Decolonizing Theory, Practising Solidarity*. Durham, NC: Duke University Press.

Morrison, Toni (1989) 'Unspeakable Things Unspoken: The Afro-American Presence in American Literature', *Michigan Quarterly Review* winter: 1–34.

Murch, Donna (2010) *Living for the City: Migration, Education, and the Rise of the Black Panther Party in Oakland, California*. Chapel Hill, NC: University of North Carolina Press.

Perry, Kennetta Hammond (2015) *London Is the Place for Me: Black Britons, Citizenship, and the Politics of Race*. New York: Oxford University Press.

Peters, Michael (2015) 'Why is My Curriculum White?', *Educational Philosophy and Theory* 47(7): 641–46.

Rickman, Dina (2012) 'Elite Universities Get £83m from Arms Trade Firms', *Huffington Post*, available at: www.huffingtonpost.co.uk/2012/08/21/arms-companies-russell-group-universities-83m-ethical-investment-campaign-against-the-arms-trade_n_1818747.html

Rogers, Ibram (2012) *The Black Campus Movement: Black Students and the Racial Reconstitution of Higher Education, 1965–1972*. New York: Palgrave Macmillan.

Said, Edward (1978) *Orientalism*. New York: Pantheon Books.

Santos, Boaventura de Sousa (2017) *Decolonizing the University: The Challenge of Deep Cognitive Justice*. Cambridge: Cambridge Scholars.

Schaff, Julia (2016) 'Are Universities Failing Their Students on Fossil Fuel Issues?', *Times Higher Education*, available at: www.timeshighereducation.com/student/blogs/are-universities-failing-their-students-fossil-fuel-issues

Shilliam, Robbie (2015) *The Black Pacific Anti-Colonial Struggles and Oceanic Connections*. London: Bloomsbury.

—— (2016) 'Austere Curricula: Multicultural Education and Black Students', In *Austere Histories in European Societies: Social Exclusion and the Contest of Colonial Memories*, edited by Stefan Jonsson and Julia Willén. London: Routledge.

Sithole, Tendayi (2016) 'A Decolonial Critique of Multi-Inter-Transdisciplinary (MIT) Methodology', in Sabelo J. Ndlovu-Gatsheni and Siphamandla Zondi (eds) *Decolonizing the University: Knowledge Systems and Disciplines in Africa*. Durham, NC: Carolina Academic Press, pp. 107–31.

Sivanandan, Ambalavaner (1978) *Race, Class and the State: The Black Experience in Britain*. London: Institute of Race Relations.

Smith, Linda T. (2012) *Decolonizing Methodologies: Research and Indigenous Peoples*. London: Zed Books.

Spivak, Gayatri Chakravorty (1988) 'Can the Subaltern Speak?', in Cary Nelson and Lawrence Grossberg (eds) *Marxism and the Interpretation of Culture*. Chicago: University of Illinois Press, pp. 271–316.

Steinmetz, George (2014) 'British Sociology in the Metropole and the Colonies, 1940s–60s', in John Holmwood and John Scott (eds) *The Palgrave Handbook of Sociology in Britain*. Basingstoke: Palgrave, pp. 302–37.

Tilley, Lisa (2017) 'Resisting Piratic Method by Doing Research Otherwise', *Sociology* 51(10): 27–42.

Tuck, Eve and Yang, K. Wayne (2012) 'Decolonization is not a Metaphor', *Decolonization: Indigeneity, Education & Society* 1(1): 1–40.

Vaughan, Adam (2013) 'Oxford Students and Alumni to Protest over Shell Earth Sciences Funding', *The Guardian*, 9 May, available at: www.theguardian.com/environment/2013/may/09/oxford-students-alumni-protest-shell

wa Thiong'o, Ngũgĩ (1986) *Decolonising the Mind: The Politics of Language in African Literature*. London: Currey.

Wilder, Craig (2014) *Ebony and Ivy: Race, Slavery and the Troubled History of America's Universities*. New York: Bloomsbury Press.

Wilder, Gary (2015) *Freedom Time: Negritude, Decolonization, and the Future of the World*. Durham, NC: Duke University Press.

Notes

All urls last accessed 15 January 2018.

1. Swarns, Rachel L. (2016) 'Georgetown University Plans Steps to Atone for Slave Past', 1 September, available at: www.nytimes.com/2016/09/02/us/slaves-georgetown-university.html
2. Hussain, Mariya (2015) 'Why is My Curroculum White?', 11 March, available at: www.nus.org.uk/en/news/why-is-my-curriculum-white/ and #Liberate my degree campaign, available at: www.nusconnect.org.uk/campaigns/liberatemydegree
3. Black and Asian Studies, available at: www.blackandasianstudies.org/; Campaign for the Public University, available at: https://publicuniversity.org.uk/; Remaking the University, available at: http://utotherescue.blogspot.co.uk/. See also, for discussion, Holmwood, John (2011) 'The Idea of the Public University', in John Holmwood (ed.) *A Manifesto for the Public University*. London: Bloomsbury Academic.
4. Bhambra, Gurminder K. (2014) *Connected Sociologies*. London: Bloomsbury Academic.
5. Smith, Linda T. (2012) *Decolonizing Methodologies: Research and Indigenous Peoples*. London: Zed Books; Wilder, Gary (2015) *Freedom Time: Negritude, Decolonization, and the Future of the World*. Durham, NC: Duke University Press; Allen, Amy (2016) *The End of Progress: Decolonizing the Normative Foundations of Critical Theory*. New York: Columbia University Press; Tilley, Lisa (2017) 'Resisting Piratic Method by Doing Research Otherwise', *Sociology* 51(10): 27–42.
6. Bhambra 2014 op. cit.
7. Anzaldúa, Gloria (1987) *Borderlands: The New Mestiza = La Frontera*. San Francisco: Aunt Lute Books; Bhabha, Homi K. (1993) *Location of Culture*. London: Routledge.
8. Fanon, Frantz (1963) *The Wretched of the Earth*. New York: Grove Press; Césaire, Aimé (2000) *Discourse on Colonialism*, trans. Joan Pinkham and with an Introduction by Robin D.G. Kelley. New York: New York University Press; Kelley, Robin D.G. (2016) 'Black Study, Black Struggle', *Boston Review*, 24 October.
9. See, for example, wa Thiongo, Ngũgĩ (1986) *Decolonising the Mind: The Politics of Language in African Literature*. London: Currey; Lorde, Audre (2007 [1984]) 'The Master's Tools Will Never Dismantle the Master's House', in *Sister Outsider: Essays and Speeches*. Berkeley, CA: Crossing Press, pp. 110–14; hooks, bell (1994) *Teaching to Transgress: Education as Practice of Freedom*. New York: Routledge; Deloria Jr, Vine (1991) 'Research, Redskins, and Reality', *American Indian Quarterly* 15(4): 457–68; Mohanty, Chandra T. (2003) *Feminism without Borders: Decolonizing Theory, Practising Solidarity*. Durham, NC: Duke University Press; Santos, Boaventura de Sousa (2017) *Decolonizing the University: The Challenge of Deep Cognitive Justice*. Cambridge: Cambridge Scholars Publishing; Grosfoguel, Ramón, Hernández, Roberto and Velásquez, Ernesto Rosen (eds) (2017) *Decolonizing the Westernized University*. London: Lexington Books; Sefa Dei, George

J. and Kempf, Arlo (eds) (2006) *Anti-Colonialism and Education*. Rotterdam: Sense Publishers; Shefner, Jon, Dahms, Harry, Emmet Jones, Robert and Jalata, Asafa (eds) *Social Justice and the University: Globalization, Human Rights and the Future of Democracy*. Basingstoke, Palgrave Macmillan.

10. Gilroy, Paul (1992) *There Ain't No Black in the Union Jack*. London: Routledge; Gilroy, Paul (2006) *Postcolonial Melancholia*. New York: Columbia University Press; Chakrabarty, Dipesh (2000) *Provincializing Europe: Postcolonial Thought and Historical Difference*. Princeton, NJ: Princeton University Press; Centre for Contemporary Cultural Studies (1982) *The Empire Strikes Back: Race and Racism in 70s Britain*. London: Hutchinson.

11. Boyce-Davies, Carole (1995) *Moving beyond Boundaries*. New York: New York University Press; Matera, Marc (2015) *Black London: The Imperial Metropolis and Decolonization in the 20th Century*. Oakland, CA: University of California Press.

12. Sivanandan, Amabalavaner (1978) *Race, Class and the State: The Black Experience in Britain*. London: Institute of Race Relations; Perry, Kennetta Hammond (2015) *London Is the Place for Me: Black Britons, Citizenship, and the Politics of Race*. New York: Oxford University Press; Bhambra, Gurminder K. (2017) 'Locating Brexit in the Pragmatics of Race, Citizenship and Empire', in William Outhwaite (ed.) *Brexit: Sociological Responses*. London: Anthem Press.

13. Murch, Donna (2010) *Living for the City: Migration, Education, and the Rise of the Black Panther Party in Oakland, California*. Chapel Hill, NC: University of North Carolina Press; Rogers, Ibram (2012) *The Black Campus Movement: Black Students and the Racial Reconstitution of Higher Education, 1965-1972*. New York: Palgrave Macmillan.

14. Shilliam, Robbie (2016) 'Austere Curricula: Multicultural Education and Black Students', in Stefan Jonsson and Julia Willén (eds) *Austere Histories in European Societies: Social Exclusion and the Contest of Colonial Memories*. London: Routledge; Andrews, Kehinde (2013) *Resisting Racism: Race, Inequality, and the Black Supplementary School Movement*. London: Trentham Books.

15. Shilliam, Robbie (2015) *The Black Pacific Anti-Colonial Struggles and Oceanic Connections*. London: Bloomsbury, p. 13.

16. Tuck, Eve and Yang, K. Wayne (2012) 'Decolonization is not a Metaphor', *Decolonization: Indigeneity, Education & Society* 1(1): 1–40.

17. Ibid. p. 3.

18. Ibid. p. 3.

19. Ibid. p. 7.

20. See, for an example in the context of literature, Morrison, Toni (1989) 'Unspeakable Things Unspoken: The Afro-American Presence in American Literature', *Michigan Quarterly Review* winter: 1–34.

21. See, for example, Steinmetz, George (2014) 'British Sociology in the Metropole and the Colonies, 1940s–60s', in John Holmwood and John Scott (eds) *The Palgrave Handbook of Sociology in Britain*. Basingstoke: Palgrave, pp. 302–37.

22. Hargreaves, John D. (1973) 'The Idea of a Colonial University', *African Affairs* 72(286): 26–36.

23. Wilder, Craig (2014) *Ebony and Ivy: Race, Slavery and the Troubled History of America's Universities*. New York: Bloomsbury Press.

24. Peters, Michael (2015) 'Why is My Curriculum White?', *Educational Philosophy and Theory* 47(7): 641–46.

25. Said, Edward (1978) *Orientalism*. New York: Pantheon Books; Bhambra, Gurminder K. (2007) *Rethinking Modernity: Postcolonialism and the Sociological Imagination*. Basingstoke: Palgrave Macmillan; Sithole, Tendayi (2016) 'A Decolonial Critique of Multi-inter-transdisciplinary (MIT) Methodology', in Sabelo Ndlovu-Gatsheni and Siphamandla Zondi (eds) *Decolonizing the University, Knowledge Systems and Disciplines in Africa*. Durham, NC: Carolina Academic Press, pp. 107–31.

26. Ahmed, Sara (2012) *On Being Included: Racism and Diversity in Institutional Life*. Durham, NC: Duke University Press; Gebrial, Dalia and Shi, Chi Chi (2015) 'The Violence of Liberalspeak: Eulogizing Cecil Rhodes, the "Businessman" and "Munificent Benefactor"', *Discover Society* 27(December), available at: https://discoversociety.org/2015/12/01/the-violence-of-liberalspeak-eulogizing-cecil-rhodes-the-businessman-and-munificent-benefactor/

27. Spivak, Gayatri Chakravorty (1988) 'Can the Subaltern Speak?', in Cary Nelson and Lawrence Grossberg (eds) *Marxism and the Interpretation of Culture*. Chicago: University of Illinois Press, pp. 271–316.

28. Vaughan, Adam (2013) 'Oxford Students and Alumni to Protest over Shell Earth Sciences Funding', *The Guardian*, 9 May.

29. Rickman, Dina (2012) 'Elite Universities Get £83m from Arms Trade Firms', *Huffington Post*, 23 August; Schaff, Julia (2016) 'Are Universities Failing Their Students on Fossil Fuel Issues?', *Times Higher Education*, 18 November.

PART I

CONTEXTS: HISTORICAL AND DISCIPLINARY

2

Rhodes Must Fall:
Oxford and Movements for Change

Dalia Gebrial

The call to decolonise the university is not a new one. In her essay 'Feminism and Fragility', Sara Ahmed talks about the 'chipping away' of institutional change: 'Chip, chip, chip. Things splinter. Maybe we can turn that chip, chip, chip into a hammer: we might chip away at the old block.'[1] For decades, teachers and students have been chipping away at the coloniality of the university, in an attempt to make it more critical, rigorous and democratic.

The metaphor of 'chipping away at the old block' is particularly apt, because it is important to look at the role the university plays in the broader decolonisation call with sober perspective; to understand the possibilities and limitations of trying to effect change from within the academy. Of course, the university is a site of knowledge production and, most crucially, consecration; it has the power to decide which histories, knowledges and intellectual contributions are considered valuable and worthy of further critical attention and dissemination. This has knock-on effects: public discourse might seem far from the academy's sphere of influence, but 'common sense' ideas of worthy knowledge do not come out of the blue, or removed from the context of power – and the university is a key shaping force in this discursive flux.

Within decolonial movements, the centrality of knowledge production to colonialism as it existed historically and as its legacies appear today are clearly known and understood. It is within this context that decolonial workers in the academy have for years sought to bring the marginalised to the centre-stage of scholarly labour; to memorialise and elevate their perspectives, histories and struggles, which would otherwise be lost in the throes of oppression; conceiving this as one part of the broader struggle to decolonise the interlocking social, economic and political systems in which we find ourselves. Indeed, this is the central, unresolved contradiction of the call to decolonise the academy: how to use the resources and position of the institution, while recognising, accounting for and undoing its inherent exclusivity.

While this chapter cannot address this with the comprehension and directness it needs, it will use the Rhodes Must Fall in Oxford (RMFO) campaign as a case study to do three things: (1) explicate the role of formalised education in the process of knowledge production, and its importance; (2) confront how the British Empire and its legacy is both normalised and trivialised in education; and (3) call for a reorientation in the anti-racist framework from diversity to decolonisation, and explore what this might look like.

Erasing history, creating 'safety'

The RMFO campaign brought the urge to decolonise from the nooks and crannies of academic departments to sensationalised newspaper headlines and heated arguments at family dinner tables. The campaign had three broad areas in which it committed to work towards decolonisation within the University of Oxford: iconography, curriculum and representation. By making these interventions in an institution that holds such unique capital as a centre of knowledge production, the campaign aimed to bring about a knock-on effect at other institutions. It was also anticipated that Oxford University's centrality to Britain's intellectual and cultural identity would enable these interventions to ripple through the public consciousness. The demand that captured the British public's imagination, however, was one inspired by the movement's namesake in South Africa: the removal of a statue of British colonialist Cecil Rhodes – widely considered to have laid the legislative groundwork for South African apartheid – from the front of Oriel College's main building.

From the outset, the campaign's most well-known demand fell victim to the problem of narrative control. Indeed, the call came at a critical juncture in student politics; campus organising had been growing globally – from Jawaharlal Nehru University in India to Amherst College in the US. However, the counter-reaction was also growing, and had a louder, wealthier voice; newspaper columns across the political spectrum – particularly in the US and the UK – bemoaned the death of free speech and academic enquiry on campuses at the hands of over-sensitive, easily triggered student activists. This phenomenon was not limited to one or two articles; it became a meme that garnered unprecedented traction throughout the commentariat.

The need to repeat and sustain this narrative of student activists as incurious, navel-gazing millennials pampered by 1990s soft parenting – rather than an energised, highly informed generation that know they deserve better than the future of precarity and debt awaiting them upon graduation – led journalists down a 'fake news' rabbit hole. Consider this example from the tail end of 2016: reports that a leaflet produced by Oxford University Students Union (OUSU) told students to refrain from using gendered pronouns 'he' and 'she' in favour of the gender-neutral 'ze' picked up pace across the British broadsheet and tabloid media.[2] Seemingly plucked out of thin air, the union categorically denied having ever mandated against the use of gendered pronouns, or the existence of such a leaflet – stating that such a move would in fact be 'counterproductive'[3] to their initiative against misgendering.

However, the intended work of the article had already been done; a delicious anecdote to further satiate the rabid hunger of confirmation bias, racking up clicks and shares at the expense of an authentic portrayal of reality. A *Telegraph* article published the day after OUSU publicly refuted the claims said as much: 'the fact that Oxford has possibly been a victim of incorrect reporting isn't the biggest worry', it argued, because 'fact or fiction', the (categorically fictional) story was symptomatic of a 'student bubble culture of safe spacing, no-platforming and the generally surreal atmosphere of mollycoddling'.[4] The desire for evidence – the desire to strengthen and legitimise particular assumptions about students campaigning around particular things – became more important than the existence of actual evidence. Indeed, the feeling that such a culture existed universally among student activists – and that it deserved wholesale dismissal because it reflected anti-intellectual childishness – became more credible than what the students actually had to say for themselves, and what they were actually doing.

Student-led decolonisation movements have faced similar reporting tactics. To name just one example, an early 2017 *Daily Mail* article expressed panic and anger at the School of Oriental and African Studies (SOAS) student union's declared commitment to decolonisation and 'confronting the white institution'. 'Students at a University of London college', it bemoaned, 'are demanding that such seminal figures as Plato, Descartes, Immanuel Kant and Bertrand Russell' – without whose work, 'understanding philosophy' is 'all but inconceivable' – be 'dropped from the curriculum simply because they are white.[5] The statement in fact invited an academic and student-led review of the curriculum, in light of the 'histories of erasure prevalent in the curriculum' and 'with a particular focus on SOAS' colonial origins and present alternative ways of knowing'.[6] It called for greater representation of philosophers from the global South and its diaspora, and a critical engagement with the colonial context in which many canonical, white philosophers wrote. What began as an intellectual claim around curricular erasure, and indeed the very processes behind the formation of curricula, was deflected into a well-trodden story of zealously 'PC' students hysterically 'censoring' the parts of intellectual history they do not 'agree' with. It is important to note here that this discourse of unwarranted sensitivity and lack of reason was – and continues to be – almost exclusively reserved for students raising issues associated with marginalised identities and struggles.

The knee-jerk impulse to paint the RMFO campaign as yet another example of immature students unable to engage in debate, led to a very particular framing of the call for Rhodes' statue to fall. From the outset, it was posited as a call for a 'safe space' in which the history of colonialism was erased in favour of comfort; that the students were demanding the removal of Rhodes' statue, because its presence evoked trauma that caused distress. The *Telegraph*'s Harry Mount slammed the students and their 'hypersensitive, unsophisticated, uneducated [attitudes]', recommending they undergo a lesson in '[dealing] calmly with things [they] disagree with'. He summarised the alleged objectionable outlook of the students: 'don't like the politics of a visiting speaker? Well then just no-platform them. Worried about rude passages in a classic novel? Demand trigger warnings that certain scenes may cause offence.'[7] Classicist Mary Beard criticised the campaign as a 'dangerous attempt to erase the past'.[8] *Times Higher Education*, although sympathetic to the questions raised by the campaign, referred to its demands as potentially trying to '[tear] down history',[9] framing it as an issue of censorship.

The campaign was immediately inserted into pre-existing conversations around no-platforming, safe spaces and campus censorship, despite none of this language coming from its original call to action, which was working towards something much deeper. Indeed, it implied that students had – in a sense – called for the 'no-platforming' of Rhodes, out of trauma. This, of course, was the precise opposite of what the students set out to achieve: the goal was never to 'no-platform' or 'erase' Rhodes – it was to platform the coloniality he represented and its lasting impact in seminars, university lectures and public discourse, subjecting it to the critical scrutiny it has thus far eluded. However, this framing tactic allowed the media to discuss the RMFO campaign without discussing the actual demand of decolonisation.

A cursory look on the movement's own website concisely summarises its aims: to 'remedy the highly selective narrative of traditional academia – which frames the West as sole producers of universal knowledge – by integrating subjugated and local epistemologies … [creating] a more intellectually rigorous, complete academy'.[10] The argument was always that European colonialism was and continues to be a shaping force of modern history and pedagogy, and that this is overlooked – particularly in Britain – in our education system out of discomfort with the truth that it harbours and the reality it reveals. This was not a matter of 'disagreeing' with mere opinions held by Rhodes – it was about critically examining the power struggle that underpins hegemonic knowledge production, and the material structures that make this possible; about bringing them into the light, and exposing what knowledge is made invisible as well as what is made hyper-visible, by being put forward as universal, or canonical.

What does it mean for Rhodes to fall?

There is a considerable gap in Britain's public knowledge of its modern history. Indeed, the curiosity that was cultivated in the RMFO campaign – albeit incredibly fraught to say the least – led to a crucial development in this conversation. For the first time in my lifetime, heated discussions around the significance and details of the British Empire were drawn out into several weeks of front-page headlines and filled hours of broadcast media. However, most interestingly, data collected the year before concerning how British people understand and relate to the British Empire regained relevance. Some subsidiary questions in a YouGov poll about the 2014 Commonwealth Games revealed that 59 percent of British adults (aged 18–60+) view the Empire as 'more something to be proud of', with just 19 percent considering it 'more something to be ashamed of'. Forty-nine percent of surveyed adults viewed countries colonised by Britain as being 'better off for being colonized' and just 45 percent could categorically say they would not like Britain to still have an Empire.[11] Indeed, that this has not been the subject of a more extensive qualitative study, and that it was not considered news upon its initial publication, is testament to the level of importance typically given to such information.

This perception of Empire through either rose-tinted glasses – or through indifference – has several root causes; from the representation of Empire in mainstream culture (or lack thereof), to the general stigmatisation of discussing Empire in public – and particularly in public political discourse. What happens as a result is the preservation of a particular notion of both Britain's present, and of global North–South relations. The education system, from primary to higher, is a key player in what Michel Rolph-Trouillot calls 'the production of history'.[12] Indeed, as Rolph-Trouillot points out, in Europe and the US, the public's sense of what history *is* remains influenced by positivist tendencies, whereby the role of the historian is to simply 'reveal' facts about pasts that are worth revealing, in a process removed from power. This epistemological insistence on history as a positivist endeavour functions as a useful tool of coloniality in the institution, as it effaces the power relations that underpin what the 'production of history' has thus far looked like. Indeed, the question of who decides what is important to whom is profoundly unfamiliar. The final educational 'product' – the curriculum – appears in a self-justifying manner, and the processes of its construction are concealed. As such, the issue of coloniality in education is not just a question for researchers – it has ramifications far beyond educational institutions. Indeed, what happens in the institution feeds back to establish a particular notion of 'objective' historical fact, which has profound consequences for perceptions of the nation's past and its present.

Seeing how this has taken shape in the historical context of education policy in the UK, the English National Curriculum, in particular, presents a fine case study as to why such questions around the production of 'common' knowledge – and particularly 'common' historical knowledge – are important. From the ideological inception of a national 'core' curriculum in the mid-1980s, struggle over what it included and why has been rife; and nowhere was the debate more heated and fraught than in the history syllabus. Indeed, education scholars describe the struggles around what they call the 'great history debate' as 'nothing less than a public and vibrant debate over the national soul'.[13] Gavin Baldwin too identifies that 'the National Curriculum codifies the knowledge, skills and attitudes which "the nation" holds to be important, or more likely it is decided by a few that these values are good for "the nation" whatever that might be'. Within this, the 'ferocity' of debates around what a National History Curriculum must include, demonstrates 'the strength of the belief that the History Curriculum could reinforce a sense of national identity';[14] in other words, there is of course an intimate connection between national identity and collective historical remembering (and forgetting). As it currently stands, a British student can study history to A-level standard, without gaining more than a lesson's worth of time studying Empire.

Given this context, it is unsurprising that attempts to subvert or question conventional teachings of history – particularly of British history – are met with such defensive fervour. Tabloid and mid-market newspaper columns have long been racked with anxiety that 'children in state schools have been taught to be ashamed of our history', an anxiety explicitly connected to the idea that Britain's Empire – 'one of the greatest, most benign empires the world has ever known' – is being 'denigrated'[15] in the National Curriculum. When discussions around curriculum content resurfaced in 2013, there was specific focus around reworking the English literature and history syllabuses to include even greater emphasis on a particular kind of 'British' history and 'English' literature. The history proposals – which were eventually scrapped following a considerable counter-reaction from scholars – looked to shift the tone of the already minimal teaching of 'Britain and her empire' away from a 'negative and anti-British' slant, and free it from the burden of 'post-colonial guilt'.[16] Indeed, it is particularly interesting that a recurring motif in the commentary around RMFO's statue demand, was that 'history' must be protected from those who wish to 'erase' it or 'tear it down'; to interrogate the statue's presence was to threaten, somehow, 'history' itself.

Here, 'history' is not the ongoing and deeply contested process of narrative building around the past; a process over which the present has agency, and which is often – in its most mainstream form – shaped in the image of dominant ideological frameworks. Rather, 'history' is fixed, unquestionable and precious because it preserves a particular reading of the past, which reinforces a particular understanding of the present; like the statue, its objectivity rises above the emotional, hand-wringing rabble, who are declared intellectually unfit to participate in the process of its production. What this demonstrates so clearly, is that the construction of a curriculum at any education level is the product of a power struggle; however, it is not perceived as such. Rather, it appears as a 'natural' process, in which disciplinary canons and narrative framings come into being through apolitical, 'rational' means that do not themselves need to be scrutinised; indeed, the very claim to apolitical greatness is itself the defining feature of the canon.

It was this assumption that RMFO threw into question. It asked: what is omitted from curricula in all disciplines, and what does this tell us about the purpose of education as we see it? Any curriculum must, by definition, exclude – the question is what is excluded and why, and whether the purpose of our education system should be to perpetuate existing power structures and norms, or equip students with the critical tools to question them. Furthermore, RMFO made connections between these knowledge gaps, and the structural, material inequalities they engender both within the academy and, most importantly, beyond the academy. As this volume will elaborate, these interrogations are not just relevant in history departments – although their importance comes to light with particular starkness here. The significance of Empire in shaping institutions of knowledge production and disciplinary canons spans the entire academy; every discipline carries with it colonial modalities of thinking that have eluded adequate scrutiny.

Rhodes rises, who is forgotten?

In a sense, the battle over Rhodes' statue became itself emblematic of the entire struggle at hand. The statue stands on one of the busiest streets in Oxford, and yet, positioned high atop a college building, it hovers out of plain sight; much like the legacy of Empire, it occupies a position of simultaneous invisibility and hyper-visibility. It is an always present, shaping political, economic and cultural force, but goes unnamed and unseen. When it occasionally appears in the public eye, it is as a nostalgic relic of a distant, irrelevant past. The statue had been standing for over a century by the time the campaign threw it into question, yet its presence, and by extension the conditions of its emergence, remained unrecognised in any substantial form. Indeed, critics often mocked the campaign as being much ado about nothing – that the statue was hardly noticeable and therefore unimportant, while simultaneously arguing that it was of such historical significance it must be safeguarded at all costs.

When the statue was erected in 1911, it was at Rhodes' behest, and he signed away a considerable part of his fortune to Oriel's endowment; in other words, the social and capital accumulation that made the statue possible – that put Rhodes in a financial and social position to buy his place on Oriel's building – was acquired directly from the colonial exploitation of Southern Africa's black population; in a literal sense, owes its very existence to this exploitation. However, in order for the statue to stand above the glowing inscription 'by means of the generous munificence of Cecil Rhodes', the heart of what Rhodes represented – settler-colonialism and the blueprint of South African apartheid – must be forgotten. The sterile language with which he is spoken of – as a 'benefactor' and 'businessman' – actively erases the history of violence that enabled his 'generous munificence'. Where great concern was expressed over whether the removal and recontextualisation of Rhodes's statue would erase 'history', little curiosity was ever shown towards what histories were and continue to be suppressed by the statue's very existence as a glorifying tribute. Indeed, the lack of any working knowledge about Rhodes among the general public – despite his significant role in Britain's colonial history – underscores the obvious fact that statues do not exist as sites of historical learning and therefore scrutinising them does not constitute a violation of historical understanding; in fact, they can often exist to obscure full historical reckoning. It was this obstacle to reckoning that the movement was trying to dislodge; an ossified, rose-tinted, 'Great Man' theory of history that squashed the perspectives of those outside European elites and was almost perfectly embodied by the crumbling statue.

So why is this project a worthy one? In the same way that colonial violence and Rhodes' wealth are decoupled in the statue's form, despite being intrinsically connected, so is the relationship between coloniality and the making of modern Europe. Tales of industrial revolutions are forcibly separated from the colonial trade routes and colonised labour that made such rapid development possible; the Enlightenment is geographically mapped as a self-contained, European project, rather than constituted through and alongside imperialism and slavery.[17] The Enlightenment not only forged and reproduced modalities of colonial thinking, it would not have been possible without the intellectual contributions of the Islamic translations (and therefore preservation) of Greek and Persian philosophical and scientific writings, or numerical systems originating in South Asia.[18] Indeed, these twin processes of both effacing the importance of the Enlightenment's colonial emergence (presenting it as a 'pure' intellectual project, separate from its material and historical context) and the racialising of these values of 'reason' and objective knowledge pursuit as white and European are foundational principles of contemporary framings of 'East' and 'West'. Sometimes, the consequences of this colonial modality of thinking are overtly worrying. White nationalist Richard Spencer, a figurehead of the 'alt-right', which has recently gained public prominence, responded in a 2016 Al Jazeera interview to a question about why non-white people are not part of America's 'greatness':

> Only Europeans could be the first ones to go to space; only Europeans could build something as magnificent as St Paul's Cathedral; only Europeans could engage in the kind of scientific discovery that we engage with, that will to keep going, to follow reason to its very limit, even if it shatters everything you thought before; only Europeans went through these tumults of Reformations, of Enlightenments ... only Europeans can be like this.

He goes on to describe being an immigrant as someone who 'washes up on someone else's shores' and '[takes] advantage of what other people have built', making them 'pathetic'; 'I wouldn't be proud of a nation of immigrants, I would be proud of a nation of frontiersman, a nation of colonizers, a nation of conquerers.'[19] While it may seem extreme, this framework of argument – which is gaining some populist traction – relies on a common lack of knowledge not only around the intellectual and material contributions of non-Europeans to 'world' history, but of the integral role played by non-Europeans in European history itself. However, this historical reality is flattened, in favour of a reading that portrays the global South as the passive recipient of other people's innovation and development. It also relies on a lack of understanding around how colonialism's power dynamics have shaped contemporary global inequalities, and uneven access to resources, development and democratic agency. The vast majority of the time, the consequence of this gap in understanding does not rear its head in a form as ugly as Spencer's, but rather come to the fore as a sense of confusion and resentment that people who did not participate in the 'building' of modernity are unreasonably trying to participate in it on an equal footing; to 'take advantage' of it, to use Spencer's terms.

Indeed, one wonders how differently public discourse around issues such as immigration, borders, war, national identity and global inequality might be conducted if the classed and racialised dynamics of colonialism were fully integrated into everyday historical reflections and representations; and, most crucially, if the full political history of the entity known as 'Britain' was reckoned with. In particular, what would this do to prevailing understandings of, and indeed the very preoccupation with, what it means to 'belong' to Britishness and to have entitlement to public resources on the basis of this claim. Indeed, it is no coincidence that online messages directed towards the RMFO campaigners were so centred around suspicion over whether these black and brown faces really deserved to be at Oxford University, or in Britain at all.

How would the long-term realisation that 'Britain' emerged through and alongside imperialism complicate what it means to 'put Britain first', a claim of Britishness that relies on selective ideas of who was implicated in its construction and how. Indeed, how would key events such as the 1948 *Windrush*, often pointed to as the genesis of 'multicultural' Britain and, for some, the project of malignant, cheating brown and black people 'washing up' on Britain's shores, illegitimately stealing the fruits of hard-working British labourers, be re-read in light of such an education? The racial watertightness of these terms of national belonging – of invested labour or inheritance of a national claim – start to fall apart when the history of Empire is taken into account. This is of course not to argue that an educational turn would see the end of racism – which operates at a deeply structural and material level – rather, it is to propose that such a shift in consciousness could change the terms and assumptions in these defining debates of our time in a way that has powerful ramifications.

Don't diversify, decolonise

RMFO's call to decolonise was, in itself, deeply unfamiliar outside very specific academic circles. This unfamiliarity – and the fact that it could not be resolved within the bureaucratic, human resource channels typically reserved for grievances around race – was a critical part of the struggle to have the campaign's demands understood. It also raised the question as to whether the decolonial demand can ever be fully met within the institution. Indeed, at its heart, decolonisation is about recognising the roots of contemporary racism in the multiple material, political, social and cultural processes of colonialism and proceeding from this point; this involves the laborious work of structural change at several levels of society – a far cry from the administering of welfare and representation services that has typically been the response to racialised grievances.

When looking at the history of anti-racist organising in the UK, the significance of this resurgence of decolonial language comes to the fore. In his seminal essay 'The End of Anti-racism',[20] Paul Gilroy perfectly captured how the theoretical focus of, and therefore demands made by, anti-racist movements in the UK went through drastic transformations as they moved from the post-war era through the establishment of neoliberal consensus in the 1980s. Writing in 1990, Gilroy identified many of the issues that would arise out of these conceptual shifts. Moving away from collective, political and indeed resource-based demands, Gilroy identifies the rise of an ideological framework, led by a 'cadre of anti-racism professionals',[21] which forgoes mass mobilisation in favour of individualised, self-help models of change. Most crucially, Gilroy identifies this shift as itself a mechanism of power:

> Meanwhile, many of the ideological gains of Thatcherite conservatism have dovetailed neatly with the shibboleths of black nationalism – self reliance and economic betterment through thrift, hard work and individual discipline.[22]

For Gilroy, this occurs in part because of a 'crisis in organizational' forms – in other words, the shift from the movement to the individual as the primary social unit and organising category. However, more importantly, it occurs because of a 'crisis in political language', whereby race itself becomes viewed almost exclusively 'in terms of culture and identity rather than politics and history'.[23] Gilroy argues that while, of course, culture and identity are 'part of the story of racial sensibility'[24] race is not reducible to these factors; it has an historical core in processes of material and political domination. A major consequence of this language crisis has been a notable shift in anti-racist discourse, towards a concession of the idea of 'race' as a politically and historically contingent category.

This rendering of race as an identity category removed from politics and history is most apparent in the consensus that has been built around a particular kind of 'multiculturalist' framework, where race is based in essential differences and where the problem lies solely in the hierarchisation of these differences, which itself arises from the purely cultural and social hostility to such difference. These differences are not only perceived as essential and therefore insurmountable, but to attempt to surmount them is itself seen as undesirable. As such, grievances and demands – be they for recognition, representation or inclusion – are made from this position of dearly held, fixed identity categories. The overall goal becomes mere tolerance – or 'recognition' – of difference as it appears in its most minute form. This has seen the growth of 'increased diversity' as the primary, and most familiar anti-racist demand. Indeed, the breaking down of the social unit from movement to individual occurs through and alongside this shift from political to culturalist understandings of difference.

As Gilroy identifies, this move entails a process of divorcing the causes of racism from wider systemic processes. Racism itself becomes something 'peripheral to the substance of political life';[25] a circumscribed phenomenon that can be dealt with while leaving the basic economic and political structure of society intact. The core demand shifts from the end of race, to the end of 'racial discrimination', and the conceptual problem lies in the idea that such a decoupling of race and racial discrimination is possible. It conceals the history of race itself as being borne out of processes of domination that have occurred at multiple points in history, and that continue to reinvent and reshape themselves in light of contemporary needs. The preoccupation then becomes diversification – in other words, individual betterment – within existing structures, rather than the interrogation of how these structures came to be, and the inequalities that are engendered and reproduced by and within them. As such, demands within higher education institutions – particularly elite ones such as Oxford University – have been centred entirely around representation and admissions.

Framing student demands within a 'decolonisation' framework marked a reorientation away from this kind of politics. First, the call included within itself – in its very terminology – identification of the immutable importance of coloniality in any contemporary conversation around race. It centred Empire and slavery – as projects of economic, political and material, as well as cultural, domination – at the heart of its explanation of racialised inequalities, and its understanding of the kind of structural change needed. Of course, this is not to argue that the call for better provisions around representation – for example, blind admissions and investment in outreach – is not an important one that is worth making. However, it is not sufficient to express grievances about diversity and representation as a circumscribed issue; it is necessary – and more difficult – also to demand recognition of, and reparative action in light of, how and why this came to be the case, and to connect it to other, more urgent, forms of structural racism.

Furthermore, it situated what was going on in Oxford University in a broader context; in other words, it moved the responsibility of Oxford student campaigners outside the space of the university itself. This intention was conveyed in part by the movement's deliberate deployment of the name 'Rhodes Must Fall' from its South African namesake, and the conscious echoing of their critiques around the statue and decolonisation. In evoking these terms, the campaign positioned itself as not just concerned with what was occurring within the institution of Oxford University, but the role Oxford as a centre of knowledge consecration – and, historically, the heart of colonial knowledge production – plays in the wider world. This was part of a broader trend of student activists deliberately plugging themselves into a global network of anti-racist activity. Indeed, just prior to the founding of the RMFO campaign, Oxford students were holding solidarity marches and teach-ins with Black Lives Matter in the US – particularly around the time of the 2015 Ferguson protests – and organising talks by figures such as Dennis Goldberg – a prominent anti-apartheid activist, who spoke about contemporary Palestinian solidarity. This increase in anti-racist activity at Oxford University started with what Nancy Fraser would identify as a classic struggle for recognition; it began promptly after the university became the focus of a nationwide scandal for admitting only one Afro-Caribbean student in its entire undergraduate intake. However, the students did not circumscribe this event within the four walls of the institution. Over the next five years, the boundaries of the conversation morphed into a much more systemic set of demands, which recognised themselves as being at once global and local.

However, this is not to argue that the movement did not come up against its own internal struggles and conceptual limitations. As has been outlined, RMFO came into being at two crucial junctures: the prominence of 'safe space' and trauma discourse as the framing narrative of student activism, and the prevalence of diversification as the primary anti-racist demand made in educational institutions. As time went on, it became increasingly difficult to keep the movement's decolonisation demand from becoming subsumed under these categories. This is entirely unsurprising, as the process of bringing unfamiliar political language into public life is difficult and fraught. Indeed, this is why, despite these struggles, a sustained commitment to these principles of locating the historical and material core of racism is worth pursuing. However, it became difficult to not internalise the terms of the debate as they were set by the media's preoccupation with individual trauma and grievances. Questions asked by journalists were almost exclusively framed around individual students' experiences at Oxford, almost in an attempt to frame the university as having a unique, Oxford-specific problem; this framing therefore took up the bulk of airtime given to RMFO spokespeople. Indeed, even sympathetic headlines argued in support of the campaign on the basis that the statue violates the university's duty of care to students of colour because of the discomfort it creates; that Oxford cannot expect to become a hospitable place for people of colour if it continues to glorify figures such as Cecil Rhodes.

This may well be true, particularly for the university's black Southern African students. Nonetheless, framing the intervention entirely in these terms has problematic consequences. First and foremost, the integral notion of the statue being a *metaphor* for wider historical, material, cultural and economic processes – and not the issue *tout court* – starts to get lost. Second, the conversation can get easily stripped of its core of political, social and economic justice, and pushed into the realm of administering welfare provisions (which is of course falsely divorced from the former). Crucially, as Robin Kelley writes, 'managing trauma does not require dismantling structural racism'.[26] In this way, focusing political energy into framing things like the Rhodes statue as a 'trigger' or a violation of safe space – although media-friendly – ultimately backfires on core, long-term anti-racist aims. While trauma is often an entry point into understanding these issues, and can be an introductory way of communicating how these structures come to light on an everyday, human level, it cannot be the basis on which a politics is developed. If for no other reason, this is because, built into the idea that RMFO existed purely to address issues around the welfare of Oxford students of colour is the assumption that issues within the university affect only those within it; however, it is far more powerful and compelling to address how these issues of a white curriculum affect – and implicate – the world outside the institution.

In other words, the movement cannot be only about students – particularly students at a university of great privilege such as Oxford – and claim an analytical framework of decoloniality. It is crucial for any student and academic-led decolonisation movement – many of which are already emerging up and down the country – not only to rigorously understand and define its terms, but also to locate the university as just one node in a network of spaces where this kind of struggle must be engaged with.

Such a movement also needs to understand its position as responding to live issues of inequality, colonialism and oppression – rather than just being a matter of legacies, or unearthing historical accounts for the sake of it. To do this kind of work in the university is to dig where you are – where you have access – rather than to view the university as the primary space where transformation happens. It is to enter the university space as a transformative force, to connect what is happening inside the institution to the outside, and to utilise its resources in the interest of social justice.

Bibliography

Ahmed, S. (2016) 'Feminism and Fragility', 26 January, available at: https://feministkilljoys.com/2016/01/26/feminism-and-fragility/

Al Jazeera English (2016) 'White Nationalist Richard Spencer Talks to Al Jazeera', video file, 9 December, available at: www.youtube.com/watch?v=ni_6sISHnqQ

Baldwin, G. (1996) 'In the Heart or on the Margins: A Personal View of National Curriculum History and Issues of Identity', in R. Andrews (ed.) *Interpreting the New National Curriculum*. London: Middlesex University Press.

Dahlgreen, W. (2014) 'The British Empire Is "Something to be Proud of"', 26 July, available at: https://yougov.co.uk/news/2014/07/26/britain-proud-its-empire/

Gilroy, P. (1990) 'The End of Anti-racism', *Journal of Ethnic and Migration Studies* 17(1): 71–83.

Gregory-Brough, J. (2016) 'OUSU Statement: The Use of Gender Neutral Pronouns', 16 December, available at: http://archive.li/AvUAF

Grove, J. (2017) 'Must Rhodes Fall?', 16 February, available at: www.timeshighereducation.com/features/must-rhodes-fall

Habib, A. (2016) 'Educational Priorities', 2 December, available at: https://soasunion.org/education/educationalpriorities/

Jenne, A. (2015) 'Mary Beard Says Drive to Remove Cecil Rhodes Statue from Oxford University Is a "Dangerous Attempt to Erase the Past"', 22 December, available at: www.independent.co.uk/news/education/education-news/mary-beard-says-drive-to-remove-cecil-rhodes-statue-from-oxford-university-is-a-dangerous-attempt-to-a6783306.html

Kelley, Robin D.G. (2016) 'Black Study, Black Struggle', *Boston Review*, 24 October, available at: bostonreview.net/forum/robin-d-g-kelley-black-study-black-struggle

Little, V. (1990) 'A National Curriculum in History: A Very Contentious Issue', *British Journal of Educational Studies* 38(4): 319–34.

Littlejohn, R. (2014) 'The Way Patriotism Is Sneered at Makes You Ashamed to Be British!' , 14 April, available at: www.dailymail.co.uk/debate/article-2604789/RICHARD-LITTLEJOHN-Makes-ashamed-British.html

Mount, H. (2016) 'Finally! Oriel College Should Have Stood Up to Rhodes Must Fall Long Ago', 29 January, available at: www.telegraph.co.uk/education/

universityeducation/12129261/Finally-Oriel-College-should-have-stood-up-to-Rhodes-Must-Fall-long-ago.html

Our Aim (2015) 24 December, available at: https://rmfoxford.wordpress.com/about/

Pells, R. (2016) 'Oxford University Students "Told to Use Gender Neutral Pronoun Ze"', 21 December, available at: www.independent.co.uk/student/news/oxford-university-students-gender-neutral-pronouns-peter-tatchell-student-union-ze-xe-a7470196.html

Petre, J. (2017) 'They Kant Be Serious! PC Students Demand White Philosophers Including Plato and Descartes be Dropped from University Syllabus', 11 January, available at: www.dailymail.co.uk/news/article-4098332/They-Kant-PC-students-demand-white-philosophers-including-Plato-Descartes-dropped-university-syllabus.html

Roberts, G. (2016) 'Oxford's "Ze" – Whether Fact or Fiction – Is a Symptom of the Wider Student Bubble', 13 December, available at: www.telegraph.co.uk/education/2016/12/13/debate-around-oxford-ze-symptom-wider-student-bubble/

Trouillot, M.R. (2015) *Silencing the Past: Power and the Production of History.* Boston, MA: Beacon Press.

Weale, S. (2016) 'Michael Gove's Claims about History Teaching Are False, Says Research', 12 September, available at: www.theguardian.com/world/2016/sep/13/michael-goves-claims-about-history-teaching-are-false-says-research

Notes

All urls last accessed March 2018.

1. Ahmed, S. (2016) 'Feminism and Fragility', 26 January, available at: https://feministkilljoys.com/2016/01/26/feminism-and-fragility/

2. Pells, R. (2016) 'Oxford University Students "Told to Use Gender Neutral Pronoun Ze"', 21 December, available at: www.independent.co.uk/student/news/oxford-university-students-gender-neutral-pronouns-peter-tatchell-student-union-ze-xe-a7470196.html

3. Gregory-Brough, J. (2016) 'OUSU Statement: The Use of Gender Neutral Pronouns', 16 December, available at: https://ousu.org/news/article/6013/OUSU-Statement-The-Use-Of-Gender-Neutral-Pronouns/

4. Roberts, G. (2016) 'Oxford's "Ze" – Whether Fact or Fiction – Is a Symptom of the Wider Student Bubble', 13 December, available at: www.telegraph.co.uk/education/2016/12/13/debate-around-oxford-ze-symptom-wider-student-bubble

5. Petre, J. (2017) 'They Kant Be Serious! PC Students Demand White Philosophers Including Plato and Descartes be Dropped from University Syllabus', 11 January, available at: www.dailymail.co.uk/news/article-4098332/They-Kant-PC-students-demand-white-philosophers-including-Plato-Descartes-dropped-university-syllabus.html

6. Habib, A. (2016) 'Educational Priorities', 2 December, available at: https://soasunion.org/education/educationalpriorities/

7. Mount, H. (2016) 'Finally! Oriel College Should Have Stood Up to Rhodes Must Fall Long Ago', 29 January, available at: www.telegraph.co.uk/education/universityeducation/12129261/Finally-Oriel-College-should-have-stood-up-to-Rhodes-Must-Fall-long-ago.html

8. Jenne, A. (2015) 'Mary Beard Says Drive to Remove Cecil Rhodes Statue from Oxford University Is a "Dangerous Attempt to Erase the Past"', 22 December, available at: www.independent.co.uk/news/education/education-news/mary-beard-says-drive-to-remove-cecil-rhodes-statue-from-oxford-university-is-a-dangerous-attempt-to-a6783306.html

9. Grove, J. (2017) 'Must Rhodes Fall?', 16 February, available at: www.timeshighereducation.com/features/must-rhodes-fall

10. Our Aim (2015) 24 December, available at: https://rmfoxford.wordpress.com/about/

11. Dahlgreen, W. (2014) 'The British Empire Is "Something to be Proud of"', 26 July, available at: https://yougov.co.uk/news/2014/07/26/britain-proud-its-empire/

12. Trouillot, M.R. (2015) *Silencing the Past: Power and the Production of History*. Boston, MA: Beacon Press.

13. Little, V. (1990) 'A National Curriculum in History: A Very Contentious Issue', *British Journal of Educational Studies* 38(4): 319–34.

14. Baldwin, G. (1996) 'In the Heart or on the Margins: A Personal View of National Curriculum History and Issues of Identity', in R. Andrews (ed.) *Interpreting the New National Curriculum*. London: Middlesex University Press, p. 136.

15. Littlejohn, R. (2014) 'The Way Patriotism Is Sneered at Makes You Ashamed to be British!', 14 April, available at: www.dailymail.co.uk/debate/article-2604789/RICHARD-LITTLEJOHN-Makes-ashamed-British.html

16. Weale, S. (2016) 'Michael Gove's Claims about History Teaching Are False, Says Research', 12 September, available at: www.theguardian.com/world/2016/sep/13/michael-goves-claims-about-history-teaching-are-false-says-research

17. Bhambra, G.K. (2009) *Rethinking Modernity: Postcolonialism and the Sociological Imagination*. Basingstoke: Palgrave Macmillan.

18. Brentjes, S. and Morrison, R.G. (2010) 'The Sciences in Islamic Societies (750–1800)', *The New Cambridge History of Islam*. Cambridge: Cambridge University Press, pp. 564–639.

19. Al Jazeera English (2016) 'White Nationalist Richard Spencer Talks to Al Jazeera', video file, 9 December. Retrieved 22 April 2017 from www.youtube.com/watch?v=ni_6sISHnqQ

20. Gilroy, P. (1990) 'The End of Anti-racism', *Journal of Ethnic and Migration Studies* 17(1): 71–83.

21. Ibid. p. 71.

22. Ibid. p. 71.

23. Ibid. p. 72.

24. Ibid. p. 72.

25. Ibid. p. 74.

26. Kelley, R.D.G. (2016) 'Black Study, Black Struggle', *Boston Review*, 24 October, available at: bostonreview.net/forum/robin-d-g-kelley-black-study-black-struggle

3

Race and the Neoliberal University: Lessons From the Public University

John Holmwood

Higher education in the UK (more specifically, England)[1] and the United States is undergoing a process of rapid change, following the application of neoliberal public policy. In each country, these changes can be traced back to the 1980s, but they have accelerated since the financial crisis of 2008. The crisis gave rise to considerable amounts of government debt in order to 'bail out' banks and other financial institutions, entailing cutbacks to other programmes of public spending to balance the books and maintain a tax regime favourable to the wealthy and big business.

The financial crisis called into question neoliberal policies of deregulation from which it derived yet had the paradoxical consequence of reinforcing those policies and, indeed, of extending them into new areas. For example, government reforms to higher education in England since 2011 have involved the introduction of marketisation with full student fees for undergraduate courses in the arts, humanities and social sciences and the removal of all public funding.[2] The intention is that students should regard their education as an investment in human capital with an eye to its returns in the labour market. Continued support for higher cost STEM (science, technology, engineering and mathematics) subjects is justified only by their significance to the economy. At the same time research is directed towards having impact for specific 'users'.

There are similar developments in the US, despite higher education being highly disaggregated, varying by state and not forming a single system as it did in the UK prior to devolution in 2000 and the reforms to English higher education after 2011. Nonetheless, in a recent book, Newfield describes reductions in public funding and a dramatic rise in the student debt burden, research increasingly directed towards commercial interests through co-sponsorship involving cross-subsidies from teaching revenues (from the humanities and social sciences), narrowing of the curriculum, reductions in teaching support (despite higher fees) and a declining quality of learning.[3] In these respects, English and US higher education are converging.[4]

Higher education as a social right

In this chapter, I look at these changes and characterise them as involving a process of the 'privatisation' of higher education as does Newfield,[5] and a shift from it being a *social right* to it being a *personal responsibility* of individuals and their families.[6] These developments are not restricted to the US and England but I will concentrate there, since these are places where the neoliberal agenda for higher education has been pushed the furthest. It might seem odd to present the US as having shifted from education as a social right to a private responsibility since many commentators regard the US as a 'laggard' welfare regime and question the extent to which social rights have ever been recognised.[7] However, in the case of higher education, it has always been a 'leader' – for example, in terms of the early development of public universities and in terms of the proportion of the age cohort graduating from university, which well exceeded that in the UK and other European countries until recently.

In this respect, Newfield sees the expansion of public higher education in the US after the Second World War as reflecting an egalitarian tradition. That tradition, he acknowledges, is deeply racialised, something to which I will return. However, he regards the development of public higher education as part of a process of democratisation that would create full participation for all. He does not say very much about the racial implications of neoliberal privatisation except to imply that it is 'structurally racist',[8] as is evident from its effects, while projecting 'neutrality' (deriving from standard market ideology). In this respect, we confront a conundrum. The idea of higher education as a personal responsibility would seem to reinforce existing socioeconomic inequalities. However, it does so under the guise of seemingly impersonal processes of the market and achievement based on merit, rather than a consequence of ascribed characteristics of 'status'. In contrast, the public university, even where it is understood as the outcome of a process of democratisation, has frequently institutionalised differential treatment on the basis of race (and, of course, also on the basis of gender).

In this context, the call to 'decolonise' the university faces the paradox that the neoliberal university claims to be 'race-blind' – indeed, it is typically held to involve competitive processes that would dissolve any ascribed characteristics involving differential treatment. From this perspective, the idea of decolonising a neoliberal university is redundant because the impersonal processes of the market recognise only legitimate differences in the capacities of individuals. Discriminatory practices against groups run counter to market efficiencies, while actions, such as affirmative action, to address past injustices are perceived as themselves discriminatory and contradicting principles of meritocratic selection.

I have written elsewhere of the racialised nature of markets[9] and, it follows that this will be true of neoliberal policies applied in higher education. The 'neutrality' of neoliberal higher education, I suggest, is a mirage. However, in arguing for public higher education as a necessary instrument for the decolonisation of the university, there is a need to confront the impact of colonialism on the meanings of democracy and membership in the political community within which higher education is located. I begin with a discussion of the rise of public higher education before addressing the problems of neoliberal higher education and its racialised character.

The rise of public higher education in the US and UK

Historically most universities began as religious or private foundations. The publicly funded university is by no means the most typical of university forms and it is not even the most prestigious. For example, the United States has a history of private foundations alongside 'land grant' universities. The latter represent the first public universities, following the Morrill Act of 1862 that provided a federal endowment of land to establish state universities. But private Ivy League colleges and liberal arts colleges preceded them and continue to be among the most prestigious in the US. Many of those private colleges were formed from endowments from wealth derived from plantation slavery. The situation was not much different for early public universities. Indeed, the very term, 'land grant' indicates that they were part of a settler-colonial project involving the extension of the US border to the west and building up local infrastructure to exploit lands from which native Americans had been dispossessed.

Indeed, while the Morrill Act was initiated in the midst of the Civil War of 1861–65 and initially applied only within northern states of the union, northern institutions were also founded on de facto racialised exclusions, as well as dispossession of Native Americans.[10] While the Civil War is usually interpreted as fought over the issue of slavery, recent revisionist histories have come to understand it as one among a number of bloody struggles, including 'Indian wars', that took place through the nineteenth century to establish the nation.[11] Land grant universities were part of a nation-building project.

Many state universities founded under the land grant system were segregated institutions that denied entry to African American students; they were part of the 'Jim Crow' arrangements that subverted equality after initial Civil War reconstruction.[12] Separate institutions for black students were founded around the same time – frequently by religious bodies – and the provisions of the Morrill Act were not extended to black students until 1890, when states that operated segregation were required to provide separate public institutions for black students. Segregated public education in the US was not ended until *Brown versus Board of Education* (1954) and the Higher Education Act of 1965, which was implemented alongside other achievements of the civil rights movement, such as the Voting Rights Act of 1965 (itself dismantled in 2014).[13] It is precisely these developments which are regarded as extending social rights and moving towards the democratisation of higher education and which we might consider as a move towards the decolonisation of higher education, however incomplete.

Notwithstanding the greater pluralism of US higher education (deriving from its federal system of government, in contrast to the highly centralised government of the UK system until devolution in 2000), and the segregated nature of its institutions, there was general agreement that what had emerged in the post-Second World War period in both countries was a differentiated set of institutions with more-or-less ordered relations among them. The distinctive feature of this complex was the central role of the 'research university', involving increasing inter-connections between the university and the wider economy and society. At the same time, the expansion of student numbers and the importance of higher education in providing credentials on the job market also gave universities an important role in securing 'equal opportunities'. Universities previously associated with elite social reproduction, such as the universities of Oxford and Cambridge in Britain and the US 'Ivy League' colleges, sought to transfer that elite status into research activities, while also presenting themselves as providing access to superior employment opportunities in a purportedly meritocratic system of recruitment.

The 1963 Robbins reforms[14] in the UK, which were responsible for a significant expansion of public higher education, also had an explicit democratic underpinning. To be sure, there was an emphasis on the role that higher education had in securing economic growth and in providing a skilled and highly trained workforce. However, the report identified four aims, or public benefits, that warranted expansion of, and public investment in, public higher education. These were the public benefit of a skilled and educated workforce (para. 25), the public benefit of higher education in producing cultivated men and women (para. 26), the public benefit of securing the advancement of learning through the combination of teaching and research within institutions (para. 27), and the public benefit of providing a common culture and standards of citizenship (para. 28). The report commented that, 'the system as a whole must be judged deficient unless it provides adequately for all of them' (para. 29).[15] Finally, the report regarded it as axiomatic that free public higher education should be 'available for all those who are qualified by ability and attainment to pursue them and who wish to do so' (para. 31).

The system that the Robbins Report inaugurated in the UK abolished existing fees and introduced means-tested grants for subsistence.[16] It also recommended an expansion of student numbers to satisfy unmet demand. While there were reputational differences among institutions, the same courses at different universities were funded to a similar extent. While there was a degree of selection in the sense that access to courses at particular universities would be determined by prior examination performance and this, in turn, contributed to the reputation of the institution in question, the system was both meritocratic in orientation and equalising in its consequences. Indeed, the expansion of free, public higher education was believed at the time to mitigate the effects of a mixed system of public and private secondary education, potentially giving rise to the decline of the latter and with it the 'sponsored' form of mobility that, according to Turner,[17] stood in contrast to the US form of 'contest' mobility (albeit that Turner neglected to address the racialised nature of the 'contest').[18]

These consequences of public higher education were less pronounced in the US, partly because of the existence of private universities that served elites as a consequence of their high fees. However, those effects were mitigated to the extent that there was also robust public higher education which offered programmes of study that were both *cheap* (because of state funding) and had *high educational value*. It is this system that Newfield (2016) argues is being dismantled by the withdrawal of public funding from state institutions and its replacement by fees (which, in turn, are rising dramatically and well above inflation).

Race and higher education

The racialised character of UK universities was much less visible than that of the US. This was because empire served to 'externalise' race as an issue of the relation between the metropole and dominions, whereas racial structures in the US were necessarily 'internal' structures of domination and exclusion. For example, in the case of the UK, higher education institutions were exported to the dominions (typically, the Scottish model of higher education was introduced by Scots-descended civil servants) and served the consolidation of Empire, especially in white settler colonies such as Australia, New Zealand, Canada and South Africa. Domestic universities in the UK also served in the education of colonial administrators.[19] However, the wider context of the Robbins reforms was the gradual dismantling of the British Empire and the UK readying itself to turn its back on a political economy of Commonwealth as a consequence of taking up membership in the European Union (EU), itself a political system founded on amnesia about the colonial heritages of its member states.[20]

In this context, it is possible to see the Robbins reforms as, in part, a 'race-blind' project of modernisation. For example, despite discussing problems of access to higher education (especially for women) there is no discussion of ethnic minority disadvantage and no mention of race.[21] Yet, alongside the debate over higher education, there was at the same time an intense debate on ('coloured') immigration, including the vituperative speeches of Enoch Powell expressing his fears of domination by those who were 'immigrant descended'. This political mobilisation gave rise to citizenship acts which turned British citizens (citizens of the UK and its colonies, and citizens of the British Commonwealth) into immigrants, while retaining an 'ancestral' claim to a now restricted British citizenship for descendants of white settlers in the dominions.

As Shilliam[22] has argued, differential treatment of members of the political community of Empire was typical of the development of the social rights of the welfare state. Rights to insurance, labour protections, education and so on, for example, were not extended throughout Empire to all citizens. This was not straightforwardly the case with higher education. Notwithstanding that the distribution of educational rights and opportunities throughout the Empire was deeply unequal, *access to UK universities was equalised in formal terms*, at least for those students who sought places and were 'qualified by ability and attainment to pursue them'. In this context, it is significant that the first move towards the reintroduction of fees in the UK was in 1981 when fees were charged for 'overseas' students as part of the first wave of neoliberal policies.[23] Many of these students so designated were from Commonwealth countries, but also caught up in a process of dividing the social right to education were the children of those who had migrated to the UK and now had to demonstrate a period of prior residence (not primarily for the purpose of education) in order to qualify as 'home' students. At the same time, EU students were to be treated as 'home' students with their rights established through residence in any member state.

This is a critical point in the argument. I am suggesting that universities in the UK and US were embedded in social structures that derive from histories of colonialism and Empire (internal in the case of the US and external in the case of the UK). Empire in the case of the UK had largely been associated with a movement of people from the metropole to colonies and dominions, but by the 1960s this was beginning to be reversed and, increasingly, citizens of the colonies and dominions were exercising their right of movement to the metropole as British subjects. In the case of the US, the 1960s marked the high point of the civil rights movement and the demand for inclusion, including within the previously segregated arrangements of the welfare state.

Instead, rather than extend social rights in this way, neoliberal public policy began to remove social rights from everyone, mobilising hostility to non-white Americans. This is associated with the Republican Party 'Southern strategy' to detach white Southern votes from the Democratic Party. Ronald Reagan's Neshoba County Fair speech in 1980 (at the scene of a lynching of Mississippi freedom summer activists in 1964) articulated this strategy in the context of neoliberalism:

> I believe in states' rights. I believe in people doing as much as they can for themselves at the community level and at the private level. And I believe that we've distorted the balance of our government today by giving powers that were never intended in the Constitution to be given to that federal establishment.[24]

These words presaged an attack on social rights of citizenship and the pathologising of welfare dependency within neoliberalism, but they derived from a primary orientation to deny the same rights to non-white citizens as were afforded to white citizens. The 'war on poverty' shifts to a 'war on the poor' and the emphasis on responsibility extends to the sentencing of offenders, with a massive increase in incarceration and a disproportionate impact on African Americans.[25]

In the UK, writers such as Goodhart[26] suggest that the problem of maintaining social rights is that they depend on social solidarity and mutual recognition. According to him, social solidarity is easier to establish and maintain in ethnically homogeneous societies and is undermined by immigration, especially where that immigration is represented as comprising 'postcolonial others'. Goodhart regrets the impact of 'neo-liberal globalization' on the white working class, but fails to extend his concerns to the disadvantages of others. What is missing is an explanation of why an inclusive politics was not pursued and also a recognition that those represented as 'postcolonial others' were previously members of a wider British political community that Empire represented.

In short, social rights, in their development, were partial, but might have been universalised and extended to others previously excluded. To do so would have been to address the racialised exclusions that they contained. In the case of higher education, this would have been to 'decolonise' the university in terms both of access and curriculum (the latter would be likely both to follow greater access as well as facilitating it, as was the case with gender and the impact of feminism, for example). In this context, then, making higher education a matter of private responsibility rather than a social right is not neutral with regard to issues of race and ethnicity. It arises precisely in the context of a restriction of social rights *in order to limit their extension*. If the white working class is collateral damage in this process, it is clear that it is ethnic minorities who are perceived as 'undeserving'.

Neoliberal higher education

What precisely does neoliberal higher education bring into being? And how can we assess its claims to be a system based on merit and individual responsibility rather than group affiliation? The break-up of public higher education in England is in its early stages, but it mirrors developments in the US, suggesting the direction of travel. As Newfield indicates, the US system of higher education is highly stratified in terms of fees, with very high fees charged at private Ivy League colleges and lower fees at public universities, albeit that fees have risen dramatically over the last decade in all universities and have risen at a rate well above inflation and the real wages of lower socioeconomic groups (itself a racialised category). There has also been an increase in for-profit providers offering lower cost degree programmes to those from disadvantaged backgrounds, especially African Americans.[27] The latter programmes have been castigated by a Senate report for malpractice and poor value.[28]

Entry to high reputation colleges is selective, with some scholarships being generated from the high fees. However, as Newfield shows, scholarships increasingly require co-funding by the recipient so that, even with scholarship support, students are facing higher levels of debt than previously because scholarship support represents just a proportion of ever-increasing fees and the balance has to be met by loans or employment. In addition, the changes in US higher education are also matched at secondary level. Places in selective institutions are based on merit, as determined by high school scores and SAT tests. However, the disparities of funding evident in higher education are also reproduced in secondary schools. Quite apart from the growth of private schooling serving wealthier families, public schools are funded by property taxes with poorer communities having less funding available to their schools than more prosperous ones.[29] Of course, the decline in public funding for higher education also reflects a similar process. Those who anticipate high income can calculate that a loan repayment is preferable to future higher taxation.[30]

Proposals that these structural disadvantages be ameliorated are held to undermine the meritocratic achievement of those who themselves benefit from the absence of a level playing field. The paradox of neoliberal 'credentialism' is that it makes participation in higher education necessary for any job beyond those paying the minimum wage, while, at the same time, the increased stratification of higher education makes place of study as important as a degree as such. The neoliberal approach is to argue for stratified fees to reflect the differential value of degrees, but that, in turn, reinforces the advantage of higher status institutions which are more academically selective. In effect, the more stratified the system the more it approaches a form of 'sponsored' mobility while reproducing an ideology of merit-based selection. Private colleges are unaffected by the degradation of public higher education, the latter merely reinforces the value of their degrees as a 'positional' good.

The system of higher education in England does not yet approximate that of the US. The most important difference is that there is a cap on the fees that can be charged to 'home' students. This has meant that universities cluster around that higher fee and few charge the lower fee that the government calculated was the base-level cost of a degree programme. It is for this reason that it has encouraged the entry of for-profit providers and teaching-only institutions. However, the Browne Report,[31] on which the reforms were based, recommended that there should be no cap in order to encourage a wider range of fees and also that those institutions charging higher fees set up a scholarship system. Even if the current political situation makes that a difficult step for the government to take, it is one that is implicit in other proposals.

For example, its interest in limiting fees is partly associated with the cost of supporting a system of income-contingent loans, in a situation where a significant proportion will not earn sufficient over the 30-year period to pay off the full amount of the loan. However, at the same time it is gathering data to be able to predict which degree programmes will be associated with high incomes, and thus to be able to use that information to restrict fee rises, or, more likely, develop programme-specific loan systems which can be privatised and through which higher fees can be set.[32]

What is clear is that the government intends that the same courses at different institutions should not receive the same funding. It also intends that there should be increased differentiation among universities and that more selective universities should be able to charge higher fees. It is in this context that we can ask questions about the position of ethnic minority students within English higher education and their prospects in the neoliberal university.

Meritocracy works differently in a wider system that is oriented towards reducing inequalities in outcomes than it does in one where inequalities are increasing. It is correct that ethnic minority students have fared worse than white English students in higher education, both in terms of access and in terms of attainment once at university. The latter is significant because, although it is evident that there are class differences in access to universities (reflecting class inequalities in school examination scores), there are no class differences in attainment for students with similar entry scores. This is not the case for BME (Black and minority ethnic) students where they have worse degree attainment than white British students with similar entry scores. This is an indictment of the current system of higher education, but it is unlikely to be overcome in the neoliberal university. In the first place, in a higher education system that is widening the stratification among institutions BME students are more likely to be recruited to lower status institutions, as well as being more likely to be targeted by for-profit providers.

In addition, the charging of market-based fees to overseas students also alters the nature of who is recruited, with an increasing proportion of self-financed students from wealthy backgrounds and a decline in the proportion supported by scholarships. This is the context in which a shift has occurred from 'affirmative' action for previously disadvantaged groups (to mitigate past advantages associated with the whiteness of institutions) to an emphasis on 'diversity',[33] with the argument that this is more consistent with merit-based selection. Increasingly, the diversity of higher education is secured by the recruitment of overseas students from elite social backgrounds (i.e. those able to pay high fees), while domestic students from ethnic minorities remain disadvantaged.[34]

Conclusion

This chapter has addressed the shift from public higher education to a neoliberal model organised around personal responsibility. The former carries the traces of its history, including the history of colonialism that has shaped all British institutions, as well as those in the US. The call to decolonise the university is a call to extend and enact social justice in education. The alternative to public higher education is a market-based system operating on neoliberal principles. This purports to be race-blind, but insofar as racialised difference and inequality is a product of social structures of disadvantage, those structures will be reproduced in any arrangements that make change a matter of personal responsibility. Personal responsibility is the ideology that maintains the status quo, not the means of challenging it.

Bibliography

Alexander, Michelle (2010) *The New Jim Crow: Mass Incarceration in the Age of Colorblindness*. New York: The New Press.

Anderson, Robert (2016) 'University Fees in Historical Perspective', *History and Policy*, 8 February, available at: www.historyandpolicy.org/policy-papers/papers/university-fees-in-historical-perspective

Berrey, Ellen (2015) *The Enigma of Diversity: The Language of Race and the Limits of Racial Justice*. Chicago, IL: University of Chicago Press.

Bhambra, Gurminder K. (2016) 'Whither Europe? Postcolonial versus Neocolonial Cosmopolitanism', *Interventions: International Journal of Postcolonial Studies* 18(2): 187–202.

Bhambra, Gurminder K. and Holmwood, John (forthcoming June 2018) *Race and the Undeserving Poor: From Abolition to Brexit*. London: Agenda Publishing.

Browne Report (2010) 'Securing a Sustainable Future for Higher Education: An Independent Review of Higher Education Funding and Student Finance', 12 October, available at: www.gov.uk/government/publications/the-browne-report-higher-education-funding-and-student-finance

Collins, Randall (1979) *The Credential Society: An Historical Sociology of Education and Stratification*. New York: Academic Press.

Cottom, Tressie McMillan (2017) *Lower Ed: The Troubling Rise of For-profit Colleges in the New Economy*. New York: New Press.

Deegan, Mary Jo (1988) *Jane Addams and the Men of the Chicago School 1892–1918*. New Brunswick, NJ: Transaction Books.

Du Bois, W.E.B. (1935) *Black Reconstruction: An Essay toward a History of the Part which Black Folk Played in the Attempt to Reconstruct Democracy in America, 1860–1880*. Philadelphia: Albert Saifer Publisher.

Esping-Andersen, Gosta (1991) *The Three Worlds of Welfare Capitalism*. London: Polity.

Goodhart, David (2013) *The British Dream: Successes and Failures of Post-War Immigration*. London: Atlantic Books.

Hahn, Steven (2016) *A Nation without Borders: The United States and its World in an Age of Civil Wars*, New York: Viking.

Harkin Report (2012) *For-profit Higher Education: The Failure to Safeguard the Federal Investment and Ensure Student Success*. 30 July, Prepared by the Committee on Health, Education, Labor, and Pensions of the United States Senate, available at: www.gpo.gov/fdsys/pkg/CPRT-112SPRT74931/pdf/CPRT-112SPRT74931.pdf

Holmwood, John and Bhambra, Gurminder K. (2012) 'The Attack on Education as a Social Right', *South Atlantic Quarterly* 111(2): 392–401.

Lammy Review (2016) *An Independent Review into the Treatment of, and Outcomes for, Black, Asian and Minority Ethnic Individuals in the Criminal Justice System*, September, available at: www.gov.uk/government/uploads/system/uploads/attachment_data/file/643001/lammy-review-final-report.pdf

McGettigan, Andrew (2013) *The Great University Gamble: Money, Markets and the Future of Higher Education*. London: Pluto Press.

Meister, Bob (2011) 'Debt and Taxes: Can the Financial Industry Save Public Universities?', *Representations* 116(1): 128–55.

Nellis, Ashley (2016) *The Color of Justice: Racial and Ethnic Disparity in State Prisons*. The Sentencing Project, 14 June, available at: www.sentencingproject.org/publications/color-of-justice-racial-and-ethnic-disparity-in-state-prisons/

Newfield, Chris (2016) *The Great Mistake: How We Wrecked Public Universities and How We Can Fix Them*. Baltimore, MD: Johns Hopkins University Press.

NPR (2016) 'Why America's Schools Have a Money Problem', 18 April, available at: www.npr.org/2016/04/18/474256366/why-americas-schools-have-a-money-problem

Robbins Report (1963) *Higher Education: Report of the Committee appointed by the Prime Minister under the Chairmanship of Lord Robbins 1961–63.* Cmnd 2154, October, available at: www.educationengland.org.uk/documents/robbins/robbins1963.html

Shilliam, Robbie (forthcoming) *Colonial Genealogies of the Deserving Poor: From Abolition to Brexit.*

Steinmetz, George (2014) 'British Sociology in the Metropole and the Colonies, 1940s–1960s', in John Holmwood and John Scott (eds) *The Palgrave Handbook of Sociology in Britain.* London: Palgrave Macmillan.

Taylor-Gooby, Peter (2004) 'Is the Future American? Or, Can Left Politics Preserve European Welfare States from Erosion through Growing "Racial" Diversity?', *Journal of Social Policy* 34(4): 661–72.

Turner, Ralph H. (1960) 'Sponsored and Contest Mobility and the School System', *American Sociological Review* 25(6): 855–67.

Universities UK (2017) 'International Students Now Worth £25 billion to UK Economy – New Research', 6 March, available at: www.universitiesuk.ac.uk/news/Pages/International-students-now-worth-25-billion-to-UK-economy--new-research.aspx

Wilder, Craig Steven (2013) *Ebony and Ivy: Race, Slavery, and the Troubled History of America's Universities.* New York: Bloomsbury Press.

Notes

All urls last accessed 5 January 2018.

1. Since 2000, education has been a matter for devolved jurisdictions; however, policies enacted in England have significant consequences for the other jurisdictions of the UK and exert pressures to converge.

2. With the exception of that implied in underwriting the system of loans where repayment is contingent on income and outstanding debt is cancelled after 30 years, and the direct support of STEM subjects where teaching costs are higher as a consequence of equipment and laboratory costs. There was no such additional support for higher cost studio-based arts courses.

3. Newfield, Chris (2016) *The Great Mistake: How We Wrecked Public Universities and How We Can Fix Them.* Baltimore, MD: Johns Hopkins University Press.

4. See Anderson, Robert (2016) 'University Fees in Historical Perspective', *History and Policy*, 8 February, available at: www.historyandpolicy.org/policy-papers/papers/university-fees-in-historical-perspective

5. Newfield 2016 op. cit.

6. See, Holmwood, John and Bhambra, Gurminder K. (2012) 'The Attack on Education as a Social Right', *South Atlantic Quarterly* 111(2): 392–401.

7. For example, Esping-Andersen, Gosta (1991) *The Three Worlds of Welfare Capitalism.* London: Polity.

8. Newfield 2016 op. cit. p. 280.

9. Bhambra, Gurminder K. and Holmwood, John (2018) 'Colonialism, Postcolonialism and the Liberal Welfare State', *New Political Economy*.

10. See Wilder, Craig Steven (2013) *Ebony and Ivy: Race, Slavery, and the Troubled History of America's Universities*. New York: Bloomsbury Press.

11. See Hahn, Steven (2016) *A Nation without Borders: The United States and its World in an Age of Civil Wars*. New York: Viking.

12. Du Bois, W.E.B. (1935) *Black Reconstruction: An Essay toward a History of the Part which Black Folk Played in the Attempt to Reconstruct Democracy in America, 1860–1880*. Philadelphia: Albert Saifer Publisher.

13. The Higher Education Act of 1965 designated 'historically black colleges', a term which was something of a misnomer, given that 'black' colleges did not exclude white students, while 'historically white colleges' in the Southern states did exclude black students. Of course, the very idea of a 'land grant' assigned to the different states in the US follows an appropriation of land and dispossession of Native Americans as part of settlement and subsequent westward expansion. Higher education was also gendered, with women frequently excluded, and associated with the development of education outside the university, as in the 'settlement house' movement in the US and the UK. See Deegan, Mary Jo (1988) *Jane Addams and the Men of the Chicago School 1892–1918*. New Brunswick, NJ: Transaction Books.

14. Robbins Report (1963) *Higher Education: Report of the Committee Appointed by the Prime Minister under the Chairmanship of Lord Robbins 1961–63*. Cmnd 2154, October, available at: www.educationengland.org.uk/documents/robbins/robbins1963.html

15. The Robbins Report saw these aims as interconnected, rather than as discrete:

   > while emphasizing that there is no betrayal of values when institutions of higher education teach what will be of some practical use, we must postulate that what is taught should be taught in such a way as to promote the general powers of the mind. The aim should be to produce not mere specialists but rather cultivated men and women. And it is the distinguishing characteristic of a healthy higher education that, even where it is concerned with practical techniques, it imparts them on a plane of generality that makes possible their application to many problems – to find the one in the many, the general characteristic in the collection of particulars. It is this that the world of affairs demands of the world of learning. And it is this, and not conformity with traditional categories, that furnishes the criterion of what institutions of higher education may properly teach. (1963: para. 26)

16. Anderson, Robert (2016) 'University Fees in Historical Perspective', *History and Policy*, 8 February, available at: www.historyandpolicy.org/policy-papers/papers/university-fees-in-historical-perspective

17. Turner, Ralph H. (1960) 'Sponsored and Contest Mobility and the School System', *American Sociological Review* 25(6): 855–67.

18. An early commentator on the phenomenon of 'credentialism' in the US, Collins, saw 'race' as integral to its dynamics; Collins, Randall (1979) *The*

Credential Society: An Historical Sociology of Education and Stratification.
New York: Academic Press.

19. Steinmetz, George (2014) 'British Sociology in the Metropole and the Colonies, 1940s–1960s', in John Holmwood and John Scott (eds) *The Palgrave Handbook of Sociology in Britain.* London: Palgrave Macmillan.

20. Bhambra, Gurminder K. (2016) 'Whither Europe? Postcolonial versus Neocolonial Cosmopolitanism', *Interventions: International Journal of Postcolonial Studies* 18(2): 187–202.

21. With the exception of one paragraph on academic freedom which refers to possible discriminatory treatment on grounds of race, sex, religion and politics (1963: para. 705).

22. Shilliam, Robbie (forthcoming 2018) *Race and the Undeserving Poor: From Abolition to Brexit.* London: Agenda Publishing.

23. These students now generate significant revenue for UK universities. The latest report by Universities UK suggests that international students paid an estimated £4.8 billion in tuition fees, accounting for 14 percent of total university income. Some 88 percent of that fee income was paid by students from outside the EU. See Universities UK (2017) 'International Students Now Worth £25 billion to UK Economy – New Research', 6 March, available at: www.universitiesuk.ac.uk/news/Pages/International-students-now-worth-25-billion-to-UK-economy---new-research.aspx

24. The speech was given on Sunday 3 August 1980. It is not listed in the Reagan Library Collection. However, a transcript from a recording was published by the *Neshoba Democrat* newspaper, available at: http://neshobademocrat.com/Content/NEWS/News/Article/Transcript-of-Ronald-Reagan-s-1980-Neshoba-County-Fair-speech/2/297/15599

25. Alexander, Michelle (2010) *The New Jim Crow: Mass Incarceration in the Age of Colorblindness.* New York: The New Press. The idea that there were more African American men in prison than in college has been discredited, but the overall figures for incarceration remain staggering. Racial disparities in sentencing are greater in north-eastern states than in southern states (ranging from a ratio of 12:1 to 5:1) and are associated with higher incarceration rates overall in southern states). See Nellis, Ashley (2016) *The Color of Justice: Racial and Ethnic Disparity in State Prisons.* The Sentencing Project, 14 June, available at: www.sentencingproject.org/publications/color-of-justice-racial-and-ethnic-disparity-in-state-prisons/. The incarceration rate in England and Wales has also risen over the same period and is the highest in Western Europe, with similar racial and ethnic disparities as the US. Lammy Review (2016) *An Independent Review into the Treatment of, and Outcomes for, Black, Asian and Minority Ethnic Individuals in the Criminal Justice System.* September, available at: www.gov.uk/government/uploads/system/uploads/attachment_data/file/643001/lammy-review-final-report.pdf

26. Goodhart, David (2013) *The British Dream: Successes and Failures of Post-War Immigration.* London: Atlantic Books; for discussion, see Taylor-Gooby, Peter (2004) 'Is the Future American? Or, Can Left Politics Preserve European Welfare States from Erosion through Growing "Racial" Diversity?', *Journal of Social Policy* 34(4): 661–72.

27. Cottom, Tressie McMillan (2017) *Lower Ed: The Troubling Rise of For-profit Colleges in the New Economy.* New York: New Press.
28. Harkin Report (2012) *For Profit Higher Education: The Failure to Safeguard the Federal Investment and Ensure Student Success.* 30 July. Prepared by the Committee on Health, Education, Labor, and Pensions of the United States Senate, available at: www.gpo.gov/fdsys/pkg/CPRT-112SPRT74931/pdf/CPRT-112SPRT74931.pdf
29. NPR (2016) 'Why America's Schools Have a Money Problem', 18 April, available at: www.npr.org/2016/04/18/474256366/why-americas-schools-have-a-money-problem
30. See Meister, Bob (2011) 'Debt and Taxes: Can the Financial Industry Save Public Universities?', *Representations* 116(1): 128–55.
31. Browne Report (2010) *Securing a Sustainable Future for Higher Education: An Independent Review of Higher Education Funding and Student Finance.* 12 October, available at: www.gov.uk/government/publications/the-browne-report-higher-education-funding-and-student-finance
32. McGettigan, Andrew (2013) *The Great University Gamble: Money, Markets and the Future of Higher Education.* London: Pluto Press.
33. Berrey, Ellen (2015) *The Enigma of Diversity: The Language of Race and the Limits of Racial Justice.* Chicago, IL: University of Chicago Press.
34. This is manifested in the debate at Cornell University on the definition of 'black' where the definition that includes students from outside the US masks the institution's failure to address the failure to recruit from local, racialised minorities. See Jaschik, Scott (2017) 'Who Counts as a Black Student', *Inside Higher Education,* 9 October, available at: www.insidehighered.com/admissions/article/2017/10/09/cornell-students-revive-debate-whom-colleges-should-count-black

4

Black/Academia

Robbie Shilliam

Campaigns to 'decolonise' the British academy are under attack and critics have provided a set of defences for academic tradition. Universities, they argue, should be sites of free thought and free speech, and the so-called 'right of students not to be offended' is detrimental to the ethos of these sites.[1] Taking offence at a white curriculum and a white institutional space is considered a form of 'cultural policing' driven by a desire to 'censor history, literature, politics and culture'. Not only a form of censorship, some point towards an almost fascistic urge by 'young minds' to 'wipe away the past' in order to avoid having to grapple with intellectually difficult questions.[2]

A key line of critique pertains to the introduction into higher learning of identity politics, wherein intellectual positions are supposed to represent and map onto ascriptive attributes, such as race. The harm of this, say some, is that identity policing begins to matter more than the free flow of political ideas.[3] Furthermore, the 'narcissism' bred by identity politics is considered degrading to intellectual inquiry by regarding all knowledge as equally competent, that is, vulgar.[4] If every viewpoint were to be included by virtue of it representing a discrete identity, of what would 'higher' learning consist and how would knowledge claims be adjudicated? Thus, at stake, critics argue, is a defence of higher learning as an unqualified space of critique, curiosity and discernment against a contaminating wave of identity politics, narcissism and vulgarism.

None of these concerns are particularly original to our present time. Take, for instance, John Searle bemoaning, in 1993, the intrusion of Black, First Nations, Feminist and Latino/a struggles into the American academy. Searle sought to defend a 'traditional canon' against what he deemed to be a 'multicultural' challenge that politicised the attributes of canonical thinkers and the contexts in which they wrote.[5] Or take philosopher Michael Oakeshott, commenting back in 1950 upon the prospective instrumentalisation of the British higher education sector.[6]

Oakeshott argued that there should be no 'ulterior purpose' to the scholarly conversation which, in the 'gift of an interval' from practical life, proceeded at its own conversational pace and for its own purposes.[7]

These various defences of the 'traditional' academy moot a higher education that existed *before* the contamination of identity, race, politicisation. And regardless of the implicit or explicit idealisation of such a space of higher learning, all critiques logically posit a temporal sensibility to their critique: the problem has been introduced into the space. Given this sensibility, I wonder where critics would place Britain's most accomplished public intellectual of the twentieth century, Professor Stuart Hall?

A Jamaican youth, Hall entered Oxford in 1951 (just after Oakeshott published his think piece) to read an undergraduate degree in English at Merton College. Hall's reflections of Oxford draw together a 'traditional' higher education experience with a vivid community of Black and colonial intellectuals discussing empire and its aftermath:

> Some of my critics believe that I wasn't concerned about the Caribbean, or about Black culture and politics, until the 1970s. It's true, perhaps, that my publications weren't centrally preoccupied with Caribbean or Black matters. But they nonetheless formed an indispensable, active seam in my intellectual inquiries, from the 1950s up to the present.[8]

However, despite a quotidian politeness at Oxford, Hall recollects that 'I was conscious all the time that I was very, very *different* because of my race and colour. And in the discourses of Englishness, race and colour remained unspeakable silences.'[9] Hall was debating an expansive Caribbean and Black politics; but it was Oxford, institutionally, that refined him to an identity. Oxford would not allow Hall to take an Oakeshott-style 'interval' from his race.

It is certainly specious to place Hall *against* the 'traditions' of the academy; but it is also disingenuous to place Hall *within* these traditions along the lines laid out by Oakeshott, Searle and, indeed, contemporary critics of efforts to decolonise the academy. Such critics – historical and contemporary – assume a space of higher learning that is constitutively discerning, critical and curious. It is a space that must be consistently defended from outside forces that would compromise, vulgarise and partialise the higher pursuit of knowledge. So, was Hall, a (self-)avowedly

Black, Caribbean intellectual, a comforting-inside or threatening-outside presence?

Hall's contemporaries shared similar experiences. Take, for instance, African and Caribbean informants for Sheila Kitzinger's 1950s study of students attending Oxbridge institutions.[10] Her interlocutors spoke of the difficulties in constructing friendships with white peers who took the activity to be a philanthropical gesture on their part: 'They speak to you very nicely, but all the time they seem to be thinking, "I wonder whether he can read?"'[11] Informants reported that the relationship would break down when the white partner became 'embarrassed by the Negro's self-consciousness'.[12]

In the 1950s, this shock of Black intellectual competency had political salience. In fact, by this point in time Black university students had become a key concern for British race relations.[13] At the time that Hall was attending Oxford, Michael Banton, who would go on to be a formative influence in the 'sociology of race' tradition, looked towards the racist reception of Black Commonwealth citizens with apprehension. 'The slights, rebuffs and discrimination – real and imagined – which they experience may afterwards cause a reaction of resentment and may lead to a rejection of British cultural values and to political nationalism.'[14] He further observed that 'leaders of public opinion' now realised that the racist treatment of students in Britain could be detrimental to the integrity of the Commonwealth and that such students had to be re-imagined as 'leaders of the rising coloured nations whose friendship is important to the imperial country'.[15]

Alternatively, Philip Garigue documented how the same movement could be interpreted as a process of critical political clarification for Black students. Garigue framed his study of the West African Student's Union in terms of the shift among participating students from a confrontation with the British 'colour bar' to a formulation of anti-colonial sentiments.[16] By addressing the 'stresses and strains that living in Britain produced', the union, in Garigue's estimation, inculcated its members with a 'new consciousness of their own value and capacity for achievement'.[17] Eyo Ndem, a Nigerian scholar who had been a representative at the 1945 Pan-African Congress in Manchester, similarly noted that the success of Black university students was important to Black residents in Britain insofar as this success challenged the general ascription of Black mental 'inferiority'.[18]

Paradoxically, by the end of the 1950s Banton was moving from an analysis of race and the diminution of empire to one defined by an abstract sociological category – the 'stranger'. By considering the 'coloured man' as 'a stranger to British ways', Banton reduced the question of race to one of rule recognition: the stranger is 'not only uncertain of the [societal] norms: he cannot read the signs'.[19] Banton was well aware that Black students were mostly British citizens under the British Nationality Act (1948). But Banton's category shift seems to entirely surrender to the racist standpoint of the white British population on their fellow citizens. Much race relations scholarship in the 1960s accepted Banton's new categorisation.[20]

It was, of course, hardly possible for a Black university student to be a stranger to British ways considering the copious amounts of colonial indoctrination that had accompanied their prior education. Indeed, Hall studied in the halls of Oxford as, in his terms, a *familiar* stranger. There is an avowed self-reflexivity here, one that exceeds the identity reductions of much white scholarship at the time. In the halls of Oxford, Hall proceeded regardless to reason with fellow colonial intellectuals on the 'values of co-operation and common ideals' torturously being negotiated at the time towards a West Indian federation.[21] This, with all the embarrassing accoutrements of 'Negro self-consciousness'.

I wonder, who exactly was producing the problem of identity politics in this era? Is it fair to depict anti-colonial politics as identity politics? Is it adequate to conceive of the space of higher education as anything less than colonially and racially inflected? And is it any wonder that Black intellectuals increasingly pursued their work outside of and besides the halls of British academia?

In 1963 Jim Rose, at the invitation of Philip Mason, director of the Institute of Race Relations (IRR), initiated a Survey of Race Relations, which eventuated in a landmark publication, *Colour and Citizenship*. Banton had provided the first article for the institute's journal, which made the case for the utility of a sociological approach to race relations.[22] But by the early 1970s the field had become politicised with the influence of civil rights, Black Power and liberation struggle. Ambalavaner Sivanandan led a 'palace coup' at the IRR which eventuated in the revamping of the institute's journal into an explicitly anti-imperial digest, *Race & Class*. The new journal never enjoyed a strictly academic home.

Hall joined the Open University in 1979, an institution that focused upon distance learning for 'non-traditional' students. The successful radicalisation of 'cultural studies' by Stuart Hall during this era is the exception that proves the rule that it was the academy rather than the Black intellectual that had a problem with identity. While Hall's project situated race and the Black presence within Britain's postcolonial malaise, the field of avowedly Black Cultural Studies gestated mainly in North America (with several Black British academics migrating to carve out careers). Consider, also, the career trajectory of Beverley Bryan, a former Black Panther and founding member of the Brixton Black Women's Group who, after receiving a PhD from the University of London, made an academic career only by re-locating to the University of the West Indies.

An academic tradition of Black thought, not on narcissism and identity, but on racism, citizenship and empire (or, as it was to be known in the United States, Black Studies) never galvanised in Britain. This is the case even excepting the longevity of the academic careers of Gus John, Suzanne Scafe, Harry Goulbourne, Malcolm Cumberbatch and others.[23] Some Black scholars also walked the line between community activism and university teaching. Take, for instance, Devon Thomas, employed by Goldsmith College's Sociology and Anthropology department in 1975 working especially in the Community Studies section and, six years later, a member of the Brixton Defence Campaign assembled after the 1981 uprisings.

Another breakaway group from the IRR, comprising Darcus Howe, Farrukh Dhondy and Linton Kwesi Johnson, published *Race Today*. The journal's tagline, 'voice of the Black Community in Britain', signalled the liminal position, vis-à-vis the academy, of mainly Black and Asian scholars who dared to critically confront the living legacies of the British Empire. Where such an intellectual tradition – or traditions – firmly coalesced was indeed outside of academia proper, in community-based institutions and initiatives. There, Black history and Black education was galvanised in the 1970s autonomously and alongside the work of Hall et al.[24] Some from those early days still write, teach and organise in a community setting, such as Cecil Gutzmore who, with Jackie Lewis, holds weekly education sessions in Brixton under the auspices of the Pan-African Society Community Forum. Additionally, Len Garrison's work in Black community education led to the opening of the Black Cultural Archives in 1981, which now enjoys its own building and exhibition space in Windrush Square.

Indeed, the work of Black intellectuals has never been ephemeral but often aimed at building institutional capacities in fora that lie beside the academy. John LaRose and Jessica Huntley (a member of the Black Parents movement) became co-directors of the International Book Fairs of Radical Black and Third World Books, which ran from 1982 to 1995. New Beacon Books and Bogle-L'Ouverture Publications – as well as more recent fora such as Dr Lez Henry's Nu-Beyond – testify to the vitality of extra-academic Black publishing. Bogle-L'Ouverture provided readers with the commanding thoughts of Walter Rodney as he 'grounded' with his brethren and sistren in the dungles of Kingston, Jamaica rather than inside the gates of the Mona Campus of the University of the West Indies (UWI). Previously, the campus had been part of the collegiate system of the University of London and its quotidian acronym was not UWI but UC (University College). Rastafari preferred the term 'U Blind'.

Meanwhile, in Britain, countless reasoning circles of Rastafari – in political spaces such as the United Black People's Improvement Organization (UBPIO) – sharpened analyses of racism, colonialism and Black redemption. Winston Trew was a member of Fasimbas, an early Black Power congregation operating in the early 1970s, around the same time as the UBPIO. Trew, with others, was politically targeted by police, abused and falsely charged. In the book that details – and seeks to make intellectual sense of – the 'Oval 4' case, Trew strongly makes the argument that they were 'Black for a cause, not just because'.[25] Most Black intellectual work has not been primarily concerned with what we would nowadays call 'identity politics'. Such work could not afford to be vulgar or narcissistic as the stakes at play were only too real.

Compare to academia. In the same year that Jim Rose embarked on the national survey of race relations, the Robbins Report announced the expansion of higher education in an age that he considered had set for itself the ideal of 'equality of opportunity'. Yet despite Lord Robbins' 'natural egalitarianism',[26] his 1963 report was silent upon the challenges posed to these principles by the structural racism of British society which, as I have demonstrated, were also inflected within the academy.[27] Nonetheless, racist events of national significance historically book-ended the report. One year prior, the Commonwealth Immigration Act recused the rights of Commonwealth citizens to move unimpeded across the British realms. And one year after, the infamous Smethwick election in Birmingham was fought by the (winning) conservative candidate on the platform: 'If you want a nigger for a neighbour vote Liberal or Labour'.

There are many careful critiques of the decolonising project in academia.[28] I myself am a member and a critic. The project requires far more detailed and nuanced analyses of legacies, contexts, mechanisms and effects of the racialisation of knowledge. I might even venture to say that, occasionally, students can voice their concerns and felt injustice in ways that seem rhetorically powerful yet analytically weak. But I wonder if student politics of all shades has ever been so dissimilar. At least they are acting in good faith.

The greater irony is that criticism of the decolonising project has gained more traction than the project itself. There is, then, something of a far more heinous nature going on. I would suggest that some of the political class look upon the changes to Britain's (and the West's) population pyramid with trepidation. They see the base of the pyramid growing relentlessly blacker, browner, poorer. They seek to preserve the whiteness of elite cultural reproduction in sites that are currently most detached from the pyramid's base. Theirs is a melancholic, reactive mood to an inevitability born of empire, namely, that the fantasy of a pristine West could not hold for too long. *That* is the identity politics that we should be critically addressing.

Consider the following. All ethnic groups, as listed in the UK census, are over-represented in university student populations vis-à-vis their percentage of the general UK population. All, except white. Black students of continental African heritage have been one of the fastest growing ethnic groups entering university and are the largest ethnic minority of the UK student population. But Black students in general are recruited into less 'prestigious' institutions at percentages higher than any other ethnicity; their experience of higher education is significantly more negative than any other ethnicity; and their attainments are significantly lower than any other ethnicity.[29]

Some have explained away these disparities by presuming that Black students arrive at the gates of university with pronounced social and cultural deficits garnered from their familial and community upbringings – that is, their blackness. I would direct their assumptions back to the image of Stuart Hall studying at Oxford. In fact, all the evidence so far points to the fact that these racialised differentials are in the main produced *within* the British academy and cannot be accounted for in terms of deficits that Black students bring with them to the gates of higher learning.[30]

The Black Parents movement, initiated in 1975 attests to the relentless and under-acknowledged work and intellect of Black women in struggles against the educational maltreatment of their children. It was only in

1985 that the Swann Report finally refuted eugenicist explanations for the under-attainment of Black students in British secondary education. Yet higher education in Britain has never had a Swann Report. Why is it so hard to consider, then, that the traditional academy might still breed identity politics, narcissism and vulgarism at the same time as it promotes critique, curiosity and discernment. Is this a paradox? Not if we understand the differentiation to be racialised.

Those non-white people who have played the identity politics game with all due seriousness are not in academia. They have, of course, already been invited into politics, business and the civic sector. They want to hold power, not books. Most of us involved in projects that seek to decolonise the academy are not interested in identity politics, nor its narcissism or vulgarity. All of us value the decolonising project for its potential to deepen academic rigour and pursue intellectual challenge. Some of us connect the project to an ethics of epistemic justice. That is, we seek to confront and repair the racialised divisions of intellectual labour imposed by colonial rule in terms of who can think adequately for whom. Some of us even conceive of the project as an interconnected contribution to global justice, the key battles of which are fought in far harsher environments than the academy.

In any case, our concerns are profound, not narcissistic or vulgar. Few of us are eugenicist statisticians who wish to see more 'black' everywhere. On the contrary: *that* is the optical obsession of those who seek to defer an engagement with colonial injustice by labelling it 'identity politics'. Yet it is their identity which is at stake, not ours. Our knowledge cultivation has continued, despite and besides the racism of the academy.

Bibliography

Andrews, Kehinde (2013) *Resisting Racism: Race, Inequality, and the Black Supplementary School Movement.* London: Trentham Books.

Anthony, Andrew (2016) 'Is Free Speech in British Universities under Threat?', *The Guardian*, 24 January, available at: www.theguardian.com/world/2016/jan/24/safe-spaces-universities-no-platform-free-speech-rhodes

Banton, Michael (1953) 'The Economic and Social Position of Negro Immigrants in Britain', *Sociological Review* 1(2): 43–62.

—— (1959a) *White and Coloured: The Behaviour of British People Towards Coloured Immigrants.* London: Jonathan Cape.

—— (1959b) 'Sociology and Race Relations', *Race* 1(1): 3–14.

D'Ancona, Matthew (2016) 'Must Rhodes Fall?', *New York Times*, 28 January, available at: www.nytimes.com/2016/01/29/opinion/must-rhodes-fall.html?_r=1

Drake, St. Clear (1955) 'The "Colour Problem" in Britain: A Study in Social Definitions', *Sociological Review* 3(2): 197–217.

Garigue, Philip (1953) 'The West African Students' Union: A Study in Culture Contact', *Africa: Journal of the International African Institute* 23(1): 55–69.

Hall, Stuart (2017) *Familiar Stranger: A Life Between Two Islands*, edited by Bill Schwarz. Durham, NC: Duke University Press.

John, Gus (2014) 'The RSA Supplementary Schools Investigation', Gus John (blog), available at: www.gusjohn.com/2014/11/the-rsa-supplementary-schools-investigation/

Kitzinger, Sheila (1960) 'Conditional Philanthropy towards Colored Students in Britain', *Phylon* 21(2): 167–72.

Malik, Kenan (2017) 'Are SOAS Students Right to "Decolonize" Their Minds from Western Philosophers?', *The Guardian*, 19 February, available at: www.theguardian.com/education/2017/feb/19/soas-philosopy-decolonize-our-minds-enlightenment-white-european-kenan-malik

Morley, Louise (1997) 'Change and Equity in Higher Education', *British Journal of Sociology of Education* 18(2): 231–42.

Ndem, Eyo B. (1957) 'The Status of Colored People in Britain', *Phylon* 18(1): 82–87.

Oakeshott, Michael (2004) 'The Idea of a University', *Academic Questions* 17(1): 23–30.

O'Brien, Denis Patrick (1988) *Lionel Robbins*. Basingstoke: Macmillan.

Richmond, Anthony H. (1955) 'The Significance of a Multi-racial Commonwealth', *Phylon* 16(4): 380–86.

Searle, John R. (1993) 'Is There a Crisis in American Higher Education?', *Bulletin of the American Academy of Arts and Sciences* 46(4): 24–47.

Shilliam, Robbie (2016a) 'Austere Curricula: Multicultural Education and Black Students', in Stefan Jonsson and Julia Willén (eds) *Austere Histories in European Societies: Social Exclusion and the Contest of Colonial Memories*. London: Routledge.

—— (2016b) 'Black Academia 1.2', Robbie Shilliam (blog), 10 July, available at: https://robbieshilliam.wordpress.com/2016/07/10/black-academia-1-2/

Trew, Winston N. (2010) *Black for a Cause … Not Just Because …* Derbyshire: Derwent Press.

Tuck, Eve and K. Wayne Yang (2012) 'Decolonization Is Not a Metaphor', *Decolonization: Indigeneity, Education & Society* 1(1), available at: decolonization.org/index.php/des/article/download/18630/15554

Vernon, Patrick (2016) 'Where Are All the Black Historians? Patrick Vernon – Social Commentator and Political Activist', Patrick Vernon (blog), available at: https://patrickvernon.org.uk/where-are-all-the-black-historians/

Waters, Chris (1997) '"Dark Strangers" in Our Midst: Discourses of Race and Nation in Britain, 1947–1963', *Journal of British Studies* 36(2): 207–38.

Williams, Joanna (2017) 'The "Decolonize the Curriculum" Movement Re-racialises Knowledge', Open Democracy, 1 March, available at: www.opendemocracy.net/wfd/joanna-williams/decolonise-curriculum-movement-re-racialises-knowledge

Notes

All urls last checked January 2018.

1. Anthony, Andrew (2016) 'Is Free Speech in British Universities under Threat?', *The Guardian*, 24 January, available at: www.theguardian.com/world/2016/jan/24/safe-spaces-universities-no-platform-free-speech-rhodes

2. D'Ancona, Matthew (2016) 'Must Rhodes Fall?', *New York Times*, 28 January, available at: www.nytimes.com/2016/01/29/opinion/must-rhodes-fall.html?_r=1

3. Malik, Kenan (2017) 'Are SOAS Students Right to "Decolonize" Their Minds from Western Philosophers?' *The Guardian*, 19 February, available at: www.theguardian.com/education/2017/feb/19/soas-philosopy-decolonize-our-minds-enlightenment-white-european-kenan-malik

4. Williams, Joanna (2017) 'The "Decolonize the Curriculum" Movement Re-racialises Knowledge', Open Democracy, 1 March, available at: www.opendemocracy.net/wfd/joanna-williams/decolonise-curriculum-movement-re-racialises-knowledge

5. Searle, John R. (1993) 'Is There a Crisis in American Higher Education?', *Bulletin of the American Academy of Arts and Sciences* 46(4): 24–47.

6. Oakeshott, Michael (2004) 'The Idea of a University', *Academic Questions* 17(1): 23–30, at pp. 29–30.

7. Oakeshott 2004 op. cit. pp. 29–30.

8. Hall, Stuart (2017) *Familiar Stranger: A Life Between Two Islands*, edited by Bill Schwarz. Durham, NC: Duke University Press, p. 169.

9. Ibid. p. 158.

10. Kitzinger, Sheila (1960) 'Conditional Philanthropy towards Colored Students in Britain', *Phylon* 21(2): 167–72.

11. Ibid. p. 170.

12. Ibid. p. 169.

13. Drake, St. Clear (1955) 'The "Colour Problem" in Britain: A Study in Social Definitions', *Sociological Review* 3 (2): 197–217, at pp. 207–8.

14. Banton, Michael (1953) 'The Economic and Social Position of Negro Immigrants in Britain', *Sociological Review* 1(2): 43–62, at p. 59.

15. Ibid. p. 57; Richmond, Anthony H. (1955) 'The Significance of a Multiracial Commonwealth', *Phylon* 16(4): 380–86.

16. Garigue, Philip (1953) 'The West African Students' Union: A Study in Culture Contact', *Africa: Journal of the International African Institute* 23(1): 55–69.

17. Ibid. p. 69.

18. Ndem, Eyo B. (1957) 'The Status of Colored People in Britain', *Phylon* 18(1): 82–87, at pp. 86–87.

19. Banton, Michael (1959a) *White and Coloured: The Behaviour of British People Towards Coloured Immigrants*. London: Jonathan Cape, p. 97.

20. Waters, Chris (1997) '"Dark Strangers" in Our Midst: Discourses of Race and Nation in Britain, 1947–1963', *Journal of British Studies* 36(2): 207–38.

21. Hall 2017 op. cit. pp. 158–69.

22. Banton, Michael (1959b) 'Sociology and Race Relations', *Race* 1(1): 3–14.

23. It is in this historical context that we should note the importance of the Black Studies programme currently being set up at Birmingham City University.

24. See John, Gus (2014) 'The RSA Supplementary Schools Investigation', Gus John (blog), available at: www.gusjohn.com/2014/11/the-rsa-supplementary-schools-investigation/; Andrews, Kehinde (2013) *Resisting Racism: Race, Inequality, and the Black Supplementary School Movement.* London: Trentham Books; Vernon, Patrick (2016) 'Where Are All the Black Historians? Patrick Vernon – Social Commentator and Political Activist', Patrick Vernon (blog), available at: https://patrickvernon.org.uk/where-are-all-the-black-historians/

25. Trew, Winston N. (2010) *Black for a Cause ... Not Just Because ...* Derbyshire: Derwent Press.

26. O'Brien, Denis Patrick (1988) *Lionel Robbins.* Basingstoke: Macmillan, p. 120.

27. Morley, Louise (1997) 'Change and Equity in Higher Education', *British Journal of Sociology of Education* 18(2): 231–42, at p. 237.

28. See, for example, Tuck, Eve and K. Wayne Yang (2012) 'Decolonization Is Not a Metaphor', *Decolonization: Indigeneity, Education & Society* 1(1), available at: decolonization.org/index.php/des/article/download/18630/15554

29. See Shilliam, Robbie (2016b) 'Black Academia 1.2', Robbie Shilliam (blog), 10 July, available at: https://robbieshilliam.wordpress.com/2016/07/10/black-academia-1-2/

30. Shilliam, Robbie (2016a) 'Austere Curricula: Multicultural Education and Black Students', in Stefan Jonsson and Julia Willén (eds) *Austere Histories in European Societies: Social Exclusion and the Contest of Colonial Memories.* London: Routledge.

5

Decolonising Philosophy

Nelson Maldonado-Torres, Rafael Vizcaíno,
Jasmine Wallace and Jeong Eun Annabel We

The persistence of the small number of philosophers and theorists of colour in the academy, both inside and outside philosophy departments, who critically engage questions of coloniality, inequalities, decolonisation and liberation, has contributed to keep the question of the decolonisation of philosophy relevant. Some of them have taken the lead in the creation of new institutional spaces and organisms, including programmes to train students of colour in philosophy, groups in large professional associations, book series and scholarly journals and even new organisations such as Philosophy Born of Struggle or the Caribbean Philosophical Association, to name only two of the most visible. Philosophers of colour in the academy also tend to engage in various forms of teaching and mentoring that prepare new generations of students in expanding the horizons of academic philosophy and in pursuing the decolonisation of the field.

While these and other efforts have been crucial in the introduction and cultivation of new readings and subfields in some philosophy departments and professional associations, it will be difficult to contest the idea that, generally speaking, philosophy as a field or a discipline in modern Western universities remains a bastion of Eurocentrism, whiteness in general, and white heteronormative male structural privilege and superiority in particular. One only has to look at curricular design and content, the overwhelming absence of people of colour in classrooms and philosophical reading lists despite the existence of a few, and to the criteria for merit and promotion in the field. It is no secret either, that this state of affairs is part of the legacy of Western imperialism, racialised slavery, white heteronormative male supremacy, and segregation, which highly elevated the value of civilisation and abstract universality, and exclusively linked them with concepts, norms and values that were considered to be of European provenance.

Because philosophy is grounded on and advances a particular arrangement of power/knowledge, it is not enough to argue that the solution to the above-mentioned issues lies in simply diversifying the field. Failing to address structural problems and deep-seated habits, diversity and inclusion strategies tend to make, at best, only a superficial impact, often putting the very people that they seek to 'help' in vulnerable positions and in peril. Because the problem is deep and widespread, and it involves other fields and institutions, not to mention established rankings, the celebrations of diversity and inclusion achievements of any given institution based on comparisons with others are often as deceiving as they are self-serving. The result is the eternal return of crisis and the ongoing production of a perverse circle that, at its most successful, leads to unending liberal interventions that make little to no difference or that make the problem worse.

In face of the eternal return of crisis and the perverse circle of Eurocentrism and white normativity, it becomes all the more necessary not simply to diversify philosophy, but to decolonise it. This involves addressing the Eurocentrism and the white male heteronormative foundations of the field, as well as the attitudes, institutional orders and day-to-day practices that allow Eurocentrism and white male heteronormativity to dominate the discipline. Far from simply diversifying philosophy and 'including' people of colour in it, decolonising philosophy requires a decolonial turn that touches on all the various aspects of philosophy as a field and as a practice.

Based on Maldonado-Torres's formulation of the term, we conceive the decolonial turn as a form of liberating and decolonising reason beyond the liberal and Enlightened emancipation of rationality, and beyond the more radical Euro-critiques that have failed to consistently challenge the legacies of Eurocentrism and white male heteronormativity (often Eurocentric critiques of Eurocentrism).[1] Otherwise put, the decolonial turn seeks to overcome hierarchies that impede true rigour and excellence in philosophical thinking. We complement Maldonado-Torres's account of the decolonial turn in philosophy, theory and critique by providing an analysis of the trajectories of academic philosophy and clarifying the relevance of decolonising philosophy and of the decolonial turn for current efforts in transforming philosophy in face of the challenges of social movements such as the Third World Liberation Front and Black

Lives Matter in the United States, and Rhodes Must Fall in South Africa and England.

After a brief analysis of the trajectory and current status of philosophy as a discipline in the modern Western research university, we provide examples of the decolonial turn and of decolonising philosophy in three areas: the engagement with (1) Asian and (2) Latin American philosophies, and (3) debates in the philosophy of race and gender. To be sure, any serious effort to decolonise philosophy cannot be satisfied with simply adding new areas to an existing arrangement of power/knowledge, leaving the Eurocentric norms that define the field as a whole in place, or reproducing such norms themselves. For example, when engaging in non-European philosophies it is important to avoid reproducing problematic conceptions of time, space and subjectivity that are embedded in the Eurocentric definition of European philosophy and its many avatars. For this reason, Asia and Latin America here are not presented as continental others of Europe, but as constructed categories and projects that themselves need to be decolonised. For us, Asia and Latin America are not mere objects of study or non-problematic sites that serve as a ground for reflection, but spatio-temporal configurations that are part of modernity/coloniality.[2] Likewise, we also approach race and gender not only as constructed social realities, but also as constructed categories themselves within what Latina philosopher María Lugones has called the colonial/modern gender system.[3] Decolonising philosophy includes the critical examination of the dominant presuppositions about all these and other basic concepts in the search for a decolonial and post-continental mode of thinking, philosophy, and critique.

Trajectories of disciplinary philosophy and the decolonial turn

Philosophy is not the only field that has to contend with the legacy of and continued investment in Eurocentrism and white male heteronormativity. The entire arrangement of the liberal arts and sciences arguably has to as well. But philosophy seems to have a special place among discourses in the liberal arts because it focuses on the roots of the university at large: reason. This includes providing criteria for identifying and demarcating the humanities, the natural sciences and the social sciences, as well as for distinguishing reason from faith, secularism from religion, and the 'primitive' and the ancient from the modern. These are central columns in the edifice that sustains modern Western rationality and the modern

Western university. The modern Western research university and liberal arts therefore owe much of their basic conceptual infrastructure to philosophical formulations of rationality, universalism, subjectivity, the relationship between the subject and object, truth and method – all of which become relevant targets of critical analysis in the decolonial turn.

It is arguably not rare, then, for philosophers to see themselves as custodians of Western critique and rationality, and with it, the Western university, especially the arts and sciences. Non-Western forms of theory and philosophy are kept out of philosophy canons and, at most, become objects of study in other fields. For example, Indigenous thought is barely recognised as philosophy and it is confined to the realm of spirituality or culture, available for study by the religious studies scholar or the anthropologist. In the United States, even those who focus on American philosophy tend to conflate this area with US pragmatism and, when not, they typically fail to question the coloniality embedded in the category of 'America'. For us, any effort to engage Indigenous theory and philosophy in the United States requires the simultaneous decolonisation of philosophy and of the idea of 'America'. While we cannot do justice to this area in this context, we hope that the reflections here contribute to a further elaboration of the imperative to critically address the approach to Indigenous thought as part of the effort to decolonise philosophy and knowledge at large.

To be sure, in the current neoliberal times, philosophy, along with a good number of other humanities and social sciences, no longer occupies the position it enjoyed when the modern Western research university was in the process of securing a space of its own in the West. At that time, coming out of the European Enlightenment, philosophy, the newly defined humanities and the emerging social sciences were extremely valuable in addressing the needs of nation-states and empires in the process of construction or expansion.[4] Today, many academics still try to defend the relevance of philosophy and the humanities by appealing to their contributions to the liberal nation-state and to the idea of cultivating civility and good citizenship. As good as this may sound, these efforts arguably reflect what one could refer to as a decadent attitude that fails to address the problems of the liberal and racial nation-state and its links to the liberal arts and sciences.[5]

There is also failure in missing the opportunity to make philosophy and the humanities relevant, not for the problematic task of trying to put a limit on neoliberalism, or to domesticate it, but for decolonising the world. Since this task involves the very decolonisation of philosophy and of the humanities, many remain invested in these areas and in the liberal project of trying to save them from the onslaught of privatisation and neoliberalism rather than take on the challenge of decolonising them. And because they rightly oppose neoliberalism, the liberal defenders of the humanities obtain a sense of satisfaction that obscures the problematic dimensions of liberalism, along with the liberal arts and sciences. When it is satisfied with contributing to, rather than critically examining, this defence of liberalism and the liberal arts and sciences, philosophy becomes, or rather continues its service as, the handmaiden of the racial liberal state.

But modern Western philosophy has not always been functional with regard to the liberal order. It has also participated in its critique. Important waves of philosophical critique took place throughout the nineteenth century and especially in the mid-twentieth century after the spread of Fascism in Europe and two world wars. However, while European philosophers learned and benefited from the critical voices that called for decolonisation in the Third World at that time,[6] they overwhelmingly chose to limit the scope of their reflections and only see Europe or the Western classical ancient world as relevant for thinking. By taking various philosophical turns (the transcendental turn, the linguistic turn and the phenomenological turn, among others) within the horizons of Western modernity, they effectively evaded active and engaging participation in a larger decolonial turn that took place primarily in the emerging 'Third World' – including the Third World inside Western metropoles – that challenged modernity/coloniality. Instead, the work of the more critical European philosophers tended to become part of a Cold War dispute between philosophical orientations that were considered to be aligned with Marxism, on the one hand, and philosophical approaches that sought refuge in scientific models, logics and mathematics, on the other. From then on, academic philosophy became strongly divided between 'continental' and 'analytic' philosophical camps.

The divide between continental and analytic philosophy became particularly acute in the United States, which after the Second World War became a new global hegemon as much with respect to its military power as to the academy. It was in the United States that McCarthyism reigned supreme for a period in the 1950s, having tremendous impact in politics as well as in cultural production and the academy. As John McCumber has shown, in the context of the Cold War, McCarthyism played a key role in getting rid of philosophers who questioned capitalism with their socio-historical analyses, and in motivating the assertion of an analytic model of philosophy which kept the field away from socio-political issues and closer to mathematics and the natural sciences.[7] This situation favoured the growth of what were presumed to be apolitical and non-ideological philosophical orientations, which does not mean that analytic philosophy is inherently apolitical or that it cannot contribute to ideology critique. This led to or confirmed the minority position of specialists in continental philosophy in philosophy departments, who sometimes had to find other institutional homes. This migration contributed to the popularity of 'theory' in the US humanities in the last part of the Cold War. To be sure, much of this 'theory', along with the continental philosophy taught in philosophy departments, was largely Eurocentric, even as it began to be used for projects that questioned Eurocentrism.

Academic philosophy during the Cold War therefore seemed positioned between the Scylla of McCarthyism and the Charybdis of Eurocentrism. The significance of this situation should not be underestimated as it took place in the context where philosophical ideas that were critical of banners of the liberal nation-state, such as rationality and freedom, were spreading in multiple parts of the globe. College youth turned out to have an important role in questioning power dynamics worldwide during the 1960s and 1970s, and some philosophical works became powerful weapons in their hands. The struggles in the growing hegemonic philosophy departments, disciplined by McCarthyism and Eurocentrism, made academic philosophy less useful than it could have been in the process of producing generations of students who sought to critically engage the world. As a result, many students were forced to do philosophy outside of philosophy departments, and the more radical among them (e.g. the Black youth that created the Black Student Union in the US, and the Third World Liberation Front at San Francisco State University and the University of California Berkeley, among others) struggled to create new, non-Eurocentric, academic units. These spaces, often considered to be from a racist point of view no more than bastions of narrow identity politics or expressions of liberal multiculturalism, have served as engines for non-Eurocentric philosophy and critique.

Today we find ourselves in a peculiar context: we are no longer in the moment of Enlightened opposition to tradition wherein philosophical critique is considered central; nor are we in the context of continued liberal nation-state formation and imperial expansion, wherein the liberal arts and sciences function as handmaidens of the state. The Cold War period of increasing dominance of scientific conceptions of philosophy in the context of growing US hegemony is also in the past. Today we find an increasingly interconnected world with massively disproportionate patterns of wealth, accelerated migration flows, and racist nativist attitudes that question the very category of 'facts'. Consider that, while philosophical pretensions of scientificism during the Cold War could have generated a significant degree of legitimacy for the field of philosophy in the struggle to keep left-wing ideology and related forms of critical analysis at bay, pretensions of scientificism these days are increasingly taken as forms of elitism by populist right-wing forces that question the validity of science and facts.

Overwhelmingly in our times, philosophy, along with the humanities, finds itself caught in a seeming opposition, which in fact is a spectrum, between the neoliberal erosion of liberal ideas of collective goods, which cannot be separated from racism, on the one hand, and racist nativist populism, on the other, which tends to combine racist views of collectivities with ideas about purely individual investment and success that are central in neoliberalism. The first, neoliberalism, questions forms of thinking and creating that do not contribute to privatisation, profit maximisation and corporate efficiency, while the second, nativist populism, questions the value of anything that undermines or even relativises the ideas and values perceived as central to the nativist view of the nation.

All along, however, philosophy has faced the challenge of quite different voices which have raised questions about the meaning and significance of colonialism and decolonisation as central to an engagement with the modern/colonial world. These voices seek not only to enrich philosophy, but also to make it relevant to the planet at large. Instead of keeping academic philosophy sequestered by liberalism and Eurocentric leftist perspectives, or menaced by neoliberalism and nativism, the decolonial turn involves a dramatic opening and transformation of philosophy. It is an encounter with various forms of theorising and critique that helps everyone in the task of creating a world where dehumanisation, genocide and the early death of specific populations are not considered or effectively operate as a norm.

Decolonising philosophy and theory in and through Asia[8]

This section reflects on decolonising philosophy and theory in and through 'Asia' by tracing notable contributions from East Asian thinkers and by suggesting challenges that must be considered in the task of decolonising philosophy. In doing so, this section avers that 'the geography of reason' (to borrow the Caribbean Philosophical Association's coinage)[9] in and through Asia is exhausted neither by the discipline of philosophy nor by a selective inclusion of only the cultural aspects of a presumed 'Asian' identity in academic projects. The section is limited to East Asian references and is far from representing the entirety of conundrums faced by decolonial struggles in the heterogeneous area that is Asia.[10] The East Asian context, however, is sure to resonate with such struggles in other areas placed outside of the West.

Decolonising philosophy in and through Asia requires understanding the significance of the history of Asian thought in the present. East Asian thinkers such as Sun Ge (China) and Ch'a Sŭng-gi (South Korea) have addressed how Asians have theorised and could theorise Asia by tracing genealogies of Eastern thought. On the question of the meanings 'Asia' produces, Sun Ge asks:

> What does Asia imply? As a member of Asia, it is not merely due to the need to respond to the voices of the post-colonial intellectuals in the West that we reflect on Asia. On the contrary, whether Asia should be taken as a perspective of instrumental value, and on which level the question of Asia should be broached, is of concern to our own history. On the basis of this, we would ask: is Asia merely a question for the Japanese or other neighbouring East Asian countries? To the Chinese who, for a century, have not established any relation of partnership with the Japanese, what does Asia mean?[11]

Sun's question reflects three important aspects relevant to this section's considerations. First, the question of what Asia means directly concerns the historical realities of those who pose this question, beyond the invitation and inclusion from the West. Second, Asia is not a monolithic reality and therefore, attempts to define Asia have different meanings and significances depending on who asks the question and from what position. Third, imperialism and colonialism have had a significant impact on the discourse regarding Asia and on the relationship among

Asian countries. This is evinced as much in the profound impact of Japanese imperialism and Japan's history of fascism in the region, as in projects of nation-state formation and Cold War reordering, to name only some of the more evident examples.

In spite of, or perhaps precisely for these reasons, Sun argues that contemporary Asian thinkers must overcome both the present rhetoric of easy commercial globalisation and hasty erasures of different kinds of Asianism by post-Second World War progressives and leftists alike. Asian thinkers, Sun proffers, must undertake the difficult task of probing both Asia as an idea (i.e. history of thought, philosophy and ideals of different Pan-Asianisms) and Asia as a history and a region (i.e. knowledge produced by the disciplines of history, regional studies and the social sciences). Taking Japan as an example, this means a deep understanding of the contexts, positions and philosophical questions of Japanese thinkers of Asianism in the past is needed, such as those of Okakura Tenshin, Watsuji Tetsuro, Miyazaki Ichisada and Takeuchi Yoshimi. Without a methodical investigation into how different disciplines and lines of thought emerged in Japan in relation to the Asia question, contemporary questions on Asia posed by Asian thinkers as a 'perspective of instrumental value'[12] reify the modern/colonial construction of time and space.

In a comparable step, Ch'a Sŭng-gi (South Korea) alerts one to the philosophical engagements of Asian thinkers with modernity and Asia in the early twentieth century, to emphasise the role tradition has served as an imaginative methodology. Ch'a has analysed colonial-era (mostly from the 1930s and 1940s) Korean anti-modern thoughts' 'criticalities' (the Korean word from which this is translated is closest in meaning to the sense used in physics, describing the boundary at which a phenomenon splits into multiple phenomena). In this analysis, Ch'a examines how 'Asian' and 'Korean' traditions and value were multiply re-signified in relation to the changing understandings of the modern world order. Ch'a's work highlights the creative ways in which Korean thinkers and writers such as Lee Byŏng-gi and Jŏng Ji-yong formed a critical relation to the coloniality of their present by seeing the problems of the present through the 'eyes of the past', rather than seeing the past from the anthropological perspective of the present.[13] The past that they conceived was not a moment that has passed or that was fixed at a distance but was continuously repeated enactments in the present. Through the practice of poetic meditation – a traditional practice reclaimed to enable becoming beyond the present – these thinkers imagined alternatives to the modern/ colonial time-space.

As Japanese imperialism intensified with the advent of the Pacific War, imperial Pan-Asianism emerged as another universalism that competed with the universalism of Western modernity. Japanese Pan-Asian multiculturalism codified the colony's irreducible distance from the metropole as the colony's 'local colour'. At the same time, it re-spatialised Asia as a homogeneous entity in order to justify Japan's imperial militarism as a step towards a world freed of modernity's colonial burdens (*gendai* in Japanese, *hyundae* in Korean) as espoused by the Kyoto school 'historical philosophers'.[14] In this context, Korean intellectuals' assertion of the temporality of tradition and the past, or of the persistence of temporalities that exceed the linear-progressive temporality of modernity, serve as critiques of the binary universalisms that justified Western and Japanese imperialism.[15] For Ch'a, the critique and enactments surrounding tradition and the past borne out of these contestations continue to bear philosophical significance for the liberation struggles of the present moment.

As the works of Sun and Ch'a demonstrate, decolonising philosophy in and through Asia requires both inter-Asian and interdisciplinary conversations, but not without potential entrapments at every turn. From this perspective, any attempt to 'represent' or encapsulate Asian philosophy or thought in modules that can be unquestioningly delivered as a fixed canon, is problematically inadequate, and yet this often occurs in East–West dialogues. The Inter-Asia project in which Sun Ge (China) and Chen Kuan-Hsing (Taiwan) participate, and similar endeavours, are attentive to what Kwŏn Myŏng-a (South Korea) has criticised as the tendency in contemporary East Asian scholarship to overlook the ways in which globalisation consolidates marginalised and regionalised subjectivities under transnational refashionings.[16] Such overviews are complicit with sub-imperialism or South–South imperialism, such as East Asian enterprise for cheap labour and resources in South East Asia and Africa.[17] Chen Kuan-Hsing has similarly offered a critical examination of the ways in which the Western academy erases local thinkers by privileging the voices of diasporic, multicultural and metropolitan postcolonial thinkers instead.[18] Critical endeavours to decolonise thought across borders must therefore continuously contest different institutions' reordering of knowledge which simultaneously represent and exclude in order to sustain the colonial circuits of knowledge production.[19]

This institutional pull to re-order knowledge production concerns not only one's interlocutors and one's methodology, but also the object of inquiry itself; Eastern philosophy (as opposed to 'Western philosophy': these are the categories of philosophy deployed in some parts of East Asia) is a minoritised field of knowledge through the colonial difference[20] even in the East Asian academy, yet it is still necessary to identify and *divest* Eastern philosophy of its colonial investments. 'Eastern philosophy' circulates *as if* colonial investments *did not* shape the genealogy itself. Overcoming the limit of its selective intellectual history is an engagement with its multiple erasures, such as the erasure of peripheralised parts of Asia in the process of consolidating the 'Eastern' tradition and the impact of the Cold War on the development of this tradition. Lauding, generalising and sampling a pre-constructed Eastern philosophy only satisfies the multiculturalist logic of inclusion rather than dismantling the colonial circuit of knowledge.

One necessary and transformative direction to pursue in order to decolonise philosophy in and through Asia is to challenge the construct of Asia itself in relation to the question of Indigeneity. What have been the integrations and erasures of Indigenous modes of thought in 'Eastern philosophy', and how do the challenges posed by Native people to the meaning of sovereignty change the genealogies and questions currently asked by thinkers dwelling on the Asia question?[21] Examinations of settler-colonialism in the East Asian context have emerged in the form of settler-colonialism studies in history and anthropology[22] and in the field of Transpacific studies,[23] which engages with Indigenous knowledge productions as political and philosophical agents. This paradigm shift needs to be substantiated in the broader field of Asian studies and Asian philosophy. Indigenous peoples of East Asia and the Pacific have been fundamental and continued subjects of colonial rule. Many of them live with the high concentration of militarisation formed during the Cold War that remains in the region, which entails that they inordinately pay for the material, ecological, and biopolitical costs of securitisation.[24] Those engaging with the question of the meaning and significance of Asia and striving to decolonise philosophy, need to further wrestle with the modern/colonial legacy of scepticism towards the validity of popular and Indigenous socio-political movements on the ground as knowledge production.

These questions and reflections are typically placed outside the horizon of efforts to 'include' Asia in the discipline of philosophy. The decolonisation of philosophy in and through Asia requires something else: a sustained engagement, not only with academic philosophers in Asia, some of whom presuppose Eurocentric approaches to philosophy as the norm, but also with thinkers who critically engage the question 'what is Asia?' and 'how can Asia be decolonised?' in relation to local histories and the *longue durée* of modernity/coloniality worldwide.

Latin American liberation philosophy: reflections on Enrique Dussel's Analectics

If 'America' is a geopolitical imaginary construct and a project of European colonial powers as Europeans sought to conquer the 'New World', 'Latin America' could be considered a project of creole elites that from its inception sought the reproduction of European institutions and values via the elimination of Indigenous populations and the exploitative use of African peoples brought in as slave labour.[25] European colonisation thus not only precedes the formation of 'Latin America', but is also the principal condition of possibility for it to emerge. This means that European institutions, including universities, have been present in Latin America all throughout its history, and they continue to exist today as strong bastions of coloniality.

Unsurprisingly, Latin American philosophers have not been well represented in academic philosophy, even in Latin America. Part of the reason for this is because Latin American philosophers overwhelmingly write in Spanish and Portuguese, languages which fell from grace as worthy of philosophical reflection just as the Spanish and Portuguese empires started to fall from hegemony within the geopolitical struggles of the modern world-system. There is also the fact that philosophical production in Latin America is often looked at as if it is either too indistinguishable from European thought, although dependent and inferior, or too different and exotic (especially Indigenous philosophies), to the point where it is not taken as legitimate philosophy. For this reason, the question of whether there is a Latin American philosophy has been an important one in the region.[26]

We cannot rehearse the debate about the existence of philosophy in Latin America here. Our interest in this context is rather the indifference of mainstream academic philosophy to the topic of Latin American philosophy, though sometimes granting that there is some kind of distinct philosophy in order to satisfy liberal calls for the diversification of established canons. This liberal approach, we argue, is a form of co-optation that treats non-Western knowledges as tokens that are expected to conform and avoid threatening the modern/colonial epistemic status of philosophy and the university in general. In this section, we wish to explore ways to decolonise philosophy by seriously engaging the radicality of 'Latin American' thought, while also taking into serious consideration the coloniality embedded in the very idea of Latin America. Given the limited extent of this chapter, we will consider contributions from one philosopher of liberation whose work has been greatly influential in the critique of Eurocentrism and the exploration of South–South philosophical debates. He also happens to be the most prolific Latin American philosopher to date: the Argentine-Mexican philosopher Enrique Dussel.

The project of liberation philosophy (*filosofía de la liberación*), as artic-ulated in Dussel's work is a concrete attempt to decolonise philosophy, which has also been described as a major project in the decolonial turn.[27] Liberation philosophy begins by deflating the pretended universalism of modern Western philosophy, placing the latter within an anthropological history of the development of the planet's thought-systems.[28] Addition-ally, Dussel connects the history of modern Western philosophy to the unfolding of the modern/colonial world. If modern Western philosophy claims to begin with René Descartes' reflections on the *ego cogito*, Dussel locates this particular contribution within the existential horizon of Europe's *ego conquiro*, the ethico-political presupposition that – from the 'Reconquista' of Al-Andalus and the encounter with Tainos in 1492 to the conquest of Aztec and Incan civilisations in the early sixteenth century – led a Christian Spanish empire out of its provincial status vis-à-vis the Muslim world.[29] The genesis of modern Western philosophy thus requires an investigation into its historical conditions of possibility, which includes an examination of conceptions of world and self that are tied to the idea of 'discovery', the justification of conquest and the natu-ralisation of slavery.

Liberation philosophy posits that without a serious attempt to dwell in the constitutive outside of modernity, philosophy as a mode of thinking (whether inside or outside of the university) would remain not only Eurocentric but also colonialist. It is important to clarify, however, that this move to think outside of modernity is not for the sake of dropping anchor in a pure position of exteriority. Against any problem-atic desire for purity, liberation philosophy simply seeks to think from the site which most obviously and directly experiences the philosophical discourse of modernity as a discourse of colonisation[30] in order to transcend the totalising project of modernity/coloniality. This task does not require the constant policing of disciplinary boundaries, as is typically the case in Eurocentric philosophy. If an example of the latter includes the self-referential *dialectics* of modernity, which assimilate the world as they expand their totalising domination from within the rhetoric of modernity, like Hegel's philosophy of history,[31] then the method of liberation philosophy is instead an *analectics* of the underside of modernity.

For Dussel, who coined the term, analectics entail a rupturing (from the rhetoric of modernity) affirmation (by and within those negated subjects) aimed towards the transformation of the modern/colonial totality to bring forth nothing less than a new world.[32] If dialectics have been deployed to challenge the internal contradictions of modernity, then they have also presupposed modernity's own ontological horizon by not dislodging its logic of identity and difference.[33] In other words, the point of departure for dialectics is internal to the rhetoric of modernity itself. Dialectics thus do not entail a real transformation of consciousness and of the world, but only the affirmation of an identity that is presumed as always-already existing. Analectics, on the other hand, dislodge the logic of identity and difference in their entirety by refusing the self-referential terms set by such rhetoric of modernity. Analectics' point of departure is not an already recognised identity with internal contradictions, but instead the zone of violence and ontological erasure, the colonial world, which the totalising system of Western modernity does *not* recognise as worthy of philosophical reflection.

This is not to say that liberation philosophy negates any potential critical rationality in modernity and its dialectics. Rather, liberation philosophy seeks to subsume such rationality into a more ample framework while negating the irrational and violent colonial side of modernity. A critical effort to depart from the underside of modernity would thus supplement any negative dialectics ('the negation of the negation') with 'the affirmation of the Exteriority of the Other', which carries with it the possibility of a truly *other* world.[34] This is the constitutive moment of the analectic method, which requires a pedagogical transformation, *knowing how to listen* to the 'revealing' word of this Other beyond the system, a lived face-to-face praxis that cannot be expressed through the language of the existing system.[35] To be sure, the other world called upon is posited not in the univocal universalist way through which the myth of modernity projects its own vision, but in a pluriversal horizon that rethinks the concept of universality itself.[36] Articulating a critique of modernity by affirming its underside, liberation philosophy thus surpasses the limitations of the philosophical discourse of modernity (the fact that its own dialectics are monological and not dialogical) in a way that also goes beyond the Eurocentrism of (post)modernity, which often is sceptical of rational discourses in their entirety while at the same time limiting the categories of rational discourse and universality to Europe. Performing a rupturing shift in the geography of reason,[37] liberation philosophy effectively calls for a *transmodern* horizon that does not discard reason but instead seeks its co-realisation through those subjects that experience modernity *as* coloniality.[38]

Liberation philosophy's engagement with the theory of the Frankfurt School serves as an example of the analectic method. Not seeking to fully reject the contributions of this community of thinkers for its Eurocentrism, liberation philosophy retains what is useful for a decolonial project while dispensing with pernicious Eurocentrisms and their related burdens. Taken from the first generation of the Frankfurt School, an emphasis on materiality (as the 'affirmation of living corporeality') and negativity (the negation of suffering), are central to the currents of liberation philosophy.[39] From the second generation of the Frankfurt School, liberation philosophy retains the turn towards discursivity and intersubjectivity (lacking in the first generation). Liberation philosophy therefore retains what is useful from both the first and second generations of the Frankfurt School. Notably, it does not dispense with negative materiality, which the leading second-generation Frankfurt School thinkers – like Jürgen Habermas – have problematically discarded in the name of a procedural formalism. And against the 'ontological Eurocentrism' of the Frankfurt School (including the third generation), liberation philosophy highlights the moment of exclusion within discursivity, the exteriority of any community of communication that launches liberatory praxis.[40] Additionally, liberation philosophy harnesses the critical discursivity of the excluded against the totalising dominant community. Far from denying the contributions of the Frankfurt School in a reactionary fashion, liberation philosophy critically approaches it from a different geopolitical and epistemological position. Liberation philosophy aims to dispense with the Frankfurt School's coloniality and subsume what is useful from it (e.g. materiality, negativity, discursivity and intersubjectivity) within a decolonial and transmodern horizon towards a non-Eurocentric *'critical philosophy with global validity'.*[41] This is one brief example of how the categorical and methodological framework presented by liberation philosophy should prove useful for those seeking the decolonisation of philosophy at distinct levels of abstraction.

To be sure, the case of liberation philosophy is just one among many critical projects that pursue the decolonisation not just of philosophy, but of all thought and life. Part of why liberation philosophy is so critical in its attempts to decolonise philosophy, however, is that it dislodges the centrality of Eurocentric philosophy from the very start. This is the moment of 'delinking'[42] or rupture that prevents the project of liberation philosophy from collapsing into a version of the liberal 'inclusion of the Other' paradigm of what is already considered 'philosophy'. Instead, liberation philosophy calls for the transformation of what philosophy is from the very start. Within the globalised modern Western research university, this means that departments of philosophy have to do much more than diversify their canons in order to get rid of their modern/colonial inheritances. A meta-philosophical re-drawing of its own being requires that philosophical discourse engage in an open dialogue with other geographies of reason, including other disciplines within the university, which have, in many ways, already been philosophising, such as ethnic studies and women and gender studies. In this sense, philosophy needs to learn to listen to the revealing views and words of those who have been considered outside of the scope of theory and reason. The decolonisation of philosophy, which is taking place alongside simultaneous decolonial efforts across disciplinary boundaries, ultimately points to the decolonisation of the university itself as a site of knowledge production. This is a transdisciplinary struggle, which will no doubt change everyone involved in the process. And yet, this epistemic struggle itself is only a small part of the broader transmodern impetus to create, as the Zapatistas from south-east Mexico say, a new world in which many worlds can fit.

Decolonising philosophical approaches to race and gender

The decolonial turn invites a critique of modernity/coloniality within the epistemic paradigms governing theories of gender and race as practised in philosophy. Identifying and critically analysing the Enlightenment concepts on which feminist theory and philosophies of race are

built – concepts like justice, equality and rights – decolonial thought
(re-)imagines the potential of transmodern engagements (Dussel) with
race and gender. Decolonial thought utilises genealogies critical of
colonialism in order to imagine alternative horizons for gender and race
theories.

Philosophical approaches to race and gender have historically focused
on a politics of redistribution and recognition as potential sites of critical
social intervention. For example, feminist theorists Simone de Beauvoir,
Luce Irigaray and bell hooks, to name just a few, have focused their
respective critiques of patriarchy on the lack of recognition extended
to women. In *The Second Sex* de Beauvoir argues that society reduces
women to their biological sex and in so doing recognises only their repro-
ductive potential.[43] Women's liberation in this account is represented
as the social recognition of women as project-making beings capable
of engaging in projects of transcendence. Irigaray's politics of recognition takes issue with canonical and masculinist philosophical theories
as well as the underlying tension of sexual difference on which these
traditions rest.[44] bell hooks' early work, *Feminist Theory: From Margin
to Center*, criticises second wave feminism for excluding black women
in the very conception of womanhood, which resulted in a failure to
recognise the unique oppressions faced by women of colour.[45] Restricted
by the power/knowledge arrangement of philosophy from the mid to
late twentieth century, these interrogations into race and gender remain
limited in their respective critiques of the liberal order. By focusing upon
the liberatory goals of recognition and redistribution, these philosophies
of race and gender were quickly subsumed by the overarching liberal
order and diverted from their original aims of decolonising theory and
power within philosophy.

As part of the ongoing growth of the decolonial turn, among related
movements, the legacies of colonial forms of redistribution and recognition in the academy have been extended by thinkers who have a
more explicit critique of liberalism. Here one can list figures such as
Linda Martín Alcoff,[46] Sylvia Wynter and Lewis Gordon.[47] They and
theorists with similar orientations have developed socio-political
theories concerned with race, ethnicity and gender without limiting
their accounts to either liberation as mere recognition or to liberal conceptions of identity.[48] They also challenge the standard conceptualisation
and separation of gender and race, inviting us to conceive decolonial
thought in terms of what Sylvia Wynter has aptly termed the 'demonic

ground' outside of our present mode of being/feeling/knowing.[49] Consideration of the 'demonic ground' is an activity that becomes crucial in the decolonial turn because it includes a meta-critique of colonialist epistemic paradigms, which is missing in mainstream analytic and continental philosophy as well as in white feminisms.

Wynter's article, 'Afterword: Beyond Miranda's Meanings: Un/silencing the "Demonic Ground" of Caliban's "Woman"', is a concrete example of a distinctly decolonial engagement with gender and race. Notably this decolonial intervention does not begin with an either/or. Using a critical genealogy of history, Wynter's analysis is one step removed from sexual or racial difference as essential difference. According to Wynter, the primary antagonism that has shaped society since the sixteenth century is not 'male' versus 'female' but 'man' versus 'native/nigger'.[50] The 'primary code of difference' does not break down in terms of a single binary like sameness and difference. In this alternative schema, 'Man' represents a new secular shift towards rationality. The category 'Man' includes, first and foremost, rational beings. In this schema, women, specifically white women, are grouped in the dominant social category, which stands in opposition to the native, who is regarded as irrational or even arational. According to Wynter's decolonial genealogy, since the sixteenth century, racial/cultural difference – what Mignolo refers to as the colonial difference – represents the primary category of social distinction internal to which there are a series of other dichotomies, including sexual difference.

Wynter's account of social difference is not, as it might first appear, a simple reordering of the all too familiar identity categories belonging to philosophies of race and of feminist theories. Wynter does not, for example, prioritise race over gender or vice versa.[51] Instead, by grouping the racial and cultural together (i.e. racial/cultural), Wynter sidesteps the tendencies of simple rankings. Colonial difference means that white European men represent the ordering principle around which the social is structured. However, insofar as Man stands in opposition to 'native/ nigger', the former also includes white, European, women. Already we can see that a politics of representation has become complicated. There is no single narrative of equality. White women, for example, embody the dominant cultural/racial category to the extent that they are European and white (and Christian and rational, at least in comparison to the 'native' and even more radically and primal for Wynter, the 'nigger'). In contrast to men, however, they still fall short of the ideal within the dominant ordering logic because they fail to *fully* embody rationality. Conversely, the struggle for women of colour – the struggle of Caliban's woman – is a struggle around the racial/cultural/rational. In Shakespeare's *The Tempest*, Caliban's woman is not only absent from the play, and therefore absent from the competition of erotic desire, but she is also structurally and ontologically absent in a way that makes the represented symbolic order of desire, of culture, and of rationality possible. As Wynter states, 'the absence of Caliban's woman, is an absence which is functional to the new secularizing schema by which the peoples of Western Europe legitimated their global expansion as well as their expropriation and/their [*sic*] marginalisation of all the other population-groups of the globe'.[52] Wynter's account suggests that a politics of representation, a politics that governs at least some important sectors of contemporary feminist theories and philosophies of race, is impossible within coloniality's symbolic order because this order depends upon the ontological exclusion of Caliban's woman, that is, the native's female companion.

Using Wynter's critical genealogy as described above, a potential method of decolonial feminist and anti-racist thought becomes clear. A decolonial approach seeks to 'de-code the system of meaning of that other discourse [whether the dominant discourse of the status quo or the critical discourses of feminist theory and philosophy of race], which has imposed this mode of silence for some five centuries'.[53] Decolonial thought goes beyond voicing the silenced narratives of Caliban's woman. Decolonial thought is a double movement that, on the one hand, seeks to unearth the demonic ground that makes the symbolic order possible, and on the other, erects new discursive horizons from the standpoint of coloniality's underside.

Wynter's intervention demonstrates the point made in a previous section: that decolonising philosophy is not fundamentally about diversifying established canons by including certain authors or themes in the discipline. Decolonising philosophy is a form of reflection that emerges from intellectual, social, artistic and related movements that challenge colonisation and that seek to advance decolonisation. For academic philosophy, this means that any effort towards diversifying the discipline needs to be prefaced by serious consideration of the complex, non-binary interrelations between subject positions (e.g. race, gender, sexuality, ability) and their entanglement in modernity/coloniality. This means that diversification cannot take place without decolonisation. Likewise, the struggle against exclusion in academic philosophy demands decolonisation, which involves the critical interrogation of existing efforts of liberal inclusion and the terms and criteria used therein. This process involves the meta-philosophical exercise of critically engaging various categories of analysis, including basic geopolitical terms (the West, Asia, Latin America), basic philosophical concepts (reason, universality, dialectics), and basic objects of social analysis (race and gender). That some of the key figures involved in decolonial thinking are often not recognised as philosophers illustrates the nature of the challenge. Fortunately, neither decolonisation nor critique nor thinking have never depended strictly upon academic philosophy. But academic philosophy could find more ways to contribute to these tasks if it seriously engages in its own critique and decolonisation. This chapter aims to be an effort, among many other efforts in myriad places and spaces, in this direction.

Bibliography

Camacho, Keith L. and Shigematsu, Setsu (2010) *Militarized Currents: Toward a Decolonized Future in Asia and the Pacific.* Minneapolis: University of Minnesota Press.

Césaire, Aimé (2000) *Discourse on Colonialism*, trans. Joan Pinkham. New York: Monthly Review Press.

Ch'a, Sŭng-gi (2009) 반근대적 상상력의 임계들:식민지 조선 담론장에서의 전통, 세계, 주체 [Criticalities of the Anti-modern Imagination: Tradition, World, and Subject in Colonial Korean Discourse]. Seoul: Pu-rŭn-yŏk-sa, 2009.

Chen, Kuan-Hsing (1998) 'The Decolonization Question', in Chen Kuan-Hsing (ed.) *Trajectories: Inter-Asia Cultural Studies.* Abingdon: Routledge.

de Beauvoir, Simone (1989) *The Second Sex*, trans. H.M. Parshley. New York: Vintage Books.

Dussel, Enrique (1974) *Método para una filosofía de la liberación: Superación analéctica de la dialéctica hegeliana.* Salamanca: Ediciones Sígueme.

—— (1985) *Philosophy of Liberation*, trans. Aquilina Martinez and Christine Morkovsky. Maryknoll, NY: Orbis Books.

—— (1995) *The Invention of the Americas: Eclipse of 'the Other' and the Myth of Modernity*, trans. Michael D. Barber. New York: Continuum.

—— (1996) *The Underside of Modernity: Apel, Ricoeur, Rorty, Taylor, and the Philosophy of Liberation*, trans. and ed. Eduardo Mendieta. Atlantic Highlands, NJ: Humanities Press.

—— (2011) 'From Critical Theory to the Philosophy of Liberation: Some Themes for a Dialogue', trans. George Ciccariello-Maher, *Transmodernity: Journal of Peripheral Cultural Production of the Luso-Hispanic World* 1(2): 16–43.

—— (2013) *Ethics of Liberation: In the Age of Globalization and Exclusion*, trans. Eduardo Mendieta et al. Durham, NC: Duke University Press.

Fanon, Frantz (2008 [1952]) *Black Skin, White Masks*, trans. Richard Philcox. New York: Grove Press.

Ferguson, Roderick A. (2012) *The Reorder of Things: The University and Its Pedagogies of Minority Difference*. Minneapolis: University of Minnesota Press.

Gordon, Lewis R. (2000) 'Du Bois's Humanistic Philosophy of Human Sciences', *Annals of the American Academy of Political and Social Sciences* 568: 265–80.

—— (2006) *Disciplinary Decadence: Living Thought in Trying Times*. Boulder, CO: Paradigm Press.

—— (2011) 'Shifting the Geography of Reason in an Age of Disciplinary Decadence', *Transmodernity: Journal of Peripheral Cultural Production of the Luso-Hispanic World* 1(2): 95–103.

hooks, bell (2015) *Feminist Theory: From Margin to Center*. New York: Routledge.

Hoskins, Janet and Nguyen, Viet Thanh (2014) *Transpacific Studies: Framing an Emerging Field*. Honolulu: University of Hawai'i Press.

Irigaray, Luce (1985) *Speculum of the Other Woman*, trans. Gillian C. Gill. Ithaca, NY: Cornell University Press.

Kwŏn, Myŏng-a (2009) 식민지 이후를 사유하다: 탈 식민화와 재식민화의 경계 [Thinking the Postcolonial: The Boundary between Decolonization and Recolonization]. Seoul: Ch'aek–se-sang.

Lee, Jin-Kyung (2010) *Service Economies: Militarism, Sex Work, and Migrant Labor in South Korea*. Minneapolis: University of Minnesota Press.

Lewallen, Ann-Elise (2016) *The Fabric of Indigeneity: Ainu Identity, Gender, and Settler Colonialism in Japan*. Santa Fe: School for Advanced Research Press; Albuquerque: University of New Mexico Press.

Lugones, María (2007) 'Heterosexualism and the Colonial/Modern Gender System', *Hypatia* 22(1): 186–209.

Maldonado-Torres, Nelson (2006) 'Toward a Critique of Continental Reason: Africana Studies and the Decolonization of Imperial Cartographies in the Americas', in Lewis Gordon and Jane Anna Gordon (eds) *Not Only the Master's Tools: Theoretical Explorations in African-American Studies*. Boulder, CO: Paradigm Press, pp. 51–84.

—— (2011a) 'Enrique Dussel's Liberation Thought in the Decolonial Turn', *Transmodernity: Journal of Peripheral Cultural Production of the Luso-Hispanic World* 1(1): 1–30.

—— (2011b) 'Thinking through the Decolonial Turn: Post-continental Interventions in Theory, Philosophy, and Critique – An Introduction', *Transmodernity: Journal of Peripheral Cultural Production of the Luso-Hispanic World* 1(2): 1–15.

—— (2017) 'The Decolonial Turn', in Juan Poblete (ed.) *New Approaches to Latin American Studies: Culture and Power*. London: Routledge, pp. 111–27.

Martín Alcoff, Linda (2005) *Visible Identities: Race, Gender, and the Self*. New York: Oxford Press.

—— (2015) *The Future of Whiteness*. Malden, MA: Polity Press.

McCumber, John (2001) *Time in the Ditch: American Philosophy and the McCarthy Era*. Evanston, IL: Northwestern University Press.

Mignolo, Walter (2000a) 'The Role of the Humanities in the Corporate University', *PMLA* 115(5): 1238–45.

—— (2000b) *Local Histories/Global Designs: Coloniality, Subaltern Knowledges, and Border Thinking*. Princeton, NJ: Princeton University Press.

—— (2002) 'The Geopolitics of Knowledge and the Colonial Difference', *Southern Atlantic Quarterly* 101(1): 57–96.

—— (2005) *The Idea of Latin America*. Malden, MA: Blackwell.

—— (2007) 'Delinking: The Rhetoric of Modernity, the Logic of Coloniality, and the Grammar of De-Coloniality', *Cultural Studies* 21(2–3): 449–514.

Morris-Suzuki, Tessa (1999) 'The Ainu: Beyond the Politics of Cultural Coexistence', *Cultural Survival* 23(4), special issue on: Visions of the Future: The Prospect for Reconciliation. www.culturalsurvival.org/publications/cultural-survival-quarterly/ainu-beyond-politics-cultural-coexistence

Sakai, Naoki and Yoo, Hyon Joo (2012) *The Trans-Pacific Imagination: Rethinking Boundary, Culture, and Society*. Singapore: World Scientific Publishing Company.

Salazar Bondy, Augusto (1996) *¿Existe una filosofía de nuestra América?* 13th edn. Mexico, DF: Siglo Veintiuno Editores.

Sandoval, Chela (2000) *Methodology of the Oppressed*. Minneapolis: University of Minnesota Press.

Saranillio, Dean Itsuji (2013) 'Why Asian Settler Colonialism Matters: A Thought Piece on Critiques, Debates, and Indigenous Difference', *Settler Colonial Studies* 3(3–4): 280–94.

Sun, Ge (2000a) 'How Does Asia Mean? (Part I)', trans. Shiu-Lun Hui and Kinchi Lau, *Inter-Asia Cultural Studies* 1(1): 13–47.

—— (2000b) 'How Does Asia Mean? (Part II)', trans. Shiu-Lun Hui and Kinchi Lau. *Inter-Asia Cultural Studies* 1(2): 319–41.

Tlostanova, Madina V. and Mignolo, Walter (2012) *Learning to Unlearn: Decolonial Reflections from Eurasia and the Americas*. Columbus: Ohio State University Press.

Tuck, Eve and Yang, K. Wayne (2012) 'Decolonization is not a Metaphor', *Decolonization: Indigeneity, Education & Society* 1(1): 1–40.

Uchida, Jun (2014) *Brokers of Empire: Japanese Settler Colonialism in Korea, 1876–1945*. Cambridge, MA: Harvard University Press.

Wallerstein, Immanuel (1991) *Unthinking Social Science: The Limits of Nineteenth-century Paradigms*. Cambridge: Polity Press.

Wynter, Sylvia (1994) 'Afterword: Beyond Miranda's Meanings: Un/Silencing the "Demonic Ground" of Caliban's Woman', in Carole Boyce Davies and Elaine Savory Fido (eds) *Out of the Kumbla: Caribbean Women and Literature*. Trenton: Africa World Press, 355–72.

—— (2003) 'Unsettling the Coloniality of Being/Power/Truth: Towards the Human, After Man, Its Overrepresentation – An Argument', *CR: The New Centennial Review* 3(3): 257–337.

Yoneyama, Lisa (2016) *Cold War Ruins: Transpacific Critique of American Justice and Japanese War Crimes*. Durham, NC: Duke University Press.

Notes

1. On the decolonial turn see Maldonado-Torres, Nelson (2017) 'The Decolonial Turn', in Juan Poblete (ed.) *New Approaches to Latin American Studies: Culture and Power*. London: Routledge, pp. 111–27; Maldonado-Torres, Nelson (2011a) 'Enrique Dussel's Liberation Thought in the Decolonial Turn', *Transmodernity: Journal of Peripheral Cultural Production of the Luso-Hispanic World* 1(1): 1–30; Maldonado-Torres, Nelson (2011b) 'Thinking through the Decolonial Turn: Post-continental Interventions in Theory, Philosophy, and Critique – An Introduction', *Transmodernity: Journal of Peripheral Cultural Production of the Luso-Hispanic World* 1(2): 1–15.

2. Maldonado-Torres, Nelson (2006) 'Toward a Critique of Continental Reason: Africana Studies and the Decolonization of Imperial Cartographies in the Americas', in Lewis Gordon and Jane Anna Gordon (eds) *Not Only the Master's Tools: Theoretical Explorations in African-American Studies*. Boulder, CO: Paradigm Press, pp. 51–84; Mignolo, Walter (2000b) *Local Histories/Global Designs: Coloniality, Subaltern Knowledges, and Border Thinking*. Princeton, NJ: Princeton University Press; Mignolo, Walter (2005) *The Idea of Latin America*. Malden, MA: Blackwell; Mignolo, Walter (2011) *The Darker Side of Western Modernity: Global Futures, Decolonial Options*. Durham, NC: Duke University Press.

3. Lugones, María (2007) 'Heterosexualism and the Colonial/Modern Gender System', *Hypatia* 22(1): 186–209.

4. Mignolo, Walter (2000a) 'The Role of the Humanities in the Corporate University', *PMLA* 115(5): 1238–45; Wallerstein, Immanuel (1991) *Unthinking Social Science: The Limits of Nineteenth-century Paradigms*. Cambridge: Polity Press.

5. We build on the approach to decadence offered in Césaire, Aimé (2000) *Discourse on Colonialism*, trans. Joan Pinkham. New York: Monthly Review Press; and Gordon, Lewis (2006) *Disciplinary Decadence: Living Thought in Trying Times*. Boulder, CO: Paradigm Press, as well as on Maldonado-Torres's account of the modern/colonial and the decolonial attitude in philosophy (see his 'Decolonial Turn', op. cit. 2017).

6. Sandoval, Chela (2000) *Methodology of the Oppressed*. Minneapolis: University of Minnesota Press.

7. McCumber, John (2001) *Time in the Ditch: American Philosophy and the McCarthy Era*. Evanston, IL: Northwestern University Press.

8. Please note that East Asian names appear in this section with their surnames first.

9. See Gordon, Lewis (2011) 'Shifting the Geography of Reason in an Age of Disciplinary Decadence', *Transmodernity: Journal of Peripheral Cultural Production of the Luso-Hispanic World* 1(2): 95–103.

10. Tlostanova, Madina V. and Mignolo, Walter (2012) *Learning to Unlearn: Decolonial Reflections from Eurasia and the Americas*. Columbus: Ohio State University Press.

11. Sun, Ge (2000b) 'How Does Asia Mean? (Part II)', trans. Shiu-Lun Hui and Kinchi Lau, *Inter-Asia Cultural Studies* 1(2): 319–41 at p. 337; Sun, Ge (2000a) 'How Does Asia Mean? (Part I)', trans. Shiu-Lun Hui and Kinchi Lau, *Inter-Asia Cultural Studies* 1(1): 13–47.

12. Sun 2000b op. cit. p. 337.

13. Ch'a, Sŭng-gi (2009) 반근대적 상상력의 임계들:식민지 조선 담론장에서의 전통, 세계, 주체 [Criticalities of the Anti-modern Imagination: Tradition, World, and Subject in Colonial Korean Discourse]. Seoul : Pu-rŭn-yŏk-sa, pp. 148, 151.

14. Jeong Eun Annabel We explores the two critiques of modernity from East Asia and Latin America and the Caribbean, and what transmodernity would entail for East Asia, Latin America and the Caribbean, in a paper she presented at the 9th Conference on East–West Intercultural Relations, 'Global South, Latin America, and the Luso-Hispanic World' 12–13 May 2017. In the paper, entitled 'Decoloniality and "Hyundae (현대)": A Dialogue in Latin American/Caribbean and East Asian Genealogies', she argues that Enrique Dussel's concept of transmodernity resonates with some aspects of overcoming modernity of the Japanese PanAsianist historical philosophy, but that these aspects were not actualized due to crucial failures of self-reflection in the latter; instead, she finds the potential reurfaced in their Korean interlocutors and post-Second World War lines of thought in East Asia that developed out of the Bandung conference.

15. Ch'a 2009 op. cit. pp. 279–80.

16. Kwŏn, Myŏng-a (2009) 식민지 이후를 사유하다: 탈식민화와 재식민화의 경계 [Thinking the Post-colonial: The Boundary between Decolonization and Recolonization]. Seoul: Ch'aek–se-sang, p. 31.

17. Lee, Jin-Kyung (2010) *Service Economies: Militarism, Sex Work, and Migrant Labor in South Korea*. Minneapolis: University of Minnesota Press.

18. Chen, Kuan-Hsing 1998) 'The Decolonization Question', in Chen Kuan-Hsing (ed.) *Trajectories: Inter-Asia Cultural Studies*. Abingdon: Routledge.

19. Ferguson, Roderick A. (2012) *The Reorder of Things: The University and Its Pedagogies of Minority Difference*. Minneapolis: University of Minnesota Press.

20. Mignolo 2000b op. cit. Mignolo, Walter (2002) 'The Geopolitics of Knowledge and the Colonial Difference', *South Atlantic Quarterly* 101(1): 57–96.

21. Tuck, Eve and Yang, K. Wayne (2012) 'Decolonization is not a Metaphor', *Decolonization: Indigeneity, Education & Society* 1(1): 1–40; Saranillio, Dean Itsuji (2013) 'Why Asian Settler Colonialism Matters: A Thought Piece on Critiques, Debates, and Indigenous Difference', *Settler Colonial Studies* 3(3–4): 280–94.

22. Uchida, Jun (2014) *Brokers of Empire: Japanese Settler Colonialism in Korea, 1876–1945*. Cambridge, MA: Harvard University Press; Lewallen, Ann-Elise (2016) *The Fabric of Indigeneity: Ainu Identity, Gender, and Settler Colonialism in Japan*. Santa Fe: School for Advanced Research Press; Albuquerque: University of New Mexico Press.

23. Camacho, Keith L. and Shigematsu, Setsu (2010) *Militarized Currents: Toward a Decolonized Future in Asia and the Pacific*. Minneapolis: University of Minnesota Press; Sakai, Naoki and Yoo, Hyon Joo (2012) *The Trans-Pacific Imagination: Rethinking Boundary, Culture, and Society*. Singapore: World Scientific Publishing Company; Hoskins, Janet and Nguyen, Viet Thanh (2014) *Transpacific Studies: Framing an Emerging Field*. Honolulu: University of Hawai'i Press; Yoneyama, Lisa (2016) *Cold War Ruins: Transpacific Critique of American Justice and Japanese War Crimes*. Durham, NC: Duke University Press.

24. We are deploying Indigenous people in Asia here to refer to those groups who self-identify as Indigenous (most often groups who have been uprooted, massacred, or confined in their territory, or with regard to their sovereignty status in relation to a dominant nation-state). The question of who is and is not Indigenous (and by whose standards) seems less conducive to the shift in thinking here than the foundational challenge posed by Indigeneity to the modern colonial world-system: various socio-political endeavours in Asia have been considered in many other terms apart from Indigenous sovereignty struggles, even though Indigeneity has most profoundly called out the groundless justifications for the modern colonial world-system behind the atrocities in Asia. See, Morris-Suzuki, Tessa (1999) 'The Ainu: Beyond the Politics of Cultural Coexistence', *Cultural Survival* 23(4), special issue on Visions of the Future: The Prospect for Reconciliation, available at: www.culturalsurvival.org/publications/cultural-survival-quarterly/ainu-beyond-politics-cultural-coexistence.

25. Mignolo 2005 op. cit.

26. See, for example, Salazar Bondy, Augusto (1996) *¿Existe una filosofía de nuestra América?* 13th edn. Mexico, DF: Siglo Veintiuno Editores.

27. Maldonado-Torres 2011a op. cit.

28. Dussel, Enrique (2013) *Ethics of Liberation: In the Age of Globalization and Exclusion*, trans. Eduardo Mendieta et al. Durham, NC: Duke University Press; Dussel, Enrique (1985) *Philosophy of Liberation*, trans. Aquilina Martinez and Christine Morkovsky. Maryknoll, NY: Orbis Books.

29. Dussel, Enrique (1995) *The invention of the Americas: Eclipse of 'the Other' and the Myth of Modernity*, trans. Michael D. Barber. New York: Continuum.

30. Césaire 2000 op. cit.

31. Dussel, Enrique (1974) *Método para una filosofía de la liberación: Superación analéctica de la dialéctica hegeliana*. Salamanca: Ediciones Sígueme.

32. Ibid. p. 182.

33. Dussel 1985 op. cit. p. 183.

34. Dussel, Enrique (1996) *The Underside of Modernity: Apel, Ricoeur, Rorty, Taylor, and the Philosophy of Liberation*, trans and ed. Eduardo Mendieta. Atlantic Highlands, NJ: Humanities Press, p. 6.

35. Dussel 1974 op. cit. pp. 184, 185, 190.

36. Dussel 1996 op. cit.

37. As already mentioned in the previous section of this essay, 'Shifting the Geography of Reason' is the motto of the Caribbean Philosophical Association, an institutional space within the currents of the global academy that is

taking concrete steps to transform the field of philosophy in particular and the structure of the university in general.

38. Dussel 1996 op. cit. p. 53.
39. Dussel, Enrique (2011) 'From Critical Theory to the Philosophy of Liberation: Some Themes for a Dialogue', trans. George Ciccariello-Maher, *Transmodernity: Journal of Peripheral Cultural Production of the Luso-Hispanic World* 1(2): 16–43, at p. 17.
40. Ibid. p. 18.
41. Ibid. p. 16.
42. Mignolo, Walter (2007) 'Delinking: The Rhetoric of Modernity, the Logic of Coloniality, and the Grammar of De-Coloniality', *Cultural Studies* 21(2–3): 449–514.
43. De Beauvoir, Simone (1989) *The Second Sex*, trans. H.M. Parshley. New York: Vintage Books.
44. Irigaray, Luce (1985) *Speculum of the Other Woman*, trans. Gillian C. Gill. Ithaca, NY: Cornell University Press.
45. hooks, bell (2015) *Feminist Theory: From Margin to Center*. New York: Routledge.
46. Martín Alcoff, Linda (2015) *The Future of Whiteness*. Malden, MA: Polity Press; Martin Alcoff, Linda (2005) *Visible Identities: Race, Gender, and the Self*. New York: Oxford Press.
47. Gordon 2006 op. cit. *Disciplinary Decadence: Living Thought in Trying Times*. Boulder, Co.: Paradigm Press; Gordon, Lewis (2000) 'Du Bois's Humanistic Philosophy of Human Sciences', *Annals of the American Academy of Political and Social Sciences* 568: 265–80.
48. See Martín Alcoff op. cit. 2015 and 2005. See also Sylvia Wynter (2003) 'Unsettling the Coloniality of Being/Power/Truth: Towards the Human, After Man, Its Overrepresentation – An Argument', *CR: The New Centennial Review* 3(3): 257–337. See also, Gordon 2000 op. cit.
49. Wynter, Sylvia (1994) 'Afterword: Beyond Miranda's Meanings: Un/Silencing the "Demonic Ground" of Caliban's Woman', in Carole Boyce Davies and Elaine Savory Fido (eds) *Out of the Kumbla: Caribbean Women and Literature*. Trenton: Africa World Press, pp. 355–72 at p. 364; Wynter, Sylvia (2003) 'Unsettling the Coloniality of Being/Power/Truth: Towards the Human, After Man, Its Overrepresentation – An Argument', *CR: The New Centennial Review* 3.3: 257–337.
50. Wynter 1994 op. cit. pp. 357–58.
51. Since Kimberlé Crenshaw's development of the term 'intersectional', social and political philosophy have remained somewhat vague in their accounts of identity. There is common agreement among most contemporary theorists that identity is a multi-dimensional phenomenon that cannot be broken down into distinct axes of oppression. In practice, however, this insight has proven difficult to develop. The salient point is that rather than rely upon a vague or problematic conception of intersectionality or identity, Wynter develops an account of intersectionality by linking together race and culture. This theoretical move both highlights the ambiguity that remains in

intersectional theories and produces a new horizon for such theories going forward.

52. Wynter 1994 op. cit. pp. 361–2.
53. Ibid. p. 363.

PART II

INSTITUTIONAL INITIATIVES

6

Asylum University: Re-situating Knowledge Exchange along Cross-border Positionalities

Kolar Aparna and Olivier Kramsch

Speaking from our recent engagements (peaking in early 2015) in student struggles on campus (as part of transnational movements resisting financialisation of knowledge production and non-transparent managerial structures of universities), alongside struggles demanding equal rights for and by newly arriving asylum-seekers and long-staying undocumented inhabitants across our borderlands (straddling the Dutch/German border), we develop what we call an 'asylum university lens'. Rather than simply being associated with confinement, asylum serves as a symbolic and powerful metaphor for speaking from a space of refuge. In a similar way, where the university is more often associated with the closed-off 'ivory tower', this reconceptualisation enables it to serve as a space of solidarity for knowledge exchange. In this way, everyday interactions of classroom debates and academic writing processes emerge as embodied conversations, relationalities (also part of conflicts, tensions and paradoxes as much as of affective ties) and transformations both on campus and outside in a global context of migration and cross-border movements of refugees. Using such a lens gives us power to call attention to the instability and uncertainty of borders and boundaries while acting and situating knowledge production from such embodied relationalities that are nevertheless sensitive to differential privileges and conflicting ambitions.

Asylum University as a position

The Asylum University (AU) emerges as a movement bringing together academics, students, activists, volunteers, citizens, 'undocumented migrants' (whose asylum application has been rejected), refugees (those waiting for the asylum procedure as well as those with 'legal status'), and just people to find ways to collaborate with each other in an informal manner. AU emerges as a movement to transform everyday processes of knowledge exchange within university walls as well as within walls of asylum procedures and walls confronted by those who are 'out-of-procedure'. Rather than being associated with confinement, asylum here serves as a symbolic and powerful metaphor for speaking from 'the margins'. Speaking from the margins gives us power to call attention to the instability and uncertainty of bounded governing structures, be it of the state or of our own university (inevitably inter-twined), while acting towards transforming these structures in ways that go beyond the emotions of fear or pity (for self and the other).

Rather than being associated with the closed-off 'ivory tower', the university serves as a space of solidarity for knowledge exchange of all kinds. Inhabiting our borderlands and commuting across this border on a daily basis (especially for one author) confronts us with the urgency to weave together worlds that are otherwise meant to stay apart. We started initially with uncertain steps (because of not knowing what to expect) into migrant-support organisations on either side of the border. We are now weaving and becoming part of relations that connect multiple (border) localities (from the Dadaab camp in Kenya to Bolzano in Italy along the Austrian/Italian border, to Copenhagen in Denmark and Aarendonk in Belgium, to name a few places where people were and still are) via practices of knowledge exchange that question the divide between spaces of encampment (like asylum centres, detention centres, refugee camps and simply waiting for legal status) and spaces of learning (classrooms). In what follows we share some key moments and contextual develop-ments around which relations central to the AU initiative emerged and continue to emerge. Building on the actions, practices and relations part of these developments, we craft what we call an 'Asylum University' lens for a futuristic vision of a university that is yet to emerge.

Reflection on political and institutional conditions leading to the emergence of AU

Some of us have been part of the Nijmegen Centre for Border Research (NCBR), which itself has been running as an informal network of students and academics interested in border studies for two decades, housed at the Human Geography Department of Radboud University, Nijmegen, in the Netherlands. Like all research centres, our centre is also part of structural political-economic inequalities and unequal top-down funding landscapes that are reproduced within research collaborations across universities. Emerging also from a discomfort with precisely such relations, we felt the need to begin our pedagogical and research interests via informal relations and engagements locally, but as always open to a cross-border dimension within the context of hospitality initiatives for asylum-seekers and refugees across our Dutch/German borderland of Nijmegen (in the Netherlands) and Kranenburg, Kleve (in Germany).[1] These relations at the same time slowly extend to other locations in Belgium, Italy and Denmark, due to people moving and small informal networks spreading, as well as research initiatives being forged via these networks.

Before the political drama of the so-called refugee crisis in Europe hit the newspapers in 2015, some of us had already been in dialogue with local migrant-support networks for asylum-seekers and refugees and were busy thinking about the role of our department and our university in relation to such existing support networks. We began to have informal meetings between volunteers, asylum-seekers, refugees, academics and students to brainstorm on what could be feasible inter-relational actions that we could take to bridge the needs and aspirations of members of this informal network. Facilitating easier access to language support and higher education were among the most urgent issues that were raised by our refugee friends. The reasons for this had not only practical consequences in terms of improving one's place in the job market and feeling socially welcome in everyday spaces of interactions, but also simply to dignify oneself, since the asylum procedure and embodied experiences were acknowledged as a demoralising process, especially for one's intellectual development. Being engaged in an intellectually stimulating environment was something urgently needed as much as the material dimensions of food, housing, documents, work, etc., as identified by some. Alongside this, academics and students present raised the importance of embodied knowledge for classroom discussions as much as within scientific knowledge production channels.

Not very long after these meetings, the student occupation of the Maagdenhuis (the management building of the University of Amsterdam)[2] led to fierce debates and a student movement under the name 'New University' that opened up spaces for critical reflections around the governing and managerial structures of universities in the Netherlands and especially University of Amsterdam, then travelling to different locations in the country and across Europe. These broader, transnational initiatives working against the accelerated corporatisation of the European university landscape dovetailed with a very localised, Slow Science movement on the Radboud campus. The main impetus of this was to find a collective solution to working conditions producing epidemic levels of burnout among university staff, notably within our management faculty (one of the authors, a self-styled 'burnout activist', was a key figure in this initiative).[3]

What is to be done?

Making space: working town/gown tensions

The first practical issue in getting to organise meetings between and across university-based academics and the refugee community and volunteers was the question of *space*. The question of *where* and *when* to have meetings became a hugely difficult organisational problem. This can be seen as a classical 'town/gown' tension in which some academics felt bound to their everyday commitments of teaching and publishing that do not permit them to make a cycle ride to the city centre for meetings. On the other hand, the university campus was unfamiliar to the refugee community since their everyday life was governed by various other priorities, such as lawyer visits, seeking support for language, work, shelter, food, etc., that were mostly concentrated in the city centre and around peripheral neighbourhoods where they live. Despite being only a 15-minute cycle ride apart, the city centre and the university campus appeared miles apart in terms of creating such shared spaces of dialogue. This meant making maps of the campus and explaining bus and cycle routes to the various buildings on campus for our refugee friends, while trying to appeal to our academic counterparts to make time to cycle to the city centre for alternative meetings. Such a compromise has never been fully attained, nevertheless after more than two years the university campus is a much more familiar place for some of our refugee friends. A cafe in the city centre, which also houses refugee-support organisations, was perceived by one academic as 'too political and informal' and as not appropriate for such formal meetings initiated by university members. Here again we came across all kinds of prejudices associated with spaces in the city centre versus how the university should create spaces of its own. This eventually raised questions of privilege and the right to the (univer)city, of who has the right to speak on behalf of whom, and the underlying differential knowledges producing and reproducing such divides.

Revalorising 'valorisation': breaking down the academic/activist divide

Speaking especially about borders and migration in our classrooms without being engaged with embodied practices outside the campus relevant to such work, raises questions of how dis/connected to everyday realities university knowledge production processes are. At a time when our managerial superstructure obsesses about 'valorisation', defined by the measurable impact of our research on society (narrowly defined by local economic firms and agents), AU broadens the scope and scale of the potential societal influence of our academic labour by engaging across a range of alternative off-campus sites: Stichting GAST (a local support organisation for asylum-seekers and undocumented migrants); cafe De Klinker (a collective of various solidarity groups housed in a previously squatted building, where, apart from other activities, an open kitchen is run in which refugees are invited to cook and sell their food for voluntary contributions); BethHamifgash (an intercultural organisation also involved in refugee support across the Dutch/German border in Kleve, Germany); Heumensoord refugee camp (one of the largest refugee camps in the Netherlands that served 3000 refugees between September 2015 and May 2016), and the pro-refugee student movement it mobilised, 'Just People';[4] Terecht cafe/Justice cafe (the temporary transformation of a former abandoned canteen on campus by students into a dynamic meeting place for informal knowledge exchange initiatives between and across the academic and non-academic communities in Nijmegen, forcefully shut down by the management board of the university for not following protocols in applying for rooms); Stadsnomaden (a running eco-village established by a few students initiated simply by parking their campers on empty, unused university land); Radboud Postcolonialism & Race Reading Group (an informally run reading group discussing texts from postcolonial studies, bringing together cross-campus academics and students as well as interested outside publics); and YouAreButYouAreNot (a collaborative process in which people from AU engage with a cultural project in Bolzano reflecting on the selective closure of the Brenner pass (along the Italian/ Austrian border since 2014) for asylum-seekers heading from Italy to Germany and other northern European countries.

Through such off-campus engagements, AU practices strive to join social activism, cultural production and academic pursuits in mutually enforcing and productive ways. Legitimising activist commitments remains an uphill struggle within Dutch academia (and in Continental Europe generally), where it is often perceived by colleagues as a mere 'hobby', something one does after the real work of pursuing objective, disinterested, value-free science. Indeed, a vital mission for AU is to break down the artificially produced barrier between 'activist' and 'academic' labour. For us, the two realms are inextricably bound and mutually reinforcing. This 'borderwork' dovetails with the complementary goal of making space at a Dutch university for unrepentantly normative social science: the possibility of taking a strong normative stand in academic teaching and research. This position is still largely an unwritten taboo in many quarters of Dutch academia, where preference is given to 'objective', normative-free scientific enquiry, largely catering to the knowledge requirements of government policymakers. In making explicit ethical and normative standpoints from the urgency of everyday life when conducting research, AU breaks this taboo.

Surfing precarity through shifting convivialities

At the same time, what continues to offer a 'third space' under the umbrella of the AU initiative that differs from other existing refugee-support initiatives is its ambition of exchanging life experiences rather than aims of 'unidirectional integration'.[5] Through classroom projects, discussions, co-writing and publishing articles with refugee comrades, and simply informally creating social networks between and across groups, a lot is achieved in terms of integration as a constant negotiation of language,[6] values, aspirations, collective identities and expectations via shared conversations. The informal interactions, friendships and conversations that emerge from these interactions continue to lay the foundations for current relations and transformations of the AU initiative, as well as the space of the surrounding campus environment in which it is embedded.[7]

Meetings are needed, to begin with, to align the ambitions and expectations of different actors and groups involved. However, aiming to come to a consensus about ways to achieve goals is not realistic.

This is because these ambitions are constantly shifting both individually and, in this case, also the contexts of actors involved including refugee-support organisations and academic research communities. Further, the uncertain landscape of refugee im/mobility in which people are being transferred from one camp to another camp at the other end of the country or people are being deported back to their countries due to rejected applications does not allow for a fixed group or 'community' that exists. This does not mean that there is no community, however, but only that relations are constantly transforming due to shifting situations. Alongside such forced and voluntary im/mobilities lies also the precariousness of academic positions, funding obligations and shifting board members of refugee-support organisations that add to an uncertain and shifting ground on which the initiative runs. In short: AU surfs its own precarity, and in the teeth of it; remaining semi-invisible and fluid in the margins of institutional hierarchies and full professorial positions, it serves as an open rebuke to the minority of university staff inhabiting ultra-safe positions at the cost of rampant insecurity for the majority.

On such shifting ground, AU's modest aim is to try to keep classroom doors open, while building informal bridges between asylum centres and refugee-support organisations, alongside keeping an eye open for an opportunity to make connections with new people interested in enabling the same. Meetings have been so far held monthly for the first year and a half in which interested academics, refugees, asylum-seekers (both those waiting for asylum procedures and those whose application was rejected), volunteers in refugee support and students came regularly together, albeit as a moving, floating group of individuals rather than a fixed group. Meetings were held alternately between rooms on campus, which some of us could informally reserve during lunch hours, and the cafe De Klinker in the city centre which housed, among others, the refugee-support organisation (Stichting GAST). This served very well since we had the freedom to move back and forth that also served to introduce each group into their own worlds of everyday inhabitance and to build trust. The meetings were mostly run, in our case, by one coordinating member who was able to assume this role due to the possibility of incorporating the initiative and its transformations as part of her PhD project. However, the content of the meetings was always collectively raised. Communication was mostly via email and word-of-mouth. Once informal social networks are built, however, they have a way of spreading and transforming on their own, for which one does not have to always rely on meetings for taking actions.

'More than just a refugee': opening the classroom to the world

When we initially started, the first challenges were around the diverse intellectual and professional aspirations within the refugee community and our own limitations in being able to open courses only within the Geography Department. Language was another issue that again is complicated since courses at the Bachelor level are taught in Dutch or English, and Master's level courses only in English. This meant that those who did not speak English or Dutch could not attend the courses and even if they did they had to struggle. This made way for ideas around creating 'whisper corners' of translation during lectures and initiating courses taught in Arabic, for instance, which have however not yet materialised in practice but remain in the pipeline. Further, the Dutch system of separating vocational training from university education makes it difficult to create shared spaces of dialogue with refugees who wish to receive training skills for a vocation and those who aspire for more intellectually demanding learning environments.

What emerged as an initially euphoric yet low-key opening of the course 'Approaches to Space and Environment' – a theoretical course on historical approaches in Human Geography relevant to urban planning – eventually led to our refugee comrades building their own social networks from this base, some continuing with their passion for topics in Human Geography, some growing to meet their own professional aspirations, with others opting out of courses altogether in pursuing careers in the theatre or the arts. What remained crucial was the effort made to demonstrate that it is possible to gain access to education even if in an informal way, and have the option open for those interested. What was equally crucial was that our refugee friends for the first time had the chance to use their minds, the dignity to engage in the world as thinking beings, rather than as 'bodies' awaiting a decision from the Dutch state as to their asylum procedure. Dutch students, on the other hand, had the opportunity to engage with fellow students from Afghanistan, Iraq, Eritrea, Syria and Congo, whose experience of war, migration and resettlement in Europe directly enriched in-class discussion in the most productive of ways.

Access to literature was initially circulated informally via email; however now, after two years, we have managed to find a way of creating temporary student accounts for those who wish to be registered for a course, allowing digital access to literature and course material. For those who complete the course we make separate certificates under the name 'Asylum University' while still mentioning the course title as part of the official Radboud University syllabus, signed by the course lecturers. Official-looking documents play a crucial role here in acknowledging the effort of participation, as well as serving to enhance one's 'legal case' for asylum, if not directly, indirectly, in demonstrating one's participation in 'society', since the state gaze starts from the assumption that asylum-seekers living for long periods in a country are not 'integrated' and do not participate in social activities with so-called 'host' populations.

Most importantly, attending courses as demonstrated by most of our refugee friends allows them not to be identified as a refugee but as a fellow student, or a fellow thinker, which is one of the most urgently needed spaces of empowerment, since most of them find it hard to break out of the label of 'refugee' wherever they go – be it at social gatherings, religious functions, everyday interactions on the streets or in personal relationships with friends and acquaintances. The classroom allows one to merge into the identity of a student regardless of one's legal status, and debunks myths of 'the refugee' for other fellow students, since interactions are shaped around the aims of learning and exchange.[8] Furthermore, in co-writing and co-publishing scientific texts together with our refugee comrades, we also debunk the myth of expertise that surrounds the academic enterprise, and invert the telescope on the subject–object relation that for so long has afflicted social-scientific method. Rather than go 'out there' to do fieldwork by interviewing 'exotic Others' (in this case refugees), we become 'co-workers in the Kingdom of culture',[9] each drawing on our own embodied experiences to produce auto-ethnographies that speak powerfully to the spatio-temporal present, as well as our collective implication in shaping that present.[10] Finally, co-writing with refugee comrades at a most fundamental level enacts a way of *doing academic work otherwise*; rather than write and/ or teach in a relation of dependency, often under the shadow of a more senior staff member for whom one often relies existentially for funding, AU co-writing inaugurates another logic of knowledge production based on respect, dignity and equality. This model is orthogonal to the individualising, neoliberal competitive logic of university life today. Its implications, we believe, are profoundly transformative.

'Silence, anonymity, confidentiality'

Since the initiative does not differentiate between 'sans papiers' and refugees 'with legal status' or 'in procedure', issues of privacy, confidentiality and trust become very sensitive and important. As university campuses are not completely outside the surveillance of immigration control and identity checks, the issue of keeping the initiative 'low-profile', 'under the radar', and silent was important, especially when we initially began in 2014 in an environment of fear due to student protests in Amsterdam against managerial structures. In order to build trust among our refugee friends, it was important to assure a safe environment where they could retain anonymity of identity. Also, it is important to avoid questions of tracking identity within state frames, such as 'Why did you leave your country?', 'What is your story of hardship?', 'Where do you live?' and so on. The core aim here is to overcome exclusionary frameworks that rely on Othering, in this case of identifying people as 'refugees', while nevertheless wanting to spread information to more people who might wish to join the initiative and courses, that is, a sensitive approach to the issue of in/visibilising the initiative. For this reason, apart for exceptional circumstances, AU does not allow the use of cameras inside the classroom (web-lectures), as this would compromise the identities of refugee students during sensitive moments of their asylum procedure.

'I am already wet, you shouldn't have to become wet because of me': confronting and overcoming fear at university

For AU, the watchwords of 'silence' and 'anonymity' took on a more sinister register as we confronted the politics of fear at the outset of the movement. It is no secret that fear is used as a management strategy in most corporations and governmental institutions. The university is no exception to that rule. As we spontaneously threw open the doors of our classrooms without seeking permission from higher levels of administration, anxious, well-meaning colleagues spoke by indirect means and through innuendo that we should 'be careful', that our jobs might be threatened if we did not show restraint, common sense and moderation. Anxiety regarding potentially high numbers of refugees flooding Radboud classrooms was thick in the air, and we were made to feel it. This fear, and its psychic effects, should not be forgotten. At one point a refugee comrade of ours, a woman from Ethiopia, blurted out to the authors: 'I am already wet, you shouldn't have to become wet because of me', suggesting that she was already tainted by a legal system that had marked her as deportable. The same, she suggested, should not happen to us simply because we wished to help her. This was a stunning, revelatory moment for AU. Could we really lose our jobs for incorporating refugees into university life? On what grounds? Where were our rights as academics? What rights did the refugee community have in demanding access to educational opportunities? We were treading on *terrae incognitae*. All we felt was a diffuse, unlocatable fear.

At this point, some of us within AU suggested formalising the movement by seeking official recognition from our academic dean. The thinking then was that if we came out from the shadows by receiving official recognition, we would no longer need to operate within the pervasive climate of suspicion and fear we were inhabiting at that time. We approached our international advisor on the matter, who, though generally supportive of our goals, counselled us to be cautious, since many university administrators would question why undocumented refugees have a right to Radboud classrooms when the normal admissions procedure rejected so many native Dutch students. We were told to move cautiously. Finally, we approached another colleague in a senior management position, an academic who had once militated in the Dutch squatter movement of the 1980s, whose heart, we hoped, still beat to the Left. This colleague heard our mission, and decided the best thing to do was not go to the dean with our idea, as he was sure it would be shot down. He would therefore do something 'typically Dutch', that is acknowledge and support what we are doing, but pretend it doesn't exist when communicating with higher levels of university governance. This, in hindsight, was a brilliant solution to our dilemma, as it gave us political cover to continue our operations, thus mitigating the cloud of fear and suspicion surrounding AU. It also gave other colleagues within our faculty the necessary political cover to come out of the woodwork to join our cause. Within the past year we have had at least half a dozen colleagues spanning several departments open their classroom doors to refugees. The movement was finally maturing, and could work more fully in the 'light of day'.

Building inter-urban and cross-border coalitions

Since our refugee comrades are constantly being transferred to camps located elsewhere or themselves choose to cross borders in response to legal procedures of asylum regimes of European Union (EU) states, it becomes important to incorporate a mobile, inter-urban and cross-border dimension to AU so as to allow for social networks to spread beyond one city and nation. Precisely due to this issue it helps to be open to building networks for spreading experiences and looking for like-minded groups who wish to initiate and run a similar movement. In our case, we were contacted by a group of students from another nearby Dutch university town (Wageningen) to share our experiences and possibly help them launch a similar movement on their campus. One of our friends attending our course while living in the camp nearby was transferred to another Dutch city, Almere. This triggered not only us but also him to begin making new contacts in Almere and Amsterdam, which is close to Almere. Our friends in the Geography Department of University of Amsterdam forwarded a call for applications for a fully funded summer school opening for refugees, for which our friend who was recently transferred got selected. Most recently, a workshop has been organised on Radboud campus with the intention of linking refugee-support organisations on either side of the Dutch/German border, thus addressing a shared, cross-border problematic that until now has been addressed only within the bounded, nation-state territorial scale of the Netherlands or Germany.[11] Our model of engaged teaching/research has now embarked on a pan-European trajectory; starting in spring 2017, AU joins a Danish-funded academic consortium charged with investigating migration, borders and refugee hospitality in six EU member states.[12] This way of building on informal, cross-border networks to create alliances and possibilities for ideas to travel is an important strategic element of our movement.

Reflection: crafting an Asylum University lens

The above reflections are neither prescriptive nor descriptive of how ambitions for *decolonising the university* 'must' take place. Rather, it is most importantly a call for rethinking everyday relations producing university life, both spatially (bridging town/gown tensions) and socially (activating relations of knowledge exchange instead of privilege and 'distant gazing' towards marginalised groups, in this case refugees and those involved in their support).

From the lens of what we call 'Asylum University', the university emerges as a place from where embodied relationalities from intertwined biographies produce an open geography of multi-locatedness and cross-border positionalities from where to think, exchange and reflect. The forced and voluntary cross-border movements of refugees and migrants, rather than only limiting and restricting those involved, challenge and push relations of solidarity to transform and travel informally, despite all the legal barriers, surveillance and fear imposed on them. Rather than being symbolised by an ivory tower, the university comes to be practised as a space embedded in a dynamic community, bringing together actors on-the-ground who are proactively responsive to transformative moments in the geopolitical landscape of our borderlands, a space that is nevertheless inevitably intertwined and overlapping with other borderlands across Europe and the world through the trajectories and biographies of cross-border movements of people. Everyday practices of university life such as teaching, writing, reading, discussing, debating, rather than a matter of fulfilling bureaucratic task-loads, become empowering acts of co-production despite all the challenges of translation (i.e. linguistic translation, but also translating embodied experiences to theoretical frames and vice versa) that come with it, and academic career trajectories come to be deeply entangled with the uncertain trajectories of actors of such 'communities of engagement'.

From such a symbolic optic one inevitably questions the artificial divide between formal and informal knowledges upon which modern universities are built. Rather than being a cause for self-congratulation, treading such a path is inevitably muddled by the messy realities of negotiating relations of reciprocity under conditions of privilege, discrimination and inequality, which often shines a light onto one's own prejudices and prejudgements in confronting and unpredictable ways. The questions that continue to haunt us are: Whose voices are more or less heard? Who is allowed to speak on behalf of whom? Why and in which language? How can one be recognised as and/or make space for recognition of voices that are made invisible in order to keep privilege, and especially white privilege in place, while at the same time respecting the right not to expose oneself? What transformative practices can be initiated to make way for a future horizon of conviviality that is not precarious? Currently operating amidst the cracks in university walls, we hope such a lens makes its way to the foundational grounds of the academy, from where we can envision a pluralistic future in which multiple subjectivities and languages produce knowledges in constant motion and contestation rather than as resolved scripts written in stone.

Acknowledgements

Our thanks to all our comrades, on both sides of our borderland.

Bibliography

Aparna, Kolar and Schapendonk, Joris (in press) 'Shifting Itineraries of Asylum Hospitality: Towards a Process Geographical Approach of Guest–Host Relations', *Geoforum*.

Aparna, Kolar, Kramsch, Olivier and Schapendonk, Joris (2016) 'Re-thinking Migration Planning Visions through a Border Lens', *RaumPlanung* 183: 20–25.

Aparna, Kolar, Mahamed, Zeinab, Deenen, Ingmar and Kramsch, Olivier (2017) 'Lost Europe', *Etnografia e ricerca qualitative: Rivista quadrimestrale* 3/2017: 435–52.

Du Bois, W.E.B. (1976 [1905]) 'Of Our Spiritual Strivings', in *The Souls of Black Folk*. New York: Buccaneer Books, pp. 15–22.

Kramsch, Olivier, Aparna, Kolar and Degu, Huda (2015) 'Languaging the Borders of Europe', *Social Sciences* 4: 1207–28.

Verkoren, Willemijn, van Leeuwen, Bart, Sent, Esther-Mirjam, Tinnevelt, Ronald and Kramsch, Olivier (2014) 'Praat mee over de toekomst van de universiteit', *Vox*, 9 April: 36–37.

Notes

1. Nijmegen is located only 9 km from the German border, across which a vibrant pro-refugee movement remains active. In this chapter we speak of initiatives that straddle these borderlands (while also extending to other sites) rather than speaking from either side.

2. The occupation ran between February and April 2015.

3. Verkoren, Willemijn, van Leeuwen, Bart, Sent, Esther-Mirjam, Tinnevelt, Ronald and Kramsch, Olivier (2014) 'Praat mee over de toekomst van de universiteit', *Vox* 9 4/14: 36–37.

4. justpeople.nl

5. Aparna, Kolar and Schapendonk, Joris (2017) 'Shifting Itineraries of Asylum Hospitality: Towards a Process Geographical Approach of Guest–Host Relations', *Geoforum*.

6. Indeed, language, especially the politics of language use in the Dutch university context, has grown into one of the core themes discussed within AU, both as *praxis* and theoretical intervention. Who gets to speak what language, in which circumstances and with what outcomes are vital issues that remain to be addressed adequately in an uneven language landscape riven with unresolved postcolonial power geometries. Thus framed, the issue of language at university transcends the mere need for refugees to integrate into the Dutch body politic by learning Dutch as quickly as possible, and opens out onto the conditions that would be appropriate to producing a truly multilingual university (for a first attempt at imagining

such a 'languaging' practice, see Kramsch, Olivier, Aparna, Kolar and Degu, Huda (2015) 'Languaging the Borders of Europe', *Social Sciences* 4: 1207–28, the fruit of collaboration with the authors of this chapter and a female AU comrade from Ethiopia).

7. The transformative influence exerted by AU radiates throughout university space in ways that produce sometimes unexpectedly felicitous pedagogical effects, especially among colleagues. Two notes from the trenches will suffice. After a geographer colleague caught wind that the authors visited the Heumensoord camp (located 10 minutes' walk from our offices) in order to speak to refugee friends there, he pondered 'I'd love to go myself, but I don't have a reason to go.' We made sure to take him there on the next occasion. Another colleague, upon hearing that a Syrian refugee from Heumensoord had joined our on-campus postcolonial reading group, mentioned how challenging it must be for us to navigate the inevitable unevenness in academic knowledge such an entry must surely produce within the group. 'Our Syrian comrade studied English literature in Aleppo', we replied, with a smile.

8. The political productivity of encounters between Dutch students and refugees was underscored in one class session moderated by the authors during which a Dutch MA student expounded at length on the fear he felt when in the presence of migrants who walked in groups in Nijmegen and did not speak Dutch. A Syrian refugee student sitting a few rows ahead of him turned around after he had finished speaking, looked him straight in the eye, and said in perfect English: 'Why did your mayor [of Nijmegen] place us in the forest, separate from normal Dutch society? This was a decision that only increased your fear of us.'

9. Du Bois, W.E.B. (1976 [1905]) 'Of Our Spiritual Strivings', in *The Souls of Black Folk*. New York: Buccaneer Books, pp. 15–22.

10. For recent examples of such collective writing, see Kramsch et al. 2015 op. cit.; Aparna, Kolar, Mahamed, Zeinab, Deenen, Ingmar and Kramsch, Olivier (in press) 'Lost Europe', *Etnografia e ricerca qualitative: Rivista quadrimestrale* 3/2017: 435–52.

11. See, Aparna, Kolar, Kramsch, Olivier and Schapendonk, Joris (2016) 'Re-thinking Migration Planning Visions Through a Border Lens', *Raum-Planung* 183: 20–25.

12. Project title: *Helping Hands: Research Network on the Everyday Border Work of European Citizens* (Danish Council for Independent Research, DFF/FKK/Humanities). Participating universities: Radboud University, University of Bergen, University of Hamburg, University of Glasgow, University of Waterloo, Malmö University and the University of Copenhagen.

7

Diversity or Decolonisation? Researching Diversity at the University of Amsterdam

Rosalba Icaza and Rolando Vázquez

The second decade of the twenty-first century is witnessing a wave of student movements across various geographies that is questioning the university. It is not just demanding equal access and more democratic and transparent management. The movements are calling for the decolonisation of the university. They are challenging the politics of knowledge of the university, including the content of what is being taught and the ways in which it is being taught. They are advocating for a university that is not oblivious to its being implicated in the colonial difference that configures today's local and global realities. The movements are confronting the university with its colonial legacies, with its participation in a politics of knowledge that reinforces and reproduces social divides. The movements to decolonise the university are opening the enormous task of transforming knowledge practices, the frameworks of understanding and pedagogical practices.

In this chapter, we offer some reflections on the work of the Diversity Commission of the University of Amsterdam (UvA). As members of this commission, chaired by Professor Gloria Wekker,[1] our mandate emerged from the UvA's student movements demanding both the democratisation and decolonisation of their university. To that effect, we were asked to study the state of diversity in the university. As a commission we implemented a novel perspective that combines intersectionality and decoloniality as grounding framework.

For the commission, the question of diversity included but was not limited to the counting of demographics. The commission adopted a multi-level approach to diversity through which it became necessary, besides the demographics, to look into governance structures, emotions and life experiences, and ways of teaching and learning. Here we will focus particularly on the research data-gathering 'toolbox' that was developed with the core aims of bringing marginalised voices within the university into the conversation on diversity and decolonisation, mapping the epistemic diversity deficits of the university in general and, most importantly, uncovering the diversity enriching practices of knowledge that exist at the university but that are undervalued or disregarded.

This chapter is divided into two broad sections: the first introduces the geopolitical context that is confronting the university with the task of decolonising itself, the second shares the experience of the Diversity Commission of the UvA.

The university and geopolitics of knowledge

Universities have unique political contexts, historical formations entangled with colonialism and nation-state formations. Universities are internally and externally heterogeneous; they might be tax funded or private or a mix of both; they might be denominational or secular and so on.[2] Despite this, research has showed that universities have in different forms, and, at different speeds and to different extents, been involved in and impacted by general trends: (a) an increasing harmonisation and standardisation of programmes and structure of fees to encourage national, regional and international mobility;[3] (b) the development of strategies to address the increased demand for spaces, and the decrease in state subsidies in the global North and global South; (c) a business ethos, international rankings culture and a highly paid administrative 'class' parallel to the increasing 'precaritisation' of teaching and the outsourcing of services such as cleaning, gardening but also proofreading and grant-writing skills.[4] Universities and research centres across the world are facing public scrutiny of the role that they have historically played in reducing diversity, instead of promoting or encouraging it, in their approaches to knowledge production and dissemination.

Student mobilisations are not a novel phenomenon. They have been theorised in various forms: as waves of contention,[5] as expressions of global uprisings[6] or of transnational liberations.[7] In the mid-2000s, student-led initiatives within the Occupy Wall Street (OWS) and the Indignados movements[8] voiced concerns about a neoliberal/corporate model of university and its pro-business ethos as producing highly indebted and unemployable graduates in the context of economic austerity. Meanwhile, in Latin America, the privatisation of higher education mushroomed but also students' mobilisations demanding the creation of popular and for indigenous people's universities.[9]

From the end of 1990s, social movements in Latin America engaged in processes of political, economic and territorial autonomy started to create their own universities as an attempt to counter state-run education and increasing privatisation trends in the region. The Indigenous Universities in Ecuador, the Social Movements Universities in Peru; the Landless Peasant Movement (MST) University in Brazil and the Universidad de la Tierra in Chiapas and Oaxaca, Mexico are some experiences of these ongoing efforts to build up epistemic autonomy in the decolonisation of learning and knowing.[10] More recently, other efforts pushing for the decolonisation of learning and the university have included the 'Decolonising our Universities' movement in Malaysia, the 'Rhodes Must Fall' process in South Africa, 'Why is My Curriculum White?' in the United Kingdom, and the student mobilisations, mainly 'the University of Colour'[11] (UoC), the New Urban Collective (NUC)[12] and 'Amsterdam United'[13] in the Netherlands that instigated the creation of the UvA Diversity Commission.

The plurality of these movements aiming at the decolonisation of learning gave the research of the UvA Diversity Commission a rich and challenging context for its research.[14] We also acknowledge the relevance for the movements to reassess present knowledge-generation practices in relation to their colonial past. Taking seriously the legacies of colonialism calls for a transformation of our frameworks of understanding and our pedagogical practices.

This seems particularly relevant in the case of the standard universities as we know them today. Universities as spaces imbued with norms and rituals[15] or as institutional contexts that involve structures and emotions[16] in which some people feel at home and others are alienated, are implicated in the epistemic violence in the modern/colonial division of a geopolitics of knowledge.[17] The decolonial perspective confronts the university with its being implicated in the colonial difference, in particular its role in the reproduction of epistemic apparatuses that perpetuate the modern/colonial divide and its contribution to an unequal global political economy of knowledge. The practices of knowledge production and reproduction at the university continue to disregard or render invisible other perspectives, particularly those of the global South, while at the same time impoverishing the epistemic plurality of the world.

The calls for the decolonisation of the university are appearing in the face of dominant global designs pushing for regulation and normalisation through international ranking systems.[18] Universities need to be conceptualised as involved in highly diverse and complex politics of place.[19] Therefore, local calls to defend the state-funded and inclusive university that have national and local state politics as their horizon are considered important but not sufficient to understand present calls for decolonisation.[20]

A decolonised education and learning means different things for different people. In the 1950s and 1960s, decolonisation meant the end of colonial rule and was linked to challenging imperialism.[21] In contemporary North America, Tuck and Yang warn about the dangers of using 'decolonisation' as an ambiguous metaphor for everything that needs to be improved in societies and schools.[22] Meanwhile, across the Americas, the decolonisation of disciplinary canons and research methodologies has had on its political and ethical horizons first peoples and indigenous self-determination.[23] It is in this context that the anthropocentric biases of education and of research methodologies have been problematised too.[24]

Recent research in Europe has investigated calls for the decolonisation of universities, detecting, despite their local specificities, a common interest in addressing the visible and less visible colonial legacies of universities, such as removing statues of former colonisers (e.g. Cecil Rhodes in South Africa) or the absence of the oeuvres of women and people of colour in curricula.[25] In North America, the appropriation of originary peoples' land by Ivy League university forefathers and the connection to enslavement has been recently addressed.[26] Interestingly, this research has remained silent about the connections between the colonial foundations of universities and today's environmental degradation.[27] This is despite the fact that women across the global North/South divide are leading decolonised education and learning practices aimed at connecting both.[28]

Universities have a variety of local specificities, but the idea of the university as we understand it today can be traced to a Western genealogy. The expansion of the university as a global system of education belongs to the history of the Western project of civilisation, that is, the history of modernity. As modern institutions, universities have been implicated in the reproduction of epistemic global divides. In our view, the movements to decolonise the university are fighting the 'arrogant ignorance' that is produced by a system of knowledge that is Eurocentric, heteronormative and anthropocentric in kind. We call it an 'arrogant ignorance' because it is an epistemology that is at one and the same time pretending to be wide-ranging, or even claiming universal validity, while remaining oblivious to the epistemic diversity of the world. The university is being confronted with the need to overcome this ignorance and acknowledge the geopolitical and genealogical location of its knowledge practices.

Under these circumstances, how can the university become an ethical institution *vis-à-vis* its extractive logics that reproduced North/South divides? Is it possible to make universities realise how they are implicated in these logics and to move from there into the promotion of forms of epistemic justice? As co-authors of this chapter, but also as teachers in universities, we understand our task as that of introducing pedagogies and research tools, forms of knowing and learning that can contribute to address these questions.[29]

Can the university contribute to the possibility of an ethical life in a world that is deeply divided between those who consume and those who are consumed, such consumption including the life of others and the life of earth? Can the university address the modern/colonial divide instead of reproducing it while neglecting it? Can university communities around the world understand how they are implicated in the constitution of the modern/colonial divide, in the production and reproduction of global epistemic inequality, in the silencing of the radical plurality of the world?

Decolonising the University of Amsterdam

In the spring of 2015, student movements occupied the UvA. They demanded the democratisation of decision making in every area of the university. The 'students of colour' and their movements raised the demand to decolonise the university with the slogan '*No democratisation without decolonisation*'. One of the outcomes of this mobilisation was the creation of the Diversity Commission that conducted research from March to September 2016 to investigate the state of diversity of people *and* knowledges perspectives at UvA.

The commission developed a conceptual and methodological framework that mobilised decolonial and intersectional perspectives[30] to research the university. On the one hand, decoloniality was introduced as 'a perspective that allows us to see how the dynamics of power differences, social exclusion and discrimination (along the axes of race, gender and geographical and economic inequality) are connected to the ongoing legacies of our colonial history'.[31] Furthermore, as a research perspective, decoloniality helped the commission to 'understand the role of the University as a modern/colonial institution in the reinforcement of Western perspectives at the expense of the plurality of knowledges of the world'.[32]

On the other hand, the commission acknowledged intersectionality as a key feminist contribution to doing research and acting for social justice. Intersectionality was then deployed as a perspective and as a praxis:

> a perspective that allows us to see how various forms of discrimination cannot be seen as separate, but need to be understood in relation to each other.... Practicing intersectionality means that we avoid the tendency to separate the axes of difference that shape society, institutions and ourselves.... intersectionality allows us to see why distinct social positions of individual students and staff determine how they experience the University.[33]

In the configuration of its theoretical and methodological framework the commission already performed a decolonising move. The conjunction of 'intersectionality' and decoloniality brought together the tradition of Black feminism and the tradition of the Latin-American Modernity/coloniality network. One of the oldest universities of Europe (1632) was for the first time going to be evaluated from and with perspectives and methodologies from across the global South, from across the colonial difference, from outside the normative perspectives of Western thought.

It is important to mention that the conjunction of intersectionality and decoloniality was not just done as theoretical work. The two frameworks were set as a common ground for conversation among the commission members. One of the first steps of the commission was to organise an internal training workshop on intersectionality and decoloniality with all the members of the commission, including all research assistants. This opened up a common field of conversation and analysis that enabled the whole research process up to the public presentation of the report.

As two of the five members of the commission, each of us led a small team to investigate different but interrelated aspects of diversity practices at UvA.[34] Rosalba Icaza's team,[35] focused on 'Meanings of Diversity', and included young Black female researchers to examine the terms that circulate around the notion of diversity in UvA. This team's objective was to make sense of the effects of these meanings in the everyday administration of teaching and research.[36]

Meanwhile, Rolando Vázquez's team,[37] focused on 'Diversity in Teaching and Learning', researched the state of knowledge and teaching practices at UvA. The objective of this team was to identify to what extent the knowledge practices at UvA enriched or impoverished diversity.[38] The rest of this chapter focuses on the work done by this team and reflects on the research process and the findings.

Researching diversity in teaching and learning at UvA

Early in the research process, the team lead by Rolando Vázquez identified as one of its main challenges that of listening to the non-normative voices within the university in order to decolonise the epistemic practices of the university. By non-normative voices this team meant students of colour, non-heterosexual, first- and second-generation immigrants, refugees, non-bodily able people, and those from poor or marginalised neighbourhoods of the city of Amsterdam.

In order to assess to what extent the university knowledge practices are diversity enriching or impoverishing, the team open two broad research areas of enquiry focusing on the *what* and the how: (a) *what* knowledge is being produced and (b) *how* is it being taught? Working from a decolonial angle, it became important to address epistemic coloniality by assessing the diversity of the content of the knowledge: *the what*, and the diversity effects of the ways of teaching and learning: *the how*. Assessing the extent to which the *what of knowledge content and the how of knowledge practices* enrich or reduce epistemic diversity contributed to revealing the importance of addressing the epistemic coloniality of the university. By 'epistemic coloniality of the university', the team meant the reproduction of monocultural and extractivist approaches to knowledge that lead to the erasure and discrediting of other knowledges, and to the negation of the epistemic diversity of the world.[39]

Responding to the challenge to focus on the non-normative voices and experiences of students and staff that have traditionally been marginalised within the university community, the research team led by Vázquez, developed 'Diversity Discussion Circles' as a participatory research methodology through which this team sought to better understand the coloniality of epistemic practices at the university.[40]

In order to better understand to what extent the UvA has been enforcing Western epistemologies and subjectivities as the norm, the team led by Vázquez developed a set of categories that were not just looking at the epistemic content, but also at the epistemic practices of teaching and learning.[41] By combining Black feminist intersectionality and decoloniality, this team elaborated a framework to assess to what extent the practices of knowing at the university are conducive to actively promote or suppress diversity across the colonial divide. The framework has three core elements: the pedagogies of positionality, the pedagogies of relationality and the pedagogies of transition. This framework also helped to underscore the decolonial deficit of the university, as it provided concrete forms to understand how epistemic practices can be decolonised.

In the rest of this text, we explain further this framework as a 'toolbox' that can contribute to other attempts across the world to decolonise the university. We do this in three steps. Our first step is to introduce what is meant by the pedagogies of positionality, relationality and transition that informed the design of the discussion circles.[42] The second step is a description of the Diversity Discussion Circles. The third step is a reflection on the main findings. Finally, we will offer some remarks on the ongoing challenge to decolonise the university.

Diversity or decolonisation?

The term 'diversity' has broadly been used to discuss the composition of population of students and staff at the university. While it is of utmost importance that universities reflect the demographic diversity of the societies they are supposed to serve, the question of demographic diversity falls short of addressing the question of decolonisation. How can the university address the role it has played in reproducing global inequalities?

As we have shown, in order to address the questions raised by decolonial critical analysis through the notion of diversity we had to re-signify the term, by extending the scope of the question and by transforming its implications. The decolonisation of the university is not just about *who* is at the university, but also about the *what* and the *how* of the university knowledge practices. In other words, we extended the question of diversity to assess the epistemic practices at the university. More specifically we look at the extent to which knowledge practices at the university lead towards the reduction or the fostering of difference.

> We understand the practices that foster diversity as those that, through their inclusive approach, nurture difference as a positive force for academic excellence. Concurrently, we understand the practices that reduce diversity as those that lead toward the reduction of difference. In short, we ask to what extent are practices of teaching and learning at the University conducive either to the reduction or the fostering of difference.[43]

Translating the question of diversity in terms of knowledge practices that reduce or foster difference, gave us the possibility to address the need to transform the politics of knowledge at the university that is so central to decolonisation. By doing this we were able to establish a framework through which it became possible to show that the need for the decolonisation of the university coincides with the need to overcome monocultural approaches to knowledge. In other words, there is no decolonisation of the university without epistemic decolonisation.

The task of decolonising the university is not an ideological position but an epistemic stance that struggles against the ignorance of monocultural approaches.[44] Under this analysis Eurocentrism is detached from being an issue of identity to become an epistemic problem, namely the problem of a monocultural approach to knowledge practices, to research, to teaching and learning. As previously discussed, Eurocentrism is seen as a form of 'arrogant ignorance', in that it is a monocultural framework that assumes itself to be the overarching framework for doing and reproducing knowledge, and for understanding our world-historical reality.[45]

By displacing the question of diversity to focus on the fostering or reduction of difference it was possible for us to assess the ways in which Eurocentric, monocultural approaches were being reproduced at the university and led to the impoverishing difference. The results help us to highlight the importance of decolonising the university, as a movement towards more complex, plural and inclusive forms of learning about and understanding of our world-historical reality and earth.[46]

Under this framework, diversity-poor and diversity-rich practices could be assessed in relation to the fostering or reduction of difference.

For this we developed a participatory methodology and an analytical framework specially designed for listening to the voices that are often sidelined in the monocultural university and to differentiate their knowledge practices. This is what we explain next.

UvA Diversity Discussion Circles

Inspired by the tradition of participatory and collaborative research in Latin America,[47] research was understood as an approach to knowledge sharing and generation that not only seeks the meaningful involvement of the individuals, groups and organisations *with whom* (not *about*) we would be producing knowledge, but also as one that actively rejects extractive epistemic practices and stimulates co-production.[48]

To that effect all the members of the research 'team' led by Icaza and Vázquez were constantly reflecting on their own positionality in order to be critically aware of the specific location from where we were sharing and co-generating knowledge, and to avoid being complicit with the reproduction of abstract, ahistorical and disembodied ideas of knowledge. Our methods and tools were constantly and critically examined in all the phases of the research, asking what purposes the research was serving: 'knowledge for what?'

We implemented a participatory methodology that consisted in creating spaces of conversation that would function as safe spaces in which students could speak freely about issues concerning diversity practices at the university. Open calls for 'Diversity Discussion Circles' were issued in different faculties and other circles were organised through student groups.

The Diversity Discussion Circles were meant to be safe spaces of encounter and dialogue. They were organised in such a way that the students who are normally not heard in the classroom or in institutional processes could have a voice to express their experiences at the university with regard to diversity. The conversations in the circles enabled us to identify existing practices that needed to be recognised as valuable for promoting diversity and other practices that needed to be made more visible as being detrimental to diversity or even directly discriminatory. The Diversity Discussion Circles put into practice decolonial concepts with a specific shift that took us away from specialised abstract language towards concrete tools and lived/embodied concepts to make visible the problems of lack of diversity within the university. For example, with

Diversity is about improving our teaching and learning experiences. Everyone should be heard on this important topic. The Discussion Circles are a platform for staff and students to voice their views, experiences, and proposals around the theme of diversity. The Diversity Commission organised a first, successful series of Discussion Circles.

By popular demand, the Commission is now going to facilitate autonomously organised Circles. You only need 5 – 15 people for a successful discussion. Give us a date and time, bring your friends and colleagues, and we'll take care of the logistics: room booking, facilitating the discussion, tea and cookies!

diversity
commission

uvadiversitycommission
at gmail dot com

Figure 7.1   One of the posters issued by the Diversity Commission[49]

this methodology we found that diversity-impoverishing approaches were not just articulated through making difference invisible. Through repeated testimonies we found that the 'exhibition' of diversity is another form of exclusion. 'The exhibition of diversity functions to reinforce exclusion and discrimination by marking bodies and knowledges as "the other".[50] The recognition of difference as a move towards plural knowledge practices has to be clearly distinguished from the exhibition of difference that functions to reinforce the axes of discrimination and the monocultural approach to knowledge.

The findings of the discussion circles were ordered in an analytical framework and matrix developed through the research process to highlight the importance of diversity practices for the decolonisation of the university. Its major categories are positionality, relationality and transition. They echo important debates in decolonial, postcolonial, Black feminist and Chicana feminist literature for the overcoming of dominant epistemologies as we explain in the following section.

Positionality, relationality and transition

Positionality is an essential tool to overcome the monocultural approach to knowledge. Eurocentrism and, in general, monocultural approaches to knowledge practices assume a universal validity and reproduce an abstract and disembodied vantage point of the knowing subject. In so doing, they negate the location of all knowledges, in particular they negate the location of the dominant position of knowledge, occluding it under universal validity claims.

Practices of positionality are those practices that, even while teaching the canon, reveal the geopolitical location of knowledge. That is, knowledge is always taught in a situated manner, allowing the students to recognise the geo-genealogy to which they are being exposed and in which they are being trained, instead of assuming an abstract position of universality, of objectivity. We found that students felt more included when exposed to knowledge practices that reveal their geo-historical position.

Epistemic practices of positionality led us to argue for a transit from closed forms of expertise to open forms of expertise, that is from forms of expertise that present themselves as ahistorical and universally valid to humble and open forms of expertise that reveal and make of the location of their knowledge an integral part of their doing.

A university that engages in positioning its knowledge practices is a university that reveals the intersectional conditions of knowledge production and that shows unequivocally how the axes of differentiation along race, class and gender have been essential for establishing the canon and, concurrently, how the canon has been essential to reproduce these axes of discrimination.

As for *relationality*, the research showed how, independently of the content of the curricula being taught, the decolonisation of the university should include a transformation of the relationships established in the classroom and across the university. The classroom is a space in which power hierarchies and forms of exclusion often get reproduced.

Changing the content of knowledge, or positioning the canon, is not enough to decolonise the university as a space that reproduces forms of exclusion. The notion of relationality brings into focus the practices of knowledge that contribute to the fostering of diversity by enabling open and dynamic forms of interaction in which the diverse backgrounds are recognised as valuable. Focusing on relationality helps to make visible how detrimental are authoritarian, one-directional forms of teaching and learning. A relational approach is not simply a participatory approach, a relational approach is one in which the diverse backgrounds and the geo-historical positioning of the different participants in the classroom are rendered valuable in a dignified way for the learning of all.

Practices of teaching and learning that are grounded on relational approaches or democratic forms of teaching can contribute to decolonising our forms of learning. Through relational practices of teaching and learning the diverse background and positionality of the students is not suppressed, but, on the contrary, becomes a tool for enriching the learning experience of all. The students whose diverse backgrounds are recognised as important feel included and empowered.

Finally, we used the notion of '*transitionality*' to speak of the knowledge practices at the university that are clearly related to the socio-historical and eco-historical conditions in which we are living. The notion of transitionality highlights the importance of enabling the students to address the question of the meaning of the knowledge they are learning. What is this knowledge for? The focus on closed expertise has also meant that the university is reproducing forms of knowledge without addressing, or without enabling the student, to address the question of meaning.

Transitionality puts emphasis on undoing the abstract position of knowledge and recognising how the university is implicated in a politics of knowledge that has a deep impact, producing and reproducing our relations to the social and to the Earth. The question of transition points towards the need for the university to actively address its own societal and ecological implications by enabling the students to bridge the epistemic border between the classroom and society, the classroom and the Earth. A pedagogy of transition is a pedagogy that never loses sight of how the knowledge addressed and reproduced impacts the social and/or the Earth.

Through the research we also learned that not all forms of discrimination at the university have to do with the invisibilisation of difference. We found that the exhibition of diversity is another form of exclusion.

Often when different backgrounds are recognised in the classroom this is done to reinforce the norm. Students experience discrimination when they are being singled out due to their difference along intersectional lines. The recognition of difference can easily be turned into forms of discrimination-as-exhibition.

The recognition of difference as enriching for teaching and learning has to go hand in hand with the positionality of knowledge, that is, with a knowledge that has been humbled, a knowledge that recognises its own limits and perceives difference as enriching and not as a curiosity. It also requires a classroom based on relationality, in which the voices in differential locations along the axes of discrimination are equally valued. As mentioned, a monocultural and authoritarian classroom will turn the recognition of difference into exhibition, furthering forms of discrimination and reinforcing modern/colonial forms of exclusion.

Final reflections

The research context of the UvA Diversity Commission is a good empirical example of how it is possible to translate student movements' demands to decolonise the university that were mostly unintelligible for the administration and the staff. In the interviews with managerial staff of the university, we found a willingness to speak of diversity coupled with diversity illiteracy. It was necessary for us to make explicit how to take seriously the fact that the demands of the student movements implied deep changes in the way the university functions and that these demands went beyond the very real need to open the university to diverse demographics. The commission elaborated a series of policy recommendations through which the university could initiate a deep process of transformation towards fulfilling its commitment to a more just world.

Importantly, the report recommended a different approach to knowledge, a different ethics and politics of knowledge that would see the university transiting from a 'closed' approach to knowledge to an 'open' approach. An open approach to knowledge is not an approach that is opposed to expertise, it is an approach that encourages geo-historically positioned forms of expertise. Students, teachers and researchers who become aware of the positionality of knowledge become humble knowledge practitioners open to dialogue with other perspectives.

By translating the student demands to decolonise the university into concrete forms to transform the knowledge practices at the university, the commission managed to make a series of concrete recommendations. The recommendations that can be read in the Diversity Commission report ranged from transforming forms of assessment and evaluation (i.e. criteria for teachers' accreditation) to the need to position the bodies of knowledge (re)produced at the university. The report managed to create a space of translation between the student demands and the different stakeholders of the university community. It showed that the demand to decolonise the university is not an ideological position but a serious demand to improve the functioning of the university at all levels. Furthermore, the commission managed to show that diversifying the university, and in particular its knowledge practices, is a necessity to achieve academic excellence and to make of the university a social actor that is open and responsive to the complexities and tensions of our interconnected world.

Through the work of the commission the student demands became substantiated and became legible to the university administration. An example of how the commission functioned as a space of translation was how it transformed the movement's demand of 'no democratisation without decolonisation' into the concrete recommendation of positioning the canon across all faculties in order to consolidate a decolonial approach to teaching and learning.

Today's student movements are confronting universities with their colonial histories, with their histories of segregation, with the reproduction of the epistemic arrogance of a dominant West. The student movements are bringing to the fore the awareness of the modern/colonial positionality of sanctioned knowledges and the recognition of the universities' own participation in the modern/colonial order.

The experience of the research done by the Diversity Commission of the University of Amsterdam highlighted the importance of discussing the decolonisation of the university in relation to not *what* the university is, but rather to *how* we do things at the university. The focus of decolonisation is leading towards a transformation of the practices of knowledge: how we teach, how we learn, how we research... Whereas there has been substantive discussion in the social sciences about decolonising research methodologies, there is still a lot to be done to decolonise our pedagogies.

The decolonisation of the university is a struggle to enrich our ways of teaching and learning by listening to the plurality of knowledges of the world. It is about the challenge of relating to difference as an opportunity to enrich our knowledge practices instead of relating to difference as something that has to be reduced, moved out of sight or exhibited.

The university is facing the challenge to listen to the marginalised voices and to undo the epistemic abyss that keeps on drawing worlds apart along the colonial difference. Decolonising the university is a necessary step for the university to become a social actor engaged with processes of environmental and social justice, engaged with the formation of citizens who are aware of their position in a globally divided world. The transformation of the university that is being led by the student movements is nurturing a university for an open and plural society.

Bibliography

Ahmed, Sara (2012) *On Being Included: Racism and Diversity in Institutional Life.* Durham, NC: Duke University Press.

Arashiro, Zuleika, Demuro, Eugenia and Barahona, Melba (2015) 'Introduction: Thinking Through Our Voices', in Zuleika Arashiro and Melba Barahona (eds) *Women in Academia Crossing North–South Borders: Gender, Race, and Displacement.* Lanham, MD: Lexington Books, pp. vii–xvii.

Barbosa da Costa, Larissa, Icaza, Rosalba and Ocampo Talero, Angélica María (2015) 'Knowledge About, Knowledge With: Dilemmas of Researching Lives, Nature and Genders Otherwise', in Wendy Harcourt and Ingrid Nelson (eds) *Practicing Feminist Political Ecology: Going Beyond the Green Economy.* London: Zed Books, pp. 260–85.

De Jong, Sara, Icaza, Rosalba, Vázquez, Rolando and Withaeckx, Sophie (eds) (2017) 'Editorial: Decolonizing the University', in Sara de Jong et al. (eds) Special Issue on Decolonizing the University, *Dutch Journal of Gender Studies* (*Tijdschrift voor Genderstudies*) 20(3): 227–31.

De Oliveira Andreotti, Vanessa (2015) 'Mapping Interpretations of Decolonization in the Context of Higher Education', *Decolonization: Indigeneity, Education & Society* 4(1): 21–40.

Escobar, Arturo (2001) 'Culture Sits in Places: Reflections on Globalism and Subaltern Strategies of Localization', *Political Geography* 20: 139–74.

Fry, Tony (2012) 'Futuring the University', *Journal of Contemporary Educational Studies* 3: 54–66.

Gitlin, Todd (2012) *Occupy Nation: The Roots, the Spirit, and the Promise of Occupy Wall Street.* New York: It Books, HarperCollins.

Grosfoguel, Ramón, Hernández, Roberto and Rosen Velásquez, Ernesto (eds) (2016) *Decolonizing the Westernized University Interventions in Philosophy of Education from Within and Without.* Lanham, MD: Lexington Books.

Harcourt, Wendy and Escobar, Arturo (eds) (2005) *Women and the Politics of Place.* Bloomfield, CT: Kumarian Press.

Harcourt, Wendy and Nelson, Ingrid (2015) *Practising Feminist Political Ecologies: Moving beyond the 'Green Economy'.* London: Zed Books.

Icaza, Rosalba (2015) 'Testimony of a Pilgrimage: (Un)learning and Re-learning with the South', in Zuleika Arashiro et al. (eds) *Women in Academia Crossing North/South Borders*. Lanham, MD: Lexington Books, pp. 1–27.

Icaza, Rosalba (2018) 'Social Struggles and the Coloniality of Gender', in Robbie Shilliam and Olivia Rutazibwa (eds) *Routledge Handbook on Postcolonial Politics*. Abingdon: Routledge, pp. 58–71.

Icaza, Rosalba and Vázquez, Rolando (2017) 'Intersectionality and Diversity in Higher Education', *Tijdschrift voor Orthopedagogiek* (Special issue on Diversity in Academia, ed. Hans Jansen) 7–8: 349–57.

Khative, Kate, Killjoy, Margaret and McGuire, Mike (eds) (2012) *We Are Many:* Reflections on Movement Strategy from Occupation to Liberation. Edinburgh: AK Press.

Koopmans, Ruud (2004) 'Protests in Time and Space: The Evolution of Waves of Contention', in David A. Snow et al., *The Blackwell Companion to Social Movements*. Malden, MA: Blackwell, pp. 19–46.

Leyva, Xochitl and Speed, Shannon (2008) 'Hacia la investigación descolonizada: nuestra experiencia de co-labor', in Xochitl Leyva, Araceli Burguete and Shannon Speed (eds) *Gobernar (en) la diversidad: experiencias indígenas desde América Latina. Hacia la investigación de colabor*. México, DF: CIESAS, FLACSO Ecuador y FLACSO Guatemala, pp. 34–59.

Leyva, Xochitl et al. (2015) *Practicas otras de conocimiento(s): entre crisis, entre guerras*. San Cristobal de las Casas, Chiapas, Mexico: Cooperativa Editorial Retos.

Mignolo, Walter (2009) 'Epistemic Disobedience, Independent Thought and De-colonial Freedom', *Theory, Culture & Society* 26(7–8): 1–23.

Mignolo, Walter and Tlostanova, Madina V. (2006) 'Theorizing from the Borders. Shifting to Geo and Body Politics of Knowledge', *European Journal of Social Theory* 9(2): 205–21.

Puwar, Nirmal (2004) *Space Invaders: Race, Gender and Bodies Out of Place*. Oxford: Berg.

Restrepo, Paula (2014) 'Legitimation of Knowledge, Epistemic Justice and the Intercultural University: Towards an Epistemology of "Living Well"', *Postcolonial Studies* 17(2): 140–54.

Santos, Boaventura de Sousa (2016) *Epistemologies of the South: Justice against Epistemicide*. Abingdon: Routledge.

Santos, Boaventura de Sousa, Nunes, João A. and Meneses, Maria Paula (2007) 'Introduction: Opening Up the Canon of Knowledge and Recognition of Difference', in Boaventura de Sousa Santos (ed.) *Another Knowledge is Possible: Beyond Northern Epistemologies*. London: Verso.

Schiffrin, Anya and Kircher, Eamon (eds) (2012) *From Cairo to Wall Street: Voices from the Global Spring*. New York: The New Press.

Shilliam, Robbie and Quỳnh N. Phạm (2016) *Meanings of Bandung: Postcolonial Orders and Decolonial Visions*. London: Rowman and Littlefield.

Smith, Linda Tuhiwai (2012) *Decolonizing Methodologies: Research and Indigenous People*, 2nd edn. London: Zed Books.

Suarez-Krabbe, Julia (2016) *Race, Rights and Rebels: Alternatives to Human Rights and Development from the Global South*. London: Rowman and Littlefield.

Tlostanova, Madina and Mignolo, Walter (2012) *Learning to Unlearn: Decolonial Reflections from Eurasia and the Americas*. Columbus: Ohio State University Press.

Tuck, Eve and Yang, K. Wayne (2012) 'Decolonization Is Not a Metaphor', *Decolonization: Indigeneity, Education & Society* 1(1).

Vázquez, Rolando (2009) 'Modernity Coloniality and Visibility: The Politics of Time', *Sociological Research Online* 14 (4) 7, available at: http://www.socresonline.org.uk/14/4/7.html

Vázquez, Rolando (2015) 'Decolonial Practices of Learning', in John Friedman et al. (eds) *Going Glocal in Higher Education: The Theory, Teaching and Measurement of Global Citizenship*. Middelburg: UCR, pp. 92–100.

Vázquez, Rolando (2017) 'Precedence, Earth and the Anthropocene: Decolonizing Design', *Design Philosophy Papers* (Special Issue: Design and the Global South) 15(1): 77–91.

Wekker, Gloria, Slootman, Marieke, Icaza, Rosalba, Jansen, Hans, Vázquez, Rolando et al. (2016) *Let's Do Diversity: Report of the Diversity Commission*. Amsterdam: University of Amsterdam.

Wilder, Craig Steven (2013) *Ebony and Ivy: Race, Slavery, and the Troubled History of America's Universities*. New York: Bloomsbury Press.

Notes

All urls last accessed January 2018.

1. UvA Diversity Commission was chaired by Emeritus Professor Gloria Wekker. The other members of the commission included Marieke Slootman and Emeritus Professor Hans Jansen. The full mandate of the commission and final report can be accessed at: http://commissiedd.nl/diversity-commission/

2. Grosfoguel, Ramón, Hernández, Roberto and Rosen Velásquez, Ernesto (eds) (2016) *Decolonizing the Westernized University Interventions in Philosophy of Education from Within and Without*. Lanham, MD: Lexington Books; Mignolo, Walter (2009) 'Epistemic Disobedience, Independent Thought and De-colonial Freedom', *Theory, Culture & Society* 26 (7–8): 1–23; Mignolo, Walter and Tlostanova, Madina V. (2006) 'Theorizing from the Borders: Shifting to Geo and Body Politics of Knowledge', *European Journal of Social Theory* 9(2): 205–21.

3. Since 1999, Europe has been involved in the Bologna process to establish the European Higher Education Area (EHEA). Recently, the five countries of the East African Community – Kenya, Rwanda, Tanzania, Uganda and Burundi – declared the region a common higher education area. Similar harmonisation efforts can be found in Latin America and the Caribbean, Asia and the Middle East. Source: 'East African Community Takes Decisive Steps Towards Harmonising HE', available at: https://thepienews.com/news/east-african-community-harmonising-higher-education/

4. Fry, Tony (2012) 'Futuring the University', *Journal of Contemporary Educational Studies* 3: 54–66.

5. Koopmans, Ruud (2004) 'Protests in Time and Space: The Evolution of Waves of Contention', in David A. Snow et al., *The Blackwell Companion to Social Movements*. Malden, MA: Blackwell, pp. 19–46.

6. Schiffrin, Anya and Kircher, Eamon (eds) (2012) *From Cairo to Wall Street: Voices from the Global Spring*. New York: The New Press.

7. Khative, Kate, Killjoy, Margaret and McGuire, Mike (eds) (2012) *We Are Many*: Reflections on Movement Strategy from Occupation to Liberation. Edinburgh: AK Press.

8. Gitlin, Todd (2012) *Occupy Nation: The Roots, the Spirit, and the Promise of Occupy Wall Street*. New York: It Books, HarperCollins; Khative et al. 2012 op. cit.

9. Barbosa da Costa, Larissa, Icaza, Rosalba and Ocampo Talero, Angélica María (2015) 'Knowledge About, Knowledge With: Dilemmas of Researching Lives, Nature and Genders Otherwise', in Wendy Harcourt and Ingrid Nelson (eds) *Practicing Feminist Political Ecology: Going Beyond the Green Economy*. London: Zed Books, pp. 260–85; Santos, Boaventura de Sousa, Nunes, João A. and Meneses, Maria Paula (2007) 'Opening Up the Canon of Knowledge and Recognition of Difference', in Boaventura de Sousa Santos (ed.) *Another Knowledge is Possible: Beyond Northern Epistemologies*. London: Verso; Santos, Boaventura de Sousa (2016) *Epistemologies of the South: Justice against Epistemicide*. Abingdon: Routledge; Smith, Linda Tuhiwai (2012) *Decolonizing Methodologies: Research and Indigenous People*, 2nd edn. London: Zed Books.

10. Barbosa da Costa et al. 2015 op. cit.; Restrepo, Paula (2014) 'Legitimation of Knowledge, Epistemic Justice and the Intercultural University: Towards an Epistemology of "Living Well", *Postcolonial Studies* 17(2): 140–54.

11. The official page of the University of Color is: http://universityofcolour.com/. Members of UoC and of the New Urban Collective have created a facebook page 'Decolonials' at: www.facebook.com/groups/922214724542062/

12. The official website of the New Urban Collective can be found at: http://nucnet.nl/. They have also created the Black Archives to document the history of Black and diasporic populations not included in universities' curricula. This initiative can be accessed at: www.theblackarchives.nl/

13. The official website of Amsterdam United can be accessed here: www.amsterdamunited.org/

14. See the call for a special issue on Decolonizing the University (eds Sara de Jong, Rosalba Icaza, Rolando Vázquez and Sophie W. Withaeckx, 2017) of the Dutch *Journal of Gender Studies* (*Tijdschrift voor Genderstudies*), available at: ww.ingentaconnect.com/content/aup/tgen/2017/00000020/00000003

15. Puwar, Nirmal (2004) *Space Invaders: Race, Gender and Bodies Out of Place*. Oxford: Berg.

16. Ahmed, Sara (2012) *On Being Included: Racism and Diversity in Institutional Life*. Durham, NC: Duke University Press.

17. Mignolo and Tlostanova 2006 op. cit.; de Jong, Sara, Icaza, Rosalba, Vázquez, Rolando and Withaeckx, Sophie W. (eds) (2017) 'Editorial: Decolonizing the University', in de Jong et al. Special Issue on Decolonizing the University, *Dutch Journal of Gender Studies* (*Tijdschrift voor Genderstudies*) 20(3): 227–31.

18. Fry 2012 op. cit.; Mignolo and Tlostanova 2006 op. cit.
19. Santos 2016 op. cit.; Escobar, Arturo (2001) 'Culture Sits in Places: Reflections on Globalism and Subaltern Strategies of Localization', *Political Geography* 20: 139–74; Harcourt, Wendy and Escobar, Arturo (eds) (2005) *Women and the Politics of Place*. Bloomfield, CT: Kumarian Press.
20. De Jong et al. 2017 op. cit.
21. Shilliam, Robbie and Quỳnh N. Phạm (2016) *Meanings of Bandung: Postcolonial Orders and Decolonial Visions*. London: Rowman and Littlefield.
22. Tuck, Eve and Yang, K. Wayne (2012) 'Decolonization Is Not a Metaphor', *Decolonization: Indigeneity, Education & Society* 1(1).
23. Icaza, Rosalba (2018) 'Social Struggles and the Coloniality of Gender', in Robbie Shilliam and Olivia Rutazibwa (eds) *Routledge Handbook on Postcolonial Politics*. Abingdon: Routledge, pp. 58–71; Leyva, Xochitl et al. (2015) *Practicas otras de conocimiento(s): entre crisis, entre guerras*. San Cristobal de las Casas, Chiapas, Mexico: Cooperativa Editorial Retos; Suarez-Krabbe, Julia (2016) *Race, Rights and Rebels: Alternatives to Human Rights and Development from the Global South*. London: Rowman and Littlefield; Smith 2012 op. cit.
24. Harcourt, Wendy and Nelson, Ingrid (2015) *Practising Feminist Political Ecologies: Moving beyond the 'Green Economy'*. London: Zed Books; Barbosa da Costa et al. 2015 op. cit.
25. Grosfoguel et al. 2016 op. cit.; Santos 2016 op. cit.; Tlostanova, Madina and Mignolo, Walter (2012) *Learning to Unlearn: Decolonial Reflections from Eurasia and the Americas*. Columbus: Ohio State University Press.
26. Wilder, Craig Steven (2013) *Ebony and Ivy: Race, Slavery, and the Troubled History of America's Universities*. New York: Bloomsbury Press.
27. Vázquez, Rolando (2017) 'Precedence, Earth and the Anthropocene: Decolonizing Design', *Design Philosophy Papers* (Special Issue: Design and the Global South) 15(1): 77–91.
28. Arashiro, Zuleika, Demuro, Eugenia and Barahona, Melba (2015) 'Introduction: Thinking Through Our Voices', in Zuleika Arashiro and Melba Barahona (eds) *Women in Academia Crossing North–South Borders: Gender, Race, and Displacement*. Lanham, MD: Lexington Books, pp. vii–xvii; Leyva et al. 2015 op. cit.
29. Barbosa et al. 2015 op. cit.; Icaza 2018 in press op. cit.; Icaza, Rosalba (2015) 'Testimony of a Pilgrimage: (Un)learning and Re-learning with the South', in Arashiro and Barahona op. cit., pp. 1–27; Icaza, Rosalba and Vázquez, Rolando (2017) 'Intersectionality and Diversity in Higher Education', *Tijdschrift voor Orthopedagogiek* (Special issue on Diversity in Academia, ed. Hans Jansen) 7–8: 349–57.
30. An extended reflection on the role that intersectionality as analytical framework played in this research can be found in Icaza and Vázquez 2017 op. cit.
31. Wekker, Gloria, Slootman, Marieke, Icaza, Rosalba, Jansen, Hans, Vázquez, Rolando et al. (2016) *Let's Do Diversity: Report of the Diversity Commission*. Amsterdam: University of Amsterdam, pp. 10–11.
32. Ibid. pp. 10–11.
33. Ibid. p. 11.

34. The UvA Diversity Commission report can be accessed at: diversity-commission-report-2016-12-10.pdf
35. Rosalba Icaza's team included Jessica de Abreu and Melissa Evora as co-researchers and co-authors of chapter 3 of the report.
36. Wekker et al. 2016 op. cit., especially chapter 3; Icaza and Vázquez 2017 op. cit.
37. The members of Vázquez's team who contributed to developing the research that is described here are Tashina Blom, Emilie van Heydoorn and Max de Ploeg.
38. Wekker et al. 2016 op. cit. especially chapter 4.
39. For an important discussion on the politics of knowledge and the epistemic diversity of the world see Santos, 2016 op. cit.
40. Wekker et al. 2016 op. cit. especially chapter 4.
41. Vázquez, Rolando (2015) 'Decolonial Practices of Learning', in John Friedman et al. (eds) *Going Glocal in Higher Education: The Theory, Teaching and Measurement of Global Citizenship*. Middelburgh: UCR, pp. 92–100.
42. Ibid.
43. Wekker et al. 2016 op. cit. p. 67.
44. Vázquez 2015 op. cit.
45. Ibid.; Vázquez 2017 op. cit.
46. Vázquez 2015 op. cit.; Vázquez 2017 op. cit.
47. Leyva, Xochitl and Speed, Shannon (2008) 'Hacia la investigación descolonizada: nuestra experiencia de co-labor', in Xochitl Leyva, Araceli Burguete and Shannon Speed (eds) *Gobernar (en) la diversidad: experiencias indígenas desde América Latina. Hacia la investigación de colabor*. México, DF: CIESAS, FLACSO Ecuador y FLACSO Guatemala, pp. 34–59.
48. Leyva et al. 2015 op. cit.
49. The visuals of the commission were designed by Bas Cornelissen.
50. Wekker et al. 2016 p. 71.

8

The Challenge for Black Studies in the Neoliberal University

Kehinde Andrews

The Black Studies undergraduate degree, launched at Birmingham City University in 2016, is the first of its kind in Europe. When people hear this, there is often a look of surprise and people are interested in why it has taken so long. We should not really be surprised; universities are institutionally racist spaces that have had a historic role in producing the knowledge that racism is based on. Curricula in higher education are so exclusionary that students have had to start a national campaign, 'Why is My Curriculum White?' to pressure universities to reflect on the role of coloniality in shaping the education we have access to.[1] Similar to 1960s America, widening participation has opened the doors to Black and Brown students who are looking at what they are having to learn and demanding change. Decentring Europe from our understandings of the world is a vital and long overdue process. By rooting Black Studies in the contributions, experiences and perspectives of Africa and its diaspora, the movement becomes part of a wider battle to decolonise the university.

When Black Studies is marginalised we should not be surprised about the paucity of Black staff on campuses. Only 1.7 percent of academic staff are Black, and this makes no distinction for whether they are UK domiciled or work full or part time,[2] and the further we look up the career ladder the fewer Black staff we find. A Black Studies undergraduate degree has taken so long because the knowledge is not valued and there are nowhere near enough people employed or being trained in universities who would be able to teach it. As proud as we are of the achievement of the Black Studies degree, we should be wary about celebrating the progress that has been made in higher education.

This chapter will explore the path to the Black Studies degree, demonstrating that it was the result of a particular set of circumstances, which would be difficult to replicate. In fact, there is no other university that could credibly offer an undergraduate degree in Black Studies, which demonstrates how deep the structural problems go. The chapter will offer a blueprint for the work that we have done, but also discuss this labour in the context of the particular set of challenges of the neoliberal university. Black Studies cannot just be about changing the face of the universities, we must struggle to rewrite the nature of what it means to be academic.

Blackness in Britain

Newman University in Birmingham was the starting point for the Black Studies movement in British academia. It should come as no surprise that Black Studies gained its foothold in one of the newest universities, far away from the elite in terms of prestige and league table position. The growth of new universities and courses has been a key element in widening participation at the student level, with Black students more likely to go to post-92 institutions.[3] Newer universities have also offered more opportunities for Black staff to be employed in academia. All the Black academics who were integral to developing Black Studies are currently working in post-92 institutions. On top of this, more work needs to be done to map the exclusions of minority staff from the key disciplines, but I can personally attest to finding it extremely difficult to find a job within sociology. Newman offered me my first opportunity for an academic post, working as a Lecturer in Childhood and Early Childhood Studies – a subject that touched the far reaches of my knowledge base. But I will always be grateful for the opportunity because I am not convinced I would ever have got a job in my discipline without that foothold. At Newman, I eventually moved over to Working with Children, Young People and Families, where we hired Lisa Palmer, also to her first academic post. It was from this base of two Black academics in the same department (a rarity), that we started to build towards Black Studies.

In 2013, we organised the first 'Blackness in Britain' conference to bring together those studying the contributions, perspectives and experiences of Africa and its diaspora. When we put out the call, we were expecting just a handful of people to attend. We were overwhelmed by the 150 people who turned up on the day, and the over 40 papers we received. We had inadvertently organised a major international conference, which had captured the imagination of scholars, students and activists. It was then that the idea of Black Studies as a movement was born, as we could not let the momentum we had built disappear.

Out of a selection of papers from the conference, we created the first edited collection of Black Studies scholars in Britain. *Blackness in Britain* came out in 2016 and is a key milestone in marking out a disciplinary territory. In addition to the edited collection I also now edit a book series for Zed Books of the same name, with the aim of publishing critical work in the field over the next few years. This academic production is vital because in order to change the university we need to consecrate new forms of knowledge. A credible research base is a vital component of Black Studies.

In 2015 we held the second Blackness in Britain conference, this time spread over three days and with international keynotes from Patricia Hill Collins, Barnor Hesse and Gus John. Once again, we had over 150 people attending, a paid-for conference this time, and around 80 papers. The importance of these kinds of gatherings of Black Studies scholars hit me with a comment from one my more sceptical students who was volunteering. When confronted with the mass of Black academics and activists she said, 'I understand why you are doing this now.'

From the successes of the conferences we have also begun the work of creating a Black Studies Association. Having a network that exists outside of a university, which brings together scholars, students, teachers and activists, will be vital to the future success of Black Studies. The emerging association will be launching a journal and organising major international Black Studies conferences on a biennial basis.

Black Studies at Birmingham City University

The second 'Blackness in Britain' conference took place at Birmingham City University (BCU), after both myself and Palmer had been hired in the sociology department. Just as with Newman, BCU is a central part of the story of how Black Studies came to be. When I was hired in 2014, I was the most senior academic in sociology, and so was tasked with leading the development of the research agenda. This was an opportunity provided because of BCU's lack of research profile in sociology when I started, again providing a space outside the elite universities to do things differently.

Black Studies became a central theme of the new research centre, the Centre for Critical Social Research. Activities such as the conference and the publications were a key part of the research agenda. Subsequently, we quickly established Black Studies as a strong research presence in the faculty. Over the past three years we have held countless research and public engagement events – big and small. The publication of high-profile work and success in gaining funding from the ESRC (Economic and Social Research Council) and AHRC (Arts and Humanities Research Council) has seen Black Studies emerge as a leading contributor to research in the faculty and a lynchpin for the next REF (Research Excellence Framework) submission. Whether we agree with the traditional routes for research recognition or not, they are vitally important in providing a long-term base for any discipline within a university. This production has allowed us to secure three funded PhDs in Black Studies from the university, enabling us to produce the next generation of scholars in the discipline.

My presence in the department also coincided with a growth of staffing in sociology. When I started, there were just five staff in the department, myself included. Since then we have doubled our number to ten. As head of the research centre I have had an influence on how the department has developed, and it is no coincidence that three out of the five new staff members were Black Studies academics. This should stand as a lesson to all those universities that are making excuses for not employing Black people: if you decolonise your knowledge base you will quickly decolonise your staffing. Indeed, having five Black members of staff in one department is unique in British academia. The expertise in the department is the only reason that we can offer a Black Studies degree, and also why no other university in the country would be able to do so. To teach a full degree you need a range of staff and expertise, not just a bit of diversity on the reading list. Most universities would struggle to find five Black academics, interested in Black Studies, across the whole institution. Even our expansion of staffing is due to institutional conditions. At a time when many universities are reducing sociology departments, BCU has bucked the trend. Without this, we would not have been hiring more staff and would not have had the people to start the new degree.

In 2016, BCU also announced that it would be revalidating all of its degrees in moving to a 20-credit structure. In this move, the university was looking for innovative degree programmes and pedagogic practices. Up until this point the degree was something we had planned in the long term but with no set timeline. Revalidation was the opportunity to realise the degree and we pitched the idea to the university. This prior context is vital in understanding the university's response: Black Studies did not spring out of nowhere, we had to prove its worth as an academic discipline through our own research endeavours, and show – through the sheer number of people who came to our events – that there was substantial interest in the course. Black Studies was already high profile at the university before we formally suggested the degree. So the institutional resistance that people have often said they expected never materialised. By hiring Black staff and putting in the work to make the discipline credible, we created the conditions whereby it would have made less sense to *not* run the degree than to support it. To give credit to the faculty and the university, they have been very supportive of Black Studies.

BCU was willing to take the risk of supporting Black Studies as both a research area and a degree-level subject – a risk I cannot imagine an elite university taking given the entrenched conservatism within those hallowed halls. The post-92 institutions have spearheaded widening participation and curriculum development, because supporting minority students has had to be at the core of their work. Black and Brown students are more likely to be located in post-92 universities and, given the significant attainment gap, this is an issue for university league tables. Around half of BCU's students are from an ethnic minority so if the university does not try to address the issues of exclusions they face more serious consequences than predominantly white institutions. Something like Black Studies simply would not have been able to emerge at an elite institution. Places like Oxford University think that it is progress to mandate that their history students take one exam in 'non-British and non-European history',[4] while BCU breaks new ground by creating a degree in Black Studies. This point is crucially important because the changes in university admissions are putting a severe squeeze on post-92 universities. Since the removal of the cap on student numbers per institution, the size of the student body at Russell Group universities has gone up by 15 percent, while numbers have declined in the less prestigious institutions by over 22 percent.[5] If post-92 universities lose a foothold they will be unable to offer support for students, and unable to provide spaces for critical pedagogy.

The confluence of events that led to the formation of our Black Studies degree would be difficult to replicate elsewhere. The institution, the timing, the people involved and a large slice of good fortune all played a role in leading to where we are now. Yet our successes should make it somewhat easier for others in the future, as there is now a blueprint and a body of work for Black Studies to build on in the UK. But we should also recognise that the work we have done has not fundamentally changed the nature of British higher education. It remains true that currently no other university could credibly offer Black Studies as an undergraduate degree programme because of a lack of the staff to teach it. As much as we should be proud of what we have accomplished at BCU, there remain significant challenges and dangers ahead.

Neoliberal agenda

Part of the reason the university has been so keen to support Black Studies is because of the neoliberal agenda in higher education. The rise in fees saw the end of the cap on student places, meaning universities could take in unlimited numbers of students. It is unlikely that Black Studies would have been supported had there been the steadier recruitment that comes with a capped system, as there would have been fears that it would take students away from other courses. Without the cap, the incoming students are seen as a new source of revenue that can be freely tapped. In other words: we have a Black Studies degree as a direct result of the massive increase in fees for students.

Being the first degree of its kind is also a huge marketing boost for the university. As a post-92 institution, BCU is keen to make a name for itself in both research and teaching, and is taking the opportunity to do this through pioneering a new discipline. Better still, given all the focus on race equality, Black Studies is something that also enhances the equality credentials of the university. This is not a cynical argument as to the motivations of the university, just a realistic one. One of the central tenets of Critical Race Theory is that the interests of Black communities are advanced only when they converge with those of mainstream society.[6] It is worrying that the interests that converged to produce Black Studies are the very values that the discipline was built to oppose. We must be critically aware of what that means both for our degree and also other universities.

One of the aspects we included in the degree that chimed with the university's vision of 'employability' was to include a mandatory work placement. In the second year of the degree, students must gain experience working with a private, public or voluntary sector organisation that works to benefit Black communities. In the third and final year, the degree culminates with a project where students again work with an organisation to develop a piece of engaged research. None of this was forced on us and it does not challenge the ethos of the degree. In fact, of all the aspects of the degree this is the one that offers the best blueprint for engaging Black Studies outside the academy, creating links between campus and community. This – to borrow from Hare – 'community component' of the degree is central to its political nature. In every year of study students have to engage what they have learnt outside the boundaries of campus. In the first year, students learn the technique of ethnography in its critical form pioneered by Black sociologists like Du Bois[7] and Drakes and Cayton.[8] In the second and third years, students work directly with organisations in Black communities. The application of Black Studies to the real world is an absolutely essential part of the degree.

The problem is that the activist impulse behind this structure can easily be lost because of how we have shaped it to converge with the interests of the university. Once we are gone, the placement may become just that: a standard work placement replete with professional competencies. The Black Studies third-year project could easily become a standard dissertation with no requirement to engage outside of the university. As Black Studies is picked up across different universities, there is nothing we can do to maintain the transformative potential of the discipline. Offering a course like Black Studies can easily become a token gesture, a nod to the diversity agenda; the sprinkles of chocolate on the vanilla ice cream that is the white university. For those seeking to expand Black Studies, keeping its activist and community-centred core is vital to maintaining the critical nature of the discipline.

The work we have been doing is heavily influenced by Black Studies in America. Nathan Hare, one of the founders of the Black Studies movement in America in the late 1960s, described the process as a 'battle'.[9] At his university, San Francisco State College, the students and faculty went on a five-month-long strike in order to pressure the institution to start a Black Studies department, as part of broader changes. Grassroots community movements were involved in supporting the strike and campaigns across the country. At Cornell University, the students occupied Willard Straight Hall and ended up arming themselves because of death threats they were receiving. The shot of the students emerging from the building with shotguns and ammunition is one of the most striking from the period. Black Studies was a battle for more than just Black staff and subjects; it was an attempt to transform the educational process on campus. Hare argued that a new kind of knowledge must be produced and that:

> Black education must be education for liberation, or at least for change… All courses – whether history, literature, or mathematics – would be taught from a revolutionary ideology or perspective. Black education would become the instrument for change.[10]

With community support and mobilisation, the discipline was poised to truly transform the academy. But in the same article where he outlines the transformative principles, published just three years after the establishment of Black Studies at San Francisco State, Hare is already warning that the discipline was being co-opted. Universities were seizing on the opportunity to look pro-active by hiring Black faculty, but excluding the idea of liberation from the curriculum. Very quickly, Black Studies morphed into African American Studies, and often the radical edge was blunted. There are certainly still excellent examples of Black Studies practice taking place in African American, Africana and Black Studies departments. There is also no doubt that support for Black Studies has declined, with many courses underfunded or facing closure. However, there are also far too many examples of departments that have funding and resources (even if limited) that basically replicate the model of the academic status quo. Money is spent on conferences, travel and even furniture, with little, if any support, being offered to wider Black communities. The problem with institutionalising any movement is that you necessarily learn the institutional personality.[11] Academia is a self-referential bubble where to progress you have to talk to the same people you write for, who are all locked away in the ivory tower. It should come as no surprise that there was an institutional turn in the discipline. Black academics are only human.

Academics as a class of people are also the last group that we should expect to challenge the status quo. We romanticise the public intellectual; Michael Burawoy tried to salve the academic conscience by invoking Gramsci in his call for the 'organic public sociologist'.[12] But this interpretation could not be further from Gramsci's characterisation of the academic, who saw our role as that of 'traditional intellectuals', whose entire purpose was to replicate capitalism.[13] Anyone who is a full-time, permanent academic is incredibly privileged from day one. On a starting salary well above the average wage in the West, and a career trajectory that – if successful – can put us in the top 1 percent, or even 5 percent of earners. Even with neoliberal changes we still inhabit one of the last true professions, where we have a large degree of autonomy and professional esteem. We have also spent more time in the institutions of schooling than anyone else, and have been trained in the knowledge of the status quo. If we are honest, we are a bourgeois class who cannot be trusted to transform the nature of the beast that both nurtures and sustains us. Black Studies' original urgency and radicalism was rooted in movements off campus – the grassroots who supplied the radical foundation. Once that link was severed, the direction of travel for the discipline was set. There have been those who have valiantly fought on, but without the movements outside university it is a losing struggle.

Black Studies was a battle in America, which had community support and was a part of a political movement, yet it still succumbed to the perils of institutionalisation. In Britain the process has been markedly less turbulent. Scholars have been struggling for recognition for years, often having to leave for America to have a career. But our path to Black Studies has been through institutional mechanisms: conferences and research centres, with university support. While the institutions were previously indifferent to Black Studies and we have had to put in immense amount of labour to get to this point, we have not faced hostility in our journey to the same degree as those in the US. If there is anything that should worry us about the future of the discipline and its transformative potential, it is the lack of resistance from the institution. As much as I am grateful for the support of BCU, it is still an institution of higher education and rooted in exclusionary structures and practices. Black Studies has been won largely without the grassroots support that the American discipline had, and the message is clear: left to the academics the discipline will not achieve its transformative potential.

Colonising the master's house

Black Studies must do more than exist. Teaching a limited number of students about different knowledge cannot be the end of our endeavours. We must start by acknowledging the exclusionary framework we are in. Access to university is only for those who achieve the correct credentials from an unfair school system. The cost of university is another exclusionary force. Not just in the form of a fee loan, but the fact that the maintenance grants have disappeared and been replaced with yet more debt for students. Student accommodation is so prohibitively expensive that it must be having an impact on student choices. There is no chance I could have studied away from home in today's context of housing that costs £140 a week. We have no power over the bigger decisions being made about the sector and little influence over the managerial priorities that are handed down in the institutions. As much as we have marched for our pensions and pay, we have seen the institutions outsource basic functions like catering, security and IT to private companies, significantly harming the rights of many of the staff we work with. Not to mention the struggles that administrative staff have faced as universities have streamlined and taken on business principles. Teaching about Black people cannot be enough in this climate, in fact there is a deeper question about whether these institutions can be a place to achieve the mission that Black Studies sets out.

The university as the incubator of progressive and critical thought is a dangerous myth. The reality is that, until the 1960s, less than 5 percent of the population went to university and they were bastions of white, male privilege. In the eighteenth century, the botanist Carl Linnaeus, in his System Naturae, outlined the hierarchy of being, with 'Europaeus Albus' (white) at the top and 'Afer Niger' (black), firmly at the bottom.[14] It is no coincidence that he has a university in Sweden named after him. My colleague Nathaniel Coleman highlighted the role of Francis Galton at University College London (UCL) in promoting the eugenics movement;[15] a form of racial 'science' that was a key Nazi justification for the Holocaust.[16] Deepa Naik perfectly summed up the university's role in society when she argued at the 2016 NUS Black Students' Conference that 'the university is not racist, it *is* racism'. To use the words of Audre Lorde,[17] the university is the master's house, in that it has played an authoritative role in producing and maintaining racism. The emergence of Black Studies has not changed this function as the neoliberal agenda so neatly demonstrates. If the university is as institutionally and intractably racist as the police force then this opens up serious questions for the future of Black Studies.

Charting a role for the discipline means being clear about the kind of change that can be achieved. Black Studies is not going to influence a discipline like Social Theory, whose 2015 international conference at Cambridge included a panel on the 'future' of the subject that included only white men. More positively, we have seen some influence of Black Studies on sociology with the discourse of Blackness itself changing. No longer are we stuck in the race relations problematic, or reducing Blackness to the margin of identity. Blackness is beginning to be understood as a response to the political economy, a process of radical becoming that transcends the limits of the nation state. But it would be wrong to overstate the impact of the ideas; Black Studies will never be a staple of the academic diet outside of the discipline and except for the interested few. The reality is that the best we can probably hope for is to be ignored, left to develop alternative spaces within the academy that can produce critical knowledge and engage with communities outside. Decolonising the university may well be possible but that is not the aim of Black Studies, we aim to infiltrate it and use the resources in the service of Black communities.

Using the metaphor of the university as the master's house, just gaining access to the inside would not fundamentally challenge its role. It would be impossible to decolonise the master's house while it still sat as the centre of a slave system. Indeed, some masters were less cruel than others, however, all plantations were still sites of slavery. Similarly, there is a limit to how benevolent you can be when keeping people in bondage. So long as the system of higher education retains its role in creating the knowledge that reproduces a vastly unequal status quo, it can never truly be decolonised. Diversifying the curriculum or offering Black Studies does not change the nature of the university system. The institutional nature of oppression led Lorde to famously warn that the master's tools will never dismantle their house, and this can be seen as a call to move beyond asking for diversity to changing the knowledge and practice base of what we do. A Black Studies that replicates the pedagogy and structure of the status quo simply puts Black faces in white spaces, while leaving the master's house intact. An approach like Black Feminism, which has reshaped the relationship of the academic to both the university and wider publics, is an example of more fundamental change to the way that the house functions.[18] But to truly dismantle the master's house means to overturn and not redeem it. If we are not aiming for transformation of the house, then we need be less concerned about using the tools of the master. The struggle becomes how to subvert the tools, not how to abandon them.

Looking back historically, one of the most surprising sources of rebellion on the slave plantation was Christianity. The Bible was used to control enslaved Africans, removing their links to Africa and preaching the passages of servitude to control the masses. Reading was generally banned among the enslaved, but there were a few slave masters who allowed only the Bible to be read and disseminated, because of its role in pacifying the plantations. However, figures such as Nat Turner in America and Sam Sharpe in Jamaica were both Christian preachers who led rebellions against slavery. In both cases they used their ability to speak to the enslaved, sometimes on different plantations, to agitate and organise. This is a perfect example of subverting the master's tools, rather than outright rejecting them. Indeed, this metaphor works neatly for the role of Black Studies here. Just as the preachers were given an elevated role in the plantation system, so are academics. We can also choose to use these privileges to develop and engage with the struggle of resistance.

Black Studies is therefore not inward looking at the university; rather, it must always focus on the struggles that take place outside the academy. In this sense we are aiming to colonise the master's house; to use our positions of relative privilege to create spaces where we can take the resources from the institutions and put them in service of the Black liberation struggle. The goal is to subvert the master's tools in order to create what Robert Staples called the 'science of liberation'.[19]

The science of liberation

Using Black Studies as an alternative space inside the academy means being clear on the fundamentals and the values of the discipline. It is not enough to learn about Black people, we must be shaping our work for the purposes of liberation. There are certain elements of this that have been key in underpinning this work at BCU.

A vital part of the critique of universities is the separation of knowledge from practice. The idea of the value-free intellectual calmly analysing the social world from afar is one that must be done away with. In research terms, the idea of more engaged and community-based approaches to research have been accepted, to some extent. We must do the same for the education that we produce. Concepts of neutrality and 'balance' are code words for the maintenance of the status quo. All education is political, and that which the university propagates has played a role in producing the unjust world that we inhabit today. The politics of Black Studies must never be hidden; the programme is openly aimed at creating a new knowledge base that can support struggles of resistance. A key strand that runs through the whole degree is learning about Black political activism and pedagogical strategies that can benefit movements for social change. Students have to apply Black Studies off campus, working with organisations that engage with communities. We teach a range of politically engaged methodologies that provide students with the ability to link research to activist practice. In addition to this, we have made sure to include critical analyses of the systems of institutional power that such movements face. A strength of the degree at BCU and the staff grouping is the broadening out of knowledge to include intersectional perspectives. Black Feminism is a core of both the research and teaching, with the acknowledgement that the science of liberation must include all of those in the diaspora, regardless of gender identity, sexuality, or whether they are able-bodied.

Moving beyond academic elitism when it comes to constituting what is 'knowledge' is also vital. Given the exclusion and politics of the university, very little of the knowledge base for Black Studies can be found in the academy. Black Studies may be new to the university in Britain but has thrived in communities for decades. For example, Black Supplementary schools[20] have been organised at a grassroots level since the 1960s, teaching not just the basic school subjects but also creating spaces for Black Studies. The projects were a reaction to the racism of the mainstream schools and involved parents, community members and organisations arranging classes at evenings and weekends in order to provide education to Black children. Part of decolonising our knowledge involves expanding what it is we consider to be a credible source; for example, Malcolm X[21] has a more insightful analysis on Blackness and racism than any scholar paid by a university. Black artists have produced knowledge and methods for engaging with the world that are central to understanding Black diaspora. Black performance theory,[22] for example, will play a key role in our methods of teaching, and connecting with the arts will be an option for students in their engagement work.

Black Studies has always been an interdisciplinary project, acknowledging that disciplinary boundaries are a barrier to progress. You cannot solve social problems simply using the tools of one discipline. Mental health, for example, is a significant problem in Black communities in Britain. Black psychology may bring a different therapeutic perspective; but sociology will critique the paradigm of diagnosis and institutionalisation, as well as considering how racism itself is a factor. A historian would also be useful for putting the current position in historical perspective. We also cannot ignore the economics of mental health; of how the lack of material resources acts as a barrier to effectively tackling the mental health crisis in Black communities. A political analysis of how the state's aggressive response towards Black people and communities is also needed in order to fully account for how mental health issues are compounded. Furthermore, arts and literature could be good therapeutic sources to consider when thinking about potential solutions to mental health concerns. We may also want to consider nutrition and the politics of food. Black Studies therefore must be a space that does away with disciplinary boundaries so that we can take a holistic view of the issues and their solutions.

Having built such a space within an institution that does not necessarily share these principles, the challenge will be to see whether we can maintain the political nature of the programme. Success will depend on us making serious links to organisations off campus that can keep us to our stated principles. Left to our own devices, the institutional temptations will more than likely override our political sentiments. So, as well as explaining the basis of Black Studies and our hopes for the future, this is an open call for those who are interested to be involved in the movement for Black Studies. Our endeavours cannot simply be academic.

Bibliography

Andrews, K. (2013) *Resisting Racism: Race, Inequality and the Black Supplementary School Movement.* London: Institute of Education of Press.

Andrews, K. (2017) 'It's a Dangerous Fiction that One Exam Will Decolonise Oxford's History Degrees', *The Guardian*, 30 May.

Bauman, Z. (1989) *Modernity and the Holocaust.* Cambridge: Polity.

Bell, D. (1992) *Faces at the Bottom of the Well: The Permanence of Racism.* New York: Basic Books.

Burawoy, M. (2005) '2004 American Sociological Association Presidential Address: For a Public Sociology', *British Journal of Sociology* 56(2): 259–94.

Coleman, N. (2014) 'Eugenics: The Academy's Complicity', *Times Higher Educational Supplement,* 9 October.

DeFrantz, T. and Gonzalez, A. (eds) (2014) *Black Performance Theory.* Chapel Hill, NC: Duke University Press.

Drake, S. and Cayton, H. (1945) *Black Metropolis: A Study of Negro Life in a Northern City.* Chicago: University of Chicago Press.

Du Bois, W.E.B. (1899) *The Philadelphia Negro: A Social Study.* Philadelphia: University of Pennsylvania Press.

Goffman, E. (1961) *Asylums.* New York: Anchor Books.

Gramsci, A. (2005) *Selections from the prison Notebooks.* London: Lawrence and Wishart.

Hare, N. (1972) 'The Battle for Black Studies', *The Black Scholar* 3(9): 32–47.

Hill Collins, P. (2000) *Black Feminist Thought*. London: Routledge.

Lorde, A. (1984) *Sister Outsider*. Berkeley: The Crossing Press.

Ratcliffe, R. 2017. 'Universities Face Looming Strikes as Market Revolution Bites', *The Observer*, 18 June.

Staples, R. (1998 [1973]) 'What is Black Sociology? Toward a Sociology of Black Liberation', in J.A. Ladner (ed.) *The Death of White Sociology: Essay on Race and Culture*. Baltimore, MD: Black Classic Press, pp. 161–72.

X, M. (1970). *By Any Means Necessary*. New York: Pathfinder Press Inc.

Notes

All urls last checked January 2018.

1. Hussain, M. (2015) 'Why is My Curriculum White?', 11 March, available at: www.nus.org.uk/en/news/why-is-my-curriculum-white/
2. Higher Education Statistics Agency (2015) 'Ethnic Minority Staff by Ethnicity and Activity Standard Occupational Classification Group', available at: www.hesa.ac.uk/data-and-analysis/staff/overviews?breakdown%5B%5D=580&year=2
3. Runnymede Trust (2010) 'Ethnicity and Participation in Higher Education', Parliamentary Briefing available at: www.runnymedetrust.org/uploads/Parliamentary%20briefings/HigherEducationNovember2010.pdf
4. Andrews, K. (2017) 'It's a Dangerous Fiction that One Exam Will Decolonise Oxford's History Degrees', *The Guardian*, 30 May.
5. Ratcliffe, R. (2017) 'Universities Face Looming Strikes as Market Revolution Bites', *The Observer*, 18 June.
6. Bell, D. (1992) *Faces at the Bottom of the Well: The Permanence of Racism*. New York: Basic Books.
7. Du Bois, W.E.B. (1899) *The Philadelphia Negro: A Social Study*. Philadelphia: University of Pennsylvania Press.
8. Drake, S. and Cayton, H. (1945) *Black Metropolis: A Study of Negro Life in a Northern City*. Chicago: University of Chicago Press.
9. Hare, N. (1972) 'The Battle for Black Studies', *The Black Scholar* 3(9): 32–47.
10. Ibid. p. 33.
11. Goffman, E. (1961) *Asylums*. New York: Anchor Books.
12. Burawoy, M. (2005) '2004 American Sociological Association Presidential Address: For a Public Sociology', *British Journal of Sociology* 56(2): 259–94.
13. Gramsci, A. (2005) *Selections from the Prison Notebooks*. London: Lawrence and Wishart, p. 5.
14. Niro, Race.
15. ~~Coleman~~, N. (2014) 'Eugenics: The Academy's Complicity', *Times Higher Educational Supplement*, 9 October.
16. Bauman, Z. (1989) *Modernity and the Holocaust*. Cambridge: Polity.
17. Lorde, A. (1984) *Sister Outsider*. Berkeley: The Crossing Press.
18. Hill Collins, P. (2000) *Black Feminist Thought*. London: Routledge.

19. Staples, R. (1998 [1973]) 'What is Black Sociology? Toward a Sociology of Black Liberation', in J.A. Ladner (ed.) *The Death of White Sociology: Essay on Race and Culture*. Baltimore, MD: Black Classic Press, p. 168.
20. Andrews, K. (2013) *Resisting Racism: Race, Inequality and the Black Supplementary School Movement*. London: Institute of Education of Press.
21. X, M. (1970) *By Any Means Necessary*. New York: Pathfinder Press Inc.
22. DeFrantz, T. and Gonzalez, A. (eds) (2014) *Black Performance Theory*. Chapel Hill, NC: Duke University Press.

9

Open Initiatives for Decolonising the Curriculum

Pat Lockley

In the Random House unabridged dictionary, there are eighty-two entries under the word 'open' that could be set on separate lines, as in a poem. For me those entries are most beautiful, filled with all kinds of associations, all kinds of images.

Robert Motherwell[1]

Open Learning is an imprecise phrase to which a range of meanings can be, and is, attached. It eludes definition. But as an inscription to be carried in procession on a banner, gathering adherents and enthusiasms, it has great potential.

Norman Mackenzie[2]

Battle for open: How openness won and how it doesn't feel like a victory.

Martin Weller[3]

Men fight and lose the battle, and the thing that they fought for comes about in spite of their defeat, and when it comes turns out not to be what they meant, and other men have to fight for what they meant under another name.

William Morris[4]

Open is a lexical hydra, with each head a meaning, and with each new definition-decapitation comes two new meanings. Open is a commons with resources to be shared and a panopticommons where all actions are monitored. Open is a broad church offering acceptance and welcome, but 'openwashing'[5] is a term used to denounce the wrong types of open. Open is Janus-faced at best, at worst a cognitive dissonance of infinite thoughts.

An open definition?

Defining what open means, and then what open could offer decolonisation is key to this chapter. Open, at present, has several commonly accepted meanings[6] especially with regard to education and technology. These meanings (open as pertaining to access, open as in open source) simultaneously perform a role as both a call to arms and a shibboleth. 'Open' functions like 'green', 'fair trade' and 'free range' as both a marketing term and an exclusionary term.

A widely used technique when trying to define open is to take a historiographical approach.[7] Peter and Diemann's timeline is the most extensive.[8] This timeline does not contain Bradford Academy as the first university to explicitly admit women, Gallaudet University as the first Deaf university, any of the issues within faith-based universities, any of the historically Black colleges of the United States or the ruling of *Brown vs Board of Education* and various forms of affirmative action. If openness is about access, then these events would seem key events. If openness is ignorant of these events, does it mean openness is apolitical? So what is openness here – male, white, Western and able-bodied? Does openness tend towards serving a hegemonic public while claiming to work for everyone? One example is that the University of Berkeley took down over 20,000 open videos rather than pay to create transcriptions for deaf people.[9]

Hill, when discussing open education, suggests we gain nothing from trying to define what 'open' means and instead we should focus on what people seek to gain from using it.[10] Who or what gains from this definition of open as access? Following Spivak's view on modern historiographies

> the sophisticated vocabulary of much contemporary historiography successfully shields this cognitive failure and that this success-in-failure, this sanctioned ignorance, is inseparable from colonial domination.[11]

Is what we are seeing with 'open' as access *success-in-failure* and *sanctioned ignorance*? Are these terms synonymous with pedagogic concepts like interest-convergence[12] and Illich's *fake public goods*?[13]

Open as access

If openness is linked to a form of social justice via access then it should focus on those under-served by existing institutions. When we see access broadened, this new resource is instead taken up by those already advantaged. Whitburn argues students enrolling at the Open University have already demonstrated upward mobility before they enrol.[14] The Open University's own report on their first intake mentions a big demand from the middle class and other professional groups, which Bell and Tight consider to represent a second bite, not a second chance.[15] Andrews' commentary on the university's colonial role of placing people in the social order is likely reinforced by a form of openness which isn't targeted specifically at disadvantaged groups but instead offers opportunities to already advantaged ones.[16]

The targeting of disadvantaged groups is frequently based on reducing costs and increasing competition. Price reduction is likely to disadvantage the already disadvantaged groups who would more likely have to use these cheaper universities. The work of Cottom names this take on higher education as 'lower ed'.

> Lower Ed encompasses all credential expansion that leverages our faith in education without challenging its market imperatives and that preserves the status quo of race, class and gender inequalities.[17]

Lower prices to facilitate access are now a key selling point of openness. When the NAACP (the National Association for the Advancement of Coloured People) endorses OER[18] (open educational resources; these are teaching materials which have a more permissive copyright), it does not do so for the capability to legally remix and reuse those materials (for example, in order to remove colonialist content) but instead because OER means lower fees and textbook costs. Many US states have open textbook initiatives aiming to reduce costs for students.

Once at university, Richardson lists the many ways in which ethnic minority students are less likely to obtain good degrees.[19] Richardson's work covers research from the 1990s onwards, and so we face over 20 years of universities not addressing under-performance (even when access is achieved). Compare these quotes from Nicola Dandridge:[20]

We recognize that there is a serious issue about lack of black representation among senior staff in universities, though this is not a problem affecting universities alone, but one affecting wider society as a whole.[21]

And:

We recognize that there is a serious issue with the lack of black representation among senior staff in universities. The evidence is clear that black and minority ethnic staff continue to be underrepresented at senior levels in higher education.[22]

Six years apart and the only change seems to be an acceptance of evidence. Eighty out of 176 universities advertising jobs on jobs.ac.uk lack any statement or sentiment on diversity in their adverts.[23] The Athena Swan award (which focuses on gender equality) offered by the Equality Challenge Unit has 143 members,[24] the Race Charter award has only 36.[25] There are many forms of access, where an 'open', sometimes even a legal open, does not seem to function as expected, or at all.

MOOCs and openness

A recent development in 'open' as 'access' was the creation of MOOCs (Massive Open Online Courses) which take courses to a level of theoretically unlimited access.[26] Disadvantaged groups played a key role in the rapid expansion of MOOC provision. Daphne Koller, one of the two founders of Coursera, regularly mentions the death of a student's mother when trying to register at the University of Johannesburg, as a reason MOOCs are needed.[27] Andrew Ng (the other founder of Coursera) claims that India needs 1500 new universities to meet demand, and that he sees Coursera helping to meet that demand.[28] So who takes MOOCs? Christensen et al. report 83 percent of MOOC students have a post-secondary degree, 79.4 percent of students have a Bachelor's degree or higher and 44.2 percent indicated a level of education beyond a Bachelor degree.[29] So again, 'open as access' tends to provide a function for those already advantaged. San Jose State University (in partnership with MOOC platform Udacity) tried to use MOOCs to teach disadvantaged students. The project failed, and Sebastian Thrun (founder of Udacity) said:

These were students from difficult neighborhoods, without good access to computers, and with all kinds of challenges in their lives, it's a group for which this medium is not a good fit.[30]

Therefore, we cannot target groups except to suggest that openness fails for them. MOOCs established and continue to promote their openness on massive enrolments and accessibility. MOOCs, promoted on the perils of university admissions, predominantly educate those who already have had a university education. The imagery of theoretically disadvantaged Africans and Indians (perhaps Afro-pessimism) is key to the promotion. The global North relies on the global South's travails to justify a new benefit for them, a case of fake public goods and interest-convergence.

Within MOOC provision, there is no shortage of evidence of colonialism.[31] Specific examples include

- The biggest MOOC (in terms of students registered) was run by the British Council on IELTS guidance.[32] IELTS is an English Language proficiency test international students have to take to prove their English is of a sufficient standard.
- When a university from the United States partnered with FutureLearn, all Iranian, Sudanese, Cuban, Syrian and North Korean students were excluded.[33] The same is true of the Open University itself.[34]

What of the provision of MOOCs and their topics? The majority of MOOCs on European topics are provided by European universities, whereas the reverse holds for Asia and Africa.[35]

Table 9.1 Courses on Africa, Asia and Europe run by universities within the respective region

Area	Total courses	Ran by Universities in that region	Percentage
Africa[36]	4	1	25
Asia[37]	5	2	40
Europe[38]	8	7	87

On the production side, which university staff members are involved in creating this massive openness?

Table 9.2 Number of Black men and women producing courses for Coursera
and Futurelearn

	Men	Women	Black Men	Black Women	%
Coursera	1792	804	31	13	1.7
Futurelearn	427	405	2	7	1.1

The data in Table 9.2[39] covers all institutions, but when focusing just
on the UK and FutureLearn, only three Black academics (and those are
all women) teach on FutureLearn. This is three academics out of a total
of 524[40] (0.5 percent); in universities the percentage is 1.5 percent.[41]

MOOCs offered a platform on which they could address known
historical issues had there been the inclination. With MOOCs, we see
a provision which is primarily generated and managed by white staff
members primarily from the global North – there is no broadening,
only an increased narrowing of provision. Holmwood typifies MOOCs
as a neoliberal unbundling of universities, which could generate more
choice, but which can also be seen as the metamorphosis of universities
into a geographically footloose industry.[42] An industry whose newfound
geographic freedom manifests itself as the creation of colonial outposts
en masse? How would Alatas's idea of 'academic dependency' classify the
effect of this provision?[43] Does the provision of a free source of education
make it harder to establish services in developing countries?

Open access

Open as access also applies to research as 'open access'. Universities with
the highest percentages of Black staff are those which spend the least – in
many cases, nothing – on open access article processing charges.[44] This
means their staff's research – and ergo, careers – suffer from the absence
of the widely accepted benefits of open access.

It is widely accepted that having an article published as open access
increases citations, so that research from those universities is going to
be widespread, bringing us back to academic dependency.[45] Similarly, do
we see open access as broadening or diversifying, or merely reinforcing
the existing system?

The Directory of Open Access Journals[46] lists over 10,000 journals,
of which 70 percent are free to submit to, but in the UK, 81 percent of
journals charge a processing fee. Of the 2900 journals which charge

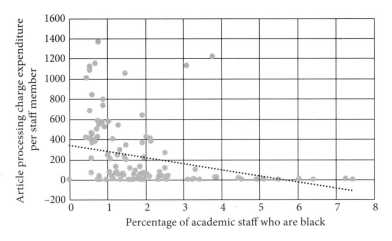

Figure 9.1 Percentage of academic staff who are Black in relation to open access article processing charges

fees, 2200 offer varied fees depending on the financial background of the author (a direct example of targeting or shaping openness). Of the 10,000 journals, 50 percent publish articles solely in English. Of the open access journals 638 are based in Africa (6%); of the 638 African journals, 585 are Egyptian (91 percent).

Open and copyleft

Openness, if based around access, could be seen as apolitical (and it appears to be apolitical in implementation), but it is not without politics; it is politicised as racist because of being ignorant of race, or if not ignorant, unwilling to specifically address issues such as race and colonialism (as well as ableness and gender), or incapable of doing so. How is this different when we look at other meanings of 'open', such as open as in 'open source'? 'Open source' was a term coined to distinguish a new practice from what was the free software movement.[47] The free software movement was started by Richard Stallman, who promoted the right to modify the source code of software. The Free Software Foundation (established by Stallman) created the general public licence (GPL). The GPL is credited with the creation of what is now known as copyleft – a copyright status which ensures an item cannot have its distribution or copyright controlled by anyone. Changes to code in GPL licensed software have to be contributed back and shared with other users. Eric Raymond popularised the term 'open source'. Open source is seen as more business friendly and allows for individuals to retain their contribution and not to have to share with others. Berry highlights other philosophical perspectives which differ between 'free' and 'open' software communities.[48]

If open is a more permissive copyright system, then does the colonial nature of copyright make openness explicitly decolonial? Copyright, as now enshrined in various trade treaties and agreements is distinctly colonial.

Smith was talking about a successful and highly respected Korean businessman who ran a publishing business called Tower Publications. Tower published textbooks for the South Korean market.... The presses at Tower reproduced tens of thousands of American textbooks, but American publishers and authors did not see any licence fees or royalty payments.

It was a familiar enough story throughout most of Asia. The price of Western textbooks as well as software was beyond the reach of most Asian students. A market in copying had sprung up. Businesses like Tower could take advantage of technologies that had made copying easier and, not having to pay licence fees to Western publishers, could produce texts at prices that Asian students could afford to buy. As Smith observed: 'American text-books were being killed'.

Korea had put a Copyright Act on its statute books in 1987, but that was where it had stayed. Copyright was not part of Korean legal practice, let alone general culture or consciousness. There were almost no copyright lawyers in Korea. Those with some knowledge of copyright had usually been trained in the US. Copyright law was for them the distant memory of lecture theatres. So far as Korean culture was concerned copyright was the most foreign of foreign transplants. Copying was regarded as a sincere form of flattery, something that should gladden authors rather than anger them.

US trade negotiators were wearily familiar with the cultural defence from Korean trade negotiators.... The Koreans were presented with a very simple choice: improve protection of US intellectual property or kiss their export markets in the US goodbye. There was nothing unlawful about the threat. In the early 1980s, the US had reformed its trade law to allow the US executive to impose trade sanctions on those countries that did not respect US intellectual property.

The head of Tower Publications spent eight or so weeks in jail. He was, as Smith pointed out, a businessman of enormous status in Korean society. Later a Korean informant also involved in the US–South Korean negotiations over intellectual property confirmed for us that the jailing of this respected figure had sent 'shock waves' throughout South Korean business and social circles. The bureaucratic elite that ran the South Korean economy had been sent a message.[49]

Copyright, and therefore, copyleft are both centred on the laws of the United States of America. Educational openness is most commonly implemented by using Creative Commons[50] licences. The most commonly used educationally is the Non-Commercial ShareAlike Attribution (often referred to as CC-NC-BY-SA).[51] The terms Non-Commercial and Attribution are part of the US Copyright Code,[52] but are not present, to give one example, in the UK Copyright, Design and Patents Act.[53] To address legal differences, Creative Commons licences have been 'ported' (in this meaning, ported means translated into a local jurisdiction) as shown in Figure 9.2.[54]

So the licences tend to the global North, version 4.0 of the licence[55] is largely expressed in the languages of the global North and these licences are no longer 'ported'. The Free Software Foundation disapproves of translations[56] and the GPL translations tend to favour the global North. Openness in copyright (when done through these licences) is therefore the colonial expansion of US law into other countries as much as the WTO (World Trade Organization) trade deal was and is. Schwartz, the ex-president of Sun Microsystems believed the GPL and other copyleft licences acted as 'technological colonialism'.[57] Hemmungs Wirtén notes that all the major copyright liberalisation protagonists are US based (they are also all male and white).[58]

Openness and the commons

Creative Commons licences create the opportunity of a freedom in the Western liberal sense,[59] but in doing so reinforce the author as individual (which is not applicable in many cultures). Brown and Nicholas note that property and intellectual property may not be distinguishable concepts in all cultures. Brown and Nicholas comment:

> Our concern is less with the economic or macropolitical aspects of digitization than with the impact of 'open access' and 'freedom of

Figure 9.2 Creative Commons international map

information' upon the tangible and intangible cultural heritage of indigenous peoples in democratic societies such as Canada and New Zealand, both countries with a colonial legacy. The nature of knowledge within these indigenous communities may be fundamentally different from that of the majority of non-indigenous cultures.[60]

Hemmungs Wirtén continues to discuss how Lange's work on the commons as analogical to the American West (and the associated acts of colonialism) ties into Locke's notion of unworked land as unowned and how this can be applied to copyright.[61] Locke's thoughts are taken up by Eric Raymond (as mentioned, key to the founding of open source) in his work 'Homesteading the Noosphere'.[62] Raymond asserts that individual ownership over a commons is key to running an open source project, and his use of the phrase 'homesteading' is close to Lange's linking of the commons to the expansion of the United States westward into Native American and Mexican lands.

The romanticism of the commons is not limited to openness. Hardt and Negri place open source and Creative Commons as a new form of peer production leading to a revolutionary commons.[63] Moe sees these licensed commons as an example Lyotard's rejection of grand narratives.[64] For Berry, however:

> it is a fragile space that seems similar to the temporary autonomous zones (TAZ) popularized by Hakim Bey. Will the creators of free culture and free software allow it to be overcoded, controlled and channelled towards consumption?
>
> Some worrying examples include: the continuing commercialization of the internet; IBM's forays into the Linux kernel; and even the colonization of blogging and photosharing.[65]

Is it autonomous, or is it merely a copyright anomie? Schweik typifies it as a 'common property regime'.[66] Most licensed works remain the property of its author, and not held in trust or in the commons. What if it isn't even a commons? Berry criticises Creative Commons for lacking commonality.

> the Creative Commons network provides only a simulacrum of a commons. It is a commons without commonalty. Under the name of the commons, we actually have a privatized, individuated

and dispersed collection of objects and resources that subsist in a technical-legal space of confusing and differential legal restrictions, ownership rights and permissions.

The Creative Commons network might enable sharing of culture goods and resources among possessive individuals and groups. But these goods are neither really shared in common, nor owned in common, nor accountable to the common itself. It is left to the whims of private individuals and groups to permit reuse. They pick and choose to draw on the commons and the freedoms and agency it confers when and where they like.[67]

In turn, Liang observes:

The concern over the expansionist tendency of intellectual property has also motivated a rearticulation of the importance of the commons of knowledge and cultural production. This is exemplified by various phenomena among the increasing popularity of non-proprietary modes such as free software and open content. A number of these concerns historically have emerged from the experience of Europe and the United States. But when one attempts to translate the terms of the intellectual property debate into the contemporary experience of countries in Asia, Latin America and Africa, it is difficult to locate any easy indexical reference to ideas such as 'the digital commons'.[68]

The commons is somehow seen as a panacea and there is an expectation of the commons as some optimised end point of a better society (even when discussing decolonial processes).[69]

Openness and open source

How would this commons not end up as colonialised as spaces outside the commons? Is this the case with the 'commons' of open source?

Figure 9.3[70] shows the percentage of commits by contributors to a project when compared to the biggest contributor to a project. The ratio of commits between first and second most common contributors to a project – 1.99 – means (albeit crudely) the main contributor is doing twice as much work as anyone else on the project. The ratio of commits between the first and hundredth ranks of contributors – 176.7 – suggests that this is far from a commons but instead a few people doing the

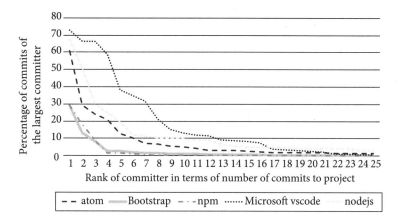

Figure 9.3   Number of commits to open source projects

majority of the work. Ghosh and Prakash find 10 percent of the authors contribute 72.3 percent of the code.[71] The recent 'heartbleed'[72] issue is an example of an incredibly important piece of open source code being looked after by a handful of people.[73] Is this, as well as failing as a commons, also not, as Terranova argues, merely a source of free labour for capitalism?[74]

Open source and the possibilities for decolonisation

Does open as permissively licensed offer anything to decolonisation? Github[75] is one of the most commonly used sites for open source and has over 67 million projects.[76] Of the 2.9 million Github repositories Google has in its big data server, only 7800[77] have codes of conduct (which indicate a form of politicisation), but there is also the 'No Code of Conduct' movement.[78] Raymond's 'cathedral and bazaar'[79] model can be seen as synonymous to Bauman's caravan parks,[80] or 'nomadic digital citizens'[81] which relates to how managing these spaces is effectively political and legal minimalism with occasional tyranny. Where does this minimalism come from? Hoofd observes that in these structures there is a reliance on everyone believing they are on the same level of privilege,[82] and that, as Emejulu and McGregor argue: 'there are no institutionalized inequalities that might undermine the agency of citizens'.[83]

Given the lack of 'codes of conduct' and a tendency to minimalism, what governs open source projects? Open source is seen as meritocratic[84] and there is a consensus that the most merit-worthy developers should run the project, however many open source projects have a 'benevolent dictator for life'[85] – usually the early developer of the project. How do people then earn this merit? On a smaller scale, it is hard to track individual attributes for code committers. Racial details are scarce but for gender, 1.5 percent of contributors to open source projects are women (that number is 28 percent when it comes to software firms).[86] Recent evidence suggests that women's code is rated as of a higher quality (it is more likely to be accepted) unless they are a newcomer, in which case a woman's code is more likely to be declined.[87] Further research would be needed to see what role race plays. Given these biases, how do projects address this? Nafus spoke to one developer:

> He glowingly enthused about the international diversity of his members, and how diversity strengthened code quality. He observed that it was 'unfortunate' that only 2 percent of members in his organization were women. We raised a number of techniques that could be used to reach out to them, including building on the formal mentoring structures within the community that already helped newcomers. His tone turned. He told us he did not believe in special help for women. He was genuinely concerned about the absence of women, and clearly valued diversity, but rejected any possible course of action. This was not because he believed our suggestions were likely to be ineffective; his obvious discomfort revealed that women's absence posed fewer problems than the method to change it.[88]

Reagle records various examples:

> When Mark Shuttleworth, leader of the Ubuntu project, repeatedly spoke of community members as 'guys', and that they need to improve their work such that it was explainable to 'girls'.[89]

Raymond's key article on source book 'The Cathedral and the Bazaar', later developed into a book, concludes on race and gender:

> after all, if one's imagination readily grants full human rights to future AI [artificial intelligence] programs, robots, dolphins, and extraterrestrial aliens, mere color and gender can't seem very important any more.[90]

Marshall notes an almost solutionist colonialism:

> We may consider the common elite programmer refusal of post-modernism, and their common assumptions of being able to solve all social problems without knowing any sociology or anthropology, or even knowing much about societies other than their own.[91]

So, in an open source system in which simultaneously the code is what matters, but there is evidence of gender discrimination and racial ignorance in what purports to be a meritocracy, what happens when dispute occurs in systems populated by nomads and tyranny? How does this relate to a notion of openness?

> In some ways the FOSS [free and open source software] movement is a closed or limited culture, and has to be. It is not open in the sense of welcoming all comers. Furthermore, if there is a dispute that is not easily resolvable by agreed technological criteria, disputes are often resolved by a 'fork.' The groups separate, and largely ignore each other from then on. That may not be possible in large interdependent social groups.[92]

Where are these repositories created? The map in Figure 9.4,[93] based on data from 2013, represents another openness originating from the global North. This is hardly surprising as of the 8500 programming languages recorded,[94] there are 128 which aren't in English (1.5 percent).

Open and open educational resources

So how does the open of open source relate to the open of open educational resources? MIT (who give their name to the Open Source MIT licence) are seen as founding the open educational movement with their Open Courseware initiative.[95] So after MIT, where do open educational resources originate from? Eighty-nine percent of OER comes from Europe and North America.[96]

So in every form of openness we have seen a tendency to an apolitical, almost ignorant nature, and a tendency to production from the global North. This may reflect post-scarcity and that, as openness is relatively new, we are observing the early days and not the finished article (should openness ever arrive at a finished meaning). Whatever potential 'open'

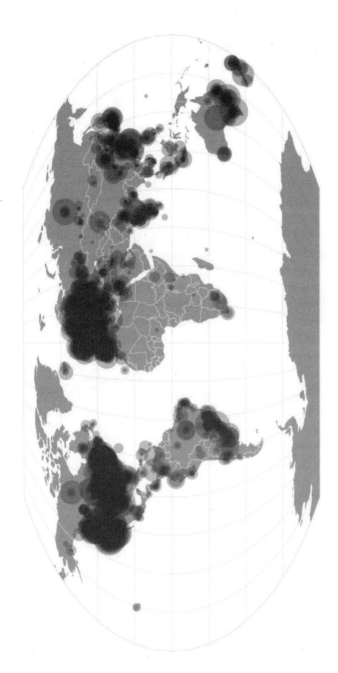

Figure 9.4 Open source contributions by location

may offer to decolonisation, it is important to remember that the possibility remains that in each form we saw colonial activities and could see that openness in itself is colonial, perhaps based on the spread of the Californian Ideology[97] with its blindness to race and its scepticism about societal change. As a meritocratic system which has done little to create meritocracy, this ignores meritocracy's own issues of marketising inequality and erasing working-class values.[98] We can see that the barriers removed could be about giving people access while removing protection for others.

The way that openness or copyright law may well have raised tuition fees should mean we exercise caution.[99] We should be aware of how we expect 'publicly funded to be publicly accessible' for copyright and not for patents and the issues this causes across the academy.[100] How well indigenous knowledge performs under openness is a genuine concern. When Africa's newest university lists its number one priority as decolonising social science through using open source materials we could see this as grounds to celebrate[101] – but how does open source prevent colonial knowledge extraction? How does this stop the commons from being colonised as if new land had been found? Ways that openness could add some form of means testing or focus remains a huge challenge. We should be careful that, in raging against perceived silos, we do not tilt at windmills, and do not ignore those in the fields doing the work.

Bibliography

Adams, R. (2017) 'British Universities Employ No Black Academics in Top Roles, Figures Show', available at: www.theguardian.com/education/2017/jan/19/british-universities-employ-no-black-academics-in-top-roles-figures-show

Alatas, S.F. (2003) 'Academic Dependency and the Global Division of Labour in the Social Sciences', *Current Sociology* 51(6): 599–613.

Altbach, P.G. (2014) 'MOOCs as Neocolonialism: Who Controls Knowledge?', *International Higher Education* 75: 5–7.

Andrews, K. (2017) 'I Compared Universities to Slave Plantations to Disturb, Not Discourage', available at: www.theguardian.com/commentisfree/2016/oct/24/universities-slave-plantations-racist

Auerbach, J. (2017) 'What a New University in Africa is Doing to Decolonize Social Sciences', available at: https://theconversation.com/what-a-new-university-in-africa-is-doing-to-decolonise-social-sciences-77181

Babcock, C. (2005) 'Sun's Schwartz Stands Against Technological Colonialism', available at: www.informationweek.com/suns-schwartz-stands-against-technological-colonialism/d/d-id/1031674

Barbrook, R. and Cameron, A. (1996) 'The Californian Ideology', *Science as Culture* 6(1): 44–72.

Bauman, Z. (2013 [2000]) *Liquid Modernity*. Cambridge: Polity.

Bell Jr, D.A. (1980) 'Brown v. Board of Education and the Interest-convergence Dilemma', *Harvard Law Review* 93: 518–33.

Bell, R. and Tight, M. (1993) *Open Universities: A British Tradition?* Buckingham: Open University Press.

Berry, D. (2004) 'The Contestation of Code: A Preliminary Investigation into the Discourse of the Free/Libre and Open Source Movements', *Critical Discourse Studies* 1(1): 65–89.

—— (2005a) 'Free as in "Free Speech" or Free as in "Free Labour"?', available at: http://freesoftwaremagazine.com/articles/free_labour/

—— (2005b) 'On the "Creative Commons": A Critique of the Commons without Commonalty', *Free Software Magazine* 5.

Brown, D. and Nicholas, G. (2012) 'Protecting Indigenous Cultural Property in the Age of Digital Democracy: Institutional and Communal Responses to Canadian First Nations and Māori Heritage Concerns', *Journal of Material Culture* 17(3): 307–24.

Chafkin, M. (2013) 'Udacity's Sebastian Thrun, Godfather of Free Online Education, Changes Course', available at: www.fastcompany.com/3021473/udacity-sebastian-thrun-uphill-climb

Christensen, G., Steinmetz, A., Alcorn, B., Bennett, A., Woods, D. and Emanuel, E.J. (2013) 'The MOOC Phenomenon: Who Takes Massive Open Online Courses and Why?' SSRN. Available at: https://papers.ssrn.com/sol3/papers.cfm?abstract_id=2350964

Cottom, T.M. (2017) *Lower Ed: The Troubling Rise of For-profit Colleges in the New Economy*. New York: The New Press.

Drahos, P. and Braithwaite, J. (2002) *Information Feudalism: Who Owns the Knowledge Economy?* Abingdon: Earthscan.

Emejulu, A. and McGregor, C. (2016) 'Towards a Radical Digital Citizenship in Digital Education', *Critical Studies in Education*. Available at: www.tandfonline.com/doi/full/10.1080/17508487.2016.1234494?scroll=top&needAccess=true

Ghosh, R.A. and Prakash, V.V. (2000) 'The Orbiten Free Software Survey', *First Monday* 5(7).

Guha, R. and Spivak, G.C. (eds) (1988) *Selected Subaltern Studies*. Oxford: Oxford University Press.

Hardt, M. and Negri, A. (2005) *Multitude: War and Democracy in the Age of Empire*. Harmondsworth: Penguin.

Havemann, L. (2016) 'Open Educational Resources', in M.A. Peters (ed.) *Encyclopaedia of Educational Philosophy and Theory*. Singapore: Springer.

Hemmungs Wirtén, E. (2006) 'Out of Sight and Out of Mind: On the Cultural Hegemony of Intellectual Property (Critique)', *Cultural Studies* 20(2–3): 282–91.

Hill, B. (2010) 'What's "Open" about Open Education', in D. Nyberg (ed.) *The Philosophy of Open Education*, International Library of the Philosophy of Education 15. London: Routledge.

Hobbs, R. (2009) 'Motherwell's *Opens*: Heidegger, Mallarmé, and Zen', in M. Collings, M. Gooding, R. Hobbs, D. Kuspit, R. Mattison, S. Ostrow and J. Yau, *Robert Motherwell: Open*. London: 21 Publishing Ltd.

Holmwood, J. (2013) 'Commercial Enclosure Whatever Happened to Open Access?', available at: ww.radicalphilosophy.com/commentary/commercial-enclosure

Hoofd, I.M. (2010) 'The Accelerated University: Activist–academic Alliances and the Simulation of Thought', *Ephemera: Theory & Politics in Organization* 10(1).

Illich, I. (1973) *Deschooling Society*. Harmondsworth: Marion Boyars.

Jaschik, S. (2017 'Analysing Black Lives Matter Without Black People Involved', available at: www.insidehighered.com/news/2017/05/30/philosophy-journal-apologizes-symposium-black-lives-matter-written-without-black

Khan, Z. (2013) 'OnlineCourses Have Great Potential, Says Coursera's Andrew Ng', available at: www.livemint.com/Specials/b8SrU2I6wjSkFyLFHfrWlO/Onlinecourseshave-great-potential-says-Coursera-s-Andrew.html

Koller, D. (2012) 'What We Are Learning from Online Education', available at: www.ted.com/talks/daphne_koller_what_we_re_learning_from_online_education/transcript?language=en

Larimer, S. (2017) 'Why UC-Berkeley Is Restricting Access to Thousands of Online Lecture Videos', www.washingtonpost.com/local/education/why-uc-berkeley-is-restricting-access-to-thousands-of-online-lecture-videos/2017/03/15/074e382a-08c0-11e7-a15f-a58d4a988474_story.html?utm_term=.67169dffc3f2

Liang, L (2014) 'Beyond Representation', in A. Schwarz and L. Eckstein (eds) (2014) *Postcolonial Piracy: Media Distribution and Cultural Production in the Global South*. London: Bloomsbury, pp. 48–77.

Littler, J. (2013) 'Meritocracy as Plutocracy: The Marketizing of "Equality" under Neoliberalism', *New Formations* 80(80): 52–72.

MacKenzie, N., Postgate, R. and Scupham, J. (1975) *Open Learning: Systems and Problems in Post-secondary Education*. Paris: UNESCO Press.

Marshall, J. (2006) 'Negri, Hardt, Distributed Governance and Open Source Software', *PORTAL Journal of Multidisciplinary International Studies* 3(1).

Moe, R. (2015) 'OER as Online Edutainment Resources: A Critical Look at Open Content, Branded Content, and How Both Affect the OER Movement', *Learning, Media and Technology* 40(3): 350–64.

Morris, W. (1888) *A Dream of John Ball*. Oxford: Kelmscott.

Nafus, D. (2012) '"Patches Don't Have Gender": What Is Not Open in Open Source Software', *New Media & Society* 14(4): 669–83.

Nafus, D., Leach, J. and Krieger, B. (2006) *Gender: Integrated Report of Findings*. FLOSSPOLS, Deliverable D 16. Cambridge, for DG INFSO, European Commission.

Noble, D.F. (1998) 'Digital Diploma Mills: The Automation of Higher Education', *Science as Culture* 7(3): 355–68.

O'Mahony, S. and Ferraro, F. (2007) 'The Emergence of Governance in an Open Source Community', *Academy of Management Journal* 50(5): 1079–106.

Opensource.com (2016) 'How Gratipay Helps Solve the "Free Rider" Problem', available at: https://opensource.com/article/16/12/how-gratipay-solves-open-sources-free-rider-problem?sc_cid=701600000011jJVAAY

O'Sullivan, M. (2008) 'Creative Commons and Contemporary Copyright: A Fitting Shoe or "a Load of Old Cobblers"?', *First Monday* 13(1).

Peter, S. and Deimann, M. (2013) 'On the Role of Openness in Education: A Historical Reconstruction', *Open Praxis* 5(1): 7–14.

Pomerantz, J. and Peek, R. (2016) 'Fifty Shades of Open', *First Monday* 21(5).

Raymond, E. (1998) 'Homesteading the Noosphere', *First Monday* 3(10).

—— (1999) 'The Cathedral and the Bazaar', *Philosophy & Technology* 12(3): 23.

Reagle, J. (2012) '"Free as in Sexist?" Free Culture and the Gender Gap', *First Monday* 18(1).

Richardson, J. (n.d.) 'The Under-attainment of Ethnic Minority Students in Higher Education: What We Know and What We Don't Know', available at: www.open.ac.uk/cicp/main/sites/www.open.ac.uk.cicp.main/files/files/ecms/web-content/290-Presentation-JR.pdf

Santos-Hermosa, G., Ferran-Ferrer, N. and Abadal, E. (2017) 'Repositories of Open Educational Resources: An Assessment of Reuse and Educational Aspects', *International Review of Research in Open and Distributed Learning* 18(5).

Schweik, C.M. and English, R. (2007) 'Tragedy of the FOSS Commons? Investigating the Institutional Designs of Free/Libre and Open Source Software Projects', *First Monday* 12(2).

Shepherd, J. (2011) '14,000 British Professors – But Only 50 Are Black', available at: www.theguardian.com/education/2011/may/27/only-50-black-british-professors

Terranova, T. (2000) 'Free Labor: Producing Culture for the Digital Economy', *Social Text* 18(2): 33–58.

Terrell, J., Kofink, A., Middleton, J., Rainear, C., Murphy-Hill, E., Parnin, C. and Stallings, J. (2017) 'Gender Differences and Bias in Open Source: Pull Request Acceptance of Women Versus Men', *PeerJ Computer Science* 3: p.e111.

Thorne, M. (2009) 'Openwashing', available at: http://michellethorne.cc/2009/03/openwashing/

Tilley, L. (2017) 'Resisting Piratic Method by Doing Research Otherwise', *Sociology* 51(1): 27–42.

Turner, C. (2017) 'Open University under Investigation after It Emerges that Cuban Students Are Banned from Institution', available at: www.telegraph.co.uk/education/2017/07/25/open-university-investigation-emerges-cuban-students-banned/

Weller, M. (2015) *Battle for Open: How Openness Won and Why It Doesn't Feel Like Victory*. London: Ubiquity Press.

Whitburn, J., Mealing, M. and Cox, C. (1976) *People in Polytechnics: A Survey of Polytechnic Staff and Students 1972–73* (No. 27). Guildford: Society for Research into Higher Education.

Wiley, D. (2016) 'Openwashing', available at: http://openwashing.org/

Notes

All urls last accessed October 2017.

1. Hobbs, R. (2009) 'Motherwell's *Opens*: Heidegger, Mallarmé, and Zen', in M. Collings, M. Gooding, R. Hobbs, D. Kuspit, R.S. Mattison, S. Ostrow and J. Yau, *Robert Motherwell: Open*. London: 21 Publishing Ltd.

2. MacKenzie, N., Postgate, R. and Scupham, J. (1975) *Open Learning: Systems and Problems in Post-secondary Education*. Paris: UNESCO Press.
3. Weller, M. (2015) *Battle for Open: How Openness Won and Why It Doesn't Feel Like Victory*. London: Ubiquity Press, p. 232.
4. Morris, W. (1888) *A Dream of John Ball*. Oxford: Kelmscott.
5. http://openwashing.org/. This domain is run by David Wiley, one of the early proponents of openness (via licensing) of educational materials; Thorne, M. (2009) 'Openwashing', available at: http://michellethorne. cc/2009/03/openwashing/; Wiley, D. (2016) 'Openwashing', available at: http://openwashing.org/
6. Holmwood, J. (2013) 'Commercial Enclosure: Whatever Happened to Open Access?', available at: www.radicalphilosophy.com/commentary/ commercial-enclosure; Pomerantz, J. and Peek, R. (2016) 'Fifty Shades of Open', *First Monday* 21(5).
7. Havemann, L. (2016) 'Open Educational Resources', in M.A. Peters (ed.) *Encyclopedia of Educational Philosophy and Theory*. Singapore: Springer Singapore; Peter, S. and Deimann, M. (2013) 'On the Role of Openness in Education: A Historical Reconstruction', *Open Praxis* 5(1): 7–14; Weller 2015 op. cit.
8. Peter and Deimann 2013 op. cit.
9. Larimer, S. (2017) 'Why UC-Berkeley Is Restricting Access to Thousands of Online Lecture Videos', available at: www.washingtonpost.com/local/ education/why-uc-berkeley-is-restricting-access-to-thousands-of-online- lecture-videos/2017/03/15/074e382a-08c0-11e7-a15f-a58d4a988474_story. html?utm_term=.67169dffc3f2
10. Hill, B. (2010) 'What's "Open" about Open Education?', in D. Nyberg (ed.) *The Philosophy of Open Education*, International Library of the Philosophy of Education 15. London: Routledge.
11. Spivak, in Guha, R. and Spivak, G.C. (eds) (1988) *Selected Subaltern Studies*. Oxford: Oxford University Press, p. 6.
12. Bell Jr, D.A. (1980) 'Brown v. Board of Education and the Interest- convergence Dilemma', *Harvard Law Review* 93: 518–33.
13. Illich, I. (1973) *Deschooling Society*. Harmondsworth: Marion Boyars, p. 46.
14. Whitburn, J., Mealing, M. and Cox, C. (1976) *People in Polytechnics: A Survey of Polytechnic Staff and Students 1972–73* (No. 27). Guildford: Society for Research into Higher Education.
15. Bell, R. and Tight, M. (1993) *Open Universities: A British Tradition?* Milton Keynes: Open University Press.
16. Andrews, K. (2017) 'I Compared Universities to Slave Plantations to Disturb, Not Discourage', available at: www.theguardian.com/commentisfree/2016/ oct/24/universities-slave-plantations-racist
17. Cottom T.M. (2017) *Lower Ed: The Troubling Rise of For-profit Colleges in the New Economy*. New York: New Press, p. 12.
18. www.naacp.org/campaigns/open-education-resources-equity-opportunities/
19. Richardson, J. (n.d.) 'The Under-attainment of Ethnic Minority Students in Higher Education: What We Know and What We Don't Know', available at: www.open.ac.uk/cicp/main/sites/www.open.ac.uk.cicp.main/files/files/ ecms/web-content/290-Presentation-JR.pdf

20. Who at the time of releasing them was head of Universities UK. She now heads the Office for Students, whose remit is widening participation and openness.

21. See Shepherd, J. (2011) '14,000 British Professors – But Only 50 Are Black', available at: www.theguardian.com/education/2011/may/27/only-50-black-british-professors

22. Adams, R. (2017) 'British Universities Employ No Black Academics in Top Roles, Figures Show', available at: www.theguardian.com/education/2017/jan/19/british-universities-employ-no-black-academics-in-top-roles-figures-show

23. I wrote some code to download job adverts from jobs.ac.uk and then read those adverts for a statement on diversity.

24. www.ecu.ac.uk/equality-charters/athena-swan/athena-swan-members/

25. www.ecu.ac.uk/equality-charters/race-equality-charter/members-award-holders/

26. The massiveness of MOOCs is built on an ability to scale content provision and so course student numbers (but not teaching support) according to user demand.

27. Koller, D. (2012) 'What We Are Learning from Online Education', available at: www.ted.com/talks/daphne_koller_what_we_re_learning_from_online_education/transcript?language=en

28. Khan, Z. (2013) 'Online Courses Have Great Potential, Says Coursera's Andrew Ng', available at: www.livemint.com/Specials/b8SrU2I6wjSkFyLFHfrWlO/Onlinecourseshave-great-potential-says-Coursera-s-Andrew.html

29. Christensen, G., Steinmetz, A., Alcorn, B., Bennett, A., Woods, D. and Emanuel, E.J. (2013) 'The MOOC Phenomenon: Who Takes Massive Open Online Courses and Why?', available at: https://papers.ssrn.com/sol3/papers.cfm?abstract_id=2350964; Cottom 2017 op. cit.

30. Chafkin, M. (2013) 'Udacity's Sebastian Thrun, Godfather of Free Online Education, Changes Course', available at: www.fastcompany.com/3021473/udacity-sebastian-thrun-uphill-climb

31. Altbach, P.G. (2014) 'MOOCs as Neocolonialism: Who Controls Knowledge?', *International Higher Education* 75: 5–7.

32. https://about.futurelearn.com/press-releases/futurelearn-delivers-the-largest-mooc-ever-as-nearly-400000-learners-convene-for-english-language-learning

33. https://about.futurelearn.com/blog/restricted-course-access

34. Turner, C. (2017) 'Open University Under Investigation after It Emerges that Cuban Students Are Banned from Institution', available at: www.telegraph.co.uk/education/2017/07/25/open-university-investigation-emerges-cuban-students-banned/

35. The sources of the data for Table 9.1 for (1) Africa, are: www.coursera.org/learn/decentralization-africa, www.coursera.org/learn/protected-areas www.futurelearn.com/courses/africa-sustainable-development, www.futurelearn.com/courses/african-philosophy; (2) Asia: www.coursera.org/learn/religions-society-china, www.coursera.org/learn/chinese-politics-2, www.coursera.org/learn/passport-to-india, www.futurelearn.com/courses/korea-global-context, www.futurelearn.com/courses/food-systems-southeast-asia;

(3) Europe: www.coursera.org/learn/eu-making-europe-work, www. coursera.org/learn/geopolitics-europe, www.coursera.org/learn/europe, www.coursera.org/learn/european-law-fundamentals, www.coursera.org/ learn/medieval-europe, www.coursera.org/learn/eu-competition-law, www. coursera.org/learn/eu-law-doing-business, www.futurelearn.com/courses/ switzerland-europe, www.futurelearn.com/courses/european-culture.

36. www.coursera.org/learn/decentralization-africa www.coursera.org/learn/ protected-areas www.futurelearn.com/courses/africa-sustainable-development www.futurelearn.com/courses/african-philosophy

37. www.coursera.org/learn/religions-society-china www.coursera.org/learn/ chinese-politics-2 www.coursera.org/learn/passport-to-india www. futurelearn.com/courses/korea-global-context www.futurelearn.com/ courses/food-systems-southeast-asia

38. www.coursera.org/learn/eu-making-europe-work www.coursera.org/learn/ geopolitics-europe www.coursera.org/learn/europe www.coursera.org/learn/ european-law-fundamentals www.coursera.org/learn/medieval-europe www. coursera.org/learn/eu-competition-law www.coursera.org/learn/eu-law-doing-business www.futurelearn.com/courses/switzerland-europe www. futurelearn.com/courses/european-culture

39. This data comes from a scraping algorithm which downloaded all staff pictures from Coursera and FutureLearn. I then manually categorised the pictures. edX is difficult to scrape and so was not used for this survey.

40. These data come from using various scraping algorithms to access data from various FutureLearn pages.

41. This is based on HESA (Higher Education Statistics Agency) data I received from their press office – 3205 Black, 201,380 overall.

42. Holmwood 2013 op. cit.

43. Alatas, S.F. (2003) 'Academic Dependency and the Global Division of Labour in the Social Sciences', *Current Sociology* 51(6): 599–613.

44. 'Article Processing Charge', Wikipedia, last edited November 2017, available at: https://en.wikipedia.org/wiki/Article_processing_charge

45. Alatas 2013 op. cit.

46. Directory of Open Access Journals, available at: https://doaj.org/csv

47. 'Free' also has a tumultuous etymology (the famous phrase to clarify its meaning is 'free as in speech but not as in beer').

48. Berry, D.M. (2004) 'The Contestation of Code: A Preliminary Investigation into the Discourse of the Free/Libre and Open Source Movements', *Critical Discourse Studies* 1(1): 65–89.

49. Drahos, P. and Braithwaite, J. (2002) *Information Feudalism: Who Owns the Knowledge Economy?* Abingdon: Earthscan.

50. https://creativecommons.org/

51. Santos-Hermosa, G., Ferran-Ferrer, N. and Abadal, E. (2017) 'Repositories of Open Educational Resources: An Assessment of Reuse and Educational Aspects', *International Review of Research in Open and Distributed Learning* 18(5).

52. Attribution: www.copyright.gov/title17/92chap1.html. Commercial: www. copyright.gov/title17/92chap12.pdf; Pomerantz and Peek 2016 op. cit.

53. Copyright, Designs and Patents Act 1988, available at: www.legislation.gov.uk/ukpga/1988/48/pdfs/ukpga_19880048_en.pdf
54. Data is from 2010; Figure 9.4 is taken from: https://en.wikipedia.org/wiki/Creative_Commons_jurisdiction_ports#/media/File:Creative_Commons_Intl_Map.svg (author: Jordan Kalilich).
55. Creative Commons, Attribution 4.0 International, available at: https://creativecommons.org/licenses/by/4.0/
56. GNU (n.d.) 'Unofficial Translations', available at: www.gnu.org/licenses/translations.en.html
57. Babcock, C. (2005) 'Sun's Schwartz Stands Against Technological Colonialism', available at: www.informationweek.com/suns-schwartz-stands-against-technological-colonialism/d/d-id/1031674
58. Hemmungs Wirtén, E. (2006) 'Out of Sight and Out of Mind: On the Cultural Hegemony of Intellectual Property (Critique)', *Cultural Studies* 20(2–3): 282–91.
59. Hemmungs Wirtén 2006 op. cit.
60. Brown, D. and Nicholas, G. (2012) 'Protecting Indigenous Cultural Property in the Age of Digital Democracy: Institutional and Communal Responses to Canadian First Nations and Māori Heritage Concerns', *Journal of Material Culture* 17(3): 307–24.
61. O'Sullivan, M. (2008) 'Creative Commons and Contemporary Copyright: A Fitting Shoe or a "Load of Old Cobblers"?', *First Monday* 13(1).
62. Raymond, E.S. (1998) 'Homesteading the Noosphere', *First Monday* 3(10).
63. Hardt, M. and Negri, A. (2005) *Multitude: War and Democracy in the Age of Empire*. Harmondsworth: Penguin.
64. Moe, R. (2015) 'OER as Online Edutainment Resources: A Critical Look at Open Content, Branded Content, and How Both Affect the OER Movement', *Learning, Media and Technology* 40(3): 350–64.
65. Berry, D. (2005a) 'Free as in "Free Speech" or Free as in "Free Labour"?', available at: http://freesoftwaremagazine.com/articles/free_labour/
66. Schweik, C.M. and English, R. (2007) 'Tragedy of the FOSS Commons? Investigating the Institutional Designs of Free/Libre and Open Source Software Projects', *First Monday* 12(2).
67. Berry, D. (2005b) 'On the "Creative Commons": A Critique of the Commons without Commonalty', *Free Software Magazine* 5.
68. Liang, L. (2014) 'Beyond Representation', in A. Schwarz and L. Eckstein (eds) *Postcolonial Piracy: Media Distribution and Cultural Production in the Global South*. London: Bloomsbury, pp. 50–51.
69. Tilley, L. (2017) 'Resisting Piratic Method by Doing Research Otherwise', *Sociology* 51(1): 27–42.
70. Data for Figure 9.5 was based on the top five octoverse projects listed on github. Data was downloaded using this tool (https://github.com/pgogy/Scriptscrape-GithubData).
71. Ghosh, R.A. and Prakash, V.V. (2000) 'The Orbiten Free Software Survey', *First Monday* 5(7).
72. Opensource.com (2016) 'How Gratipay Helps Solve the "Free Rider" Problem', available at: https://opensource.com/article/16/12/how-gratipay-solves-open-sources-free-rider-problem?sc_cid=70160000011jJVAAY

73. Heartbleed was a bug relating to how secure website access is provided and when the issue was revealed it demonstrated how vastly important open source systems (17 percent of the internet was put at risk due to heartbleed) can be in the hands of relatively poorly paid developers.

74. Terranova, T. (2000) 'Free Labor: Producing Culture for the Digital Economy', *Social Text* 18(2): 33–58.

75. www.github.com

76. octoverse.github.com

77. This data is gained from running the following SQL query 'SELECT repo_name,path FROM [bigquery-public-data:github_repos.files] where path like '%code%conduct%'' on the Github data hosted at Google Big Query.

78. See: https://github.com/domgetter/NCoC

79. Raymond, E. (1999) 'The Cathedral and the Bazaar', *Philosophy & Technology* 12(3): 23.

80. Bauman, Z. (2013) *Liquid Modernity*. Cambridge: Polity.

81. Emejulu, A. and McGregor, C. (2016) 'Towards a Radical Digital Citizenship in Digital Education', *Critical Studies in Education*. Available at: www.tandfonline.com/doi/full/10.1080/17508487.2016.1234494?scroll=top&needAccess=true

82. Hoofd, I.M. (2010) 'The Accelerated University: Activist–Academic Alliances and the Simulation of Thought', *Ephemera: Theory & Politics in Organization* 10(1).

83. Emejulu and McGregor 2016 op. cit.

84. O'Mahony, S. and Ferraro, F. (2007) 'The Emergence of Governance in an Open Source Community', *Academy of Management Journal* 50(5): 1079–106.

85. https://en.wikipedia.org/wiki/Benevolent_dictator_for_life

86. Nafus, D., Leach, J. and Krieger, B. (2006) *Gender: Integrated Report of Findings*. FLOSSPOLS, Deliverable D 16. Cambridge, for DG INFSO, European Commission.

87. Terrell, J., Kofink, A., Middleton, J., Rainear, C., Murphy-Hill, E., Parnin, C. and Stallings, J. (2017) 'Gender Differences and Bias in Open Source: Pull Request Acceptance of Women Versus Men', *PeerJ Computer Science* 3: p.e111.

88. Nafus, D. (2012) '"Patches Don't Have Gender": What Is Not Open in Open Source Software', *New Media & Society* 14(4): 669–83.

89. Reagle, J. (2012) '"Free as in Sexist?" Free Culture and the Gender Gap', *First Monday* 18(1).

90. Raymond 1999 op. cit.

91. Marshall, J. (2006) 'Negri, Hardt, Distributed Governance and Open Source Software', *PORTAL Journal of Multidisciplinary International Studies* 3(1).

92. Ibid.

93. The source for Figure. 9.4 is: http://davidfischer.github.io/gdc2/#languages/All

94. 'Non-English-based Programming Languages', Wikipedia, last edited February 2018, available at: https://en.wikipedia.org/wiki/Non-English-based_programming_languages

95. See: http://ocw.mit.edu

96. Santos-Hermosa et al. 2017 op. cit.
97. Barbrook, R. and Cameron, A. (1996) 'The Californian Ideology', *Science as Culture* 6(1): 44–72.
98. Littler, J. (2013) 'Meritocracy as Plutocracy: The Marketizing of "Equality" under Neoliberalism', *New Formations* 80(80): 52–72.
99. Noble, D.F. (1998) 'Digital Diploma Mills: The Automation of Higher Education', *Science as Culture* 7(3): 355–68.
100. Holmwood 2013 op. cit.
101. Auerbach, J. (2017) 'What a New University in Africa Is Doing to Decolonize Social Sciences', https://theconversation.com/what-a-new-university-in-africa-is-doing-to-decolonise-social-sciences-77181

PART III

DECOLONIAL REFLECTIONS

10

Meschachakanis, a Coyote Narrative: Decolonising Higher Education

Shauneen Pete

This chapter explores the decolonisation of higher education through the practice of storytelling: a decolonising strategy. Story as research methodology is a decolonising approach for it encourages a reclamation of (ab)original ways of transferring knowledges. Storytelling, as I practise it, is rooted in Indigenous ways of knowing informed by my positionality as a Cree/Salteaux/Dakota woman, scholar and university administrator. In these roles I have troubled systems of education; in much the same way as Coyote troubles community as presented in Indigenous narrative traditions.

The chapter invites the reader to join with Coyote (a trickster figure) and the author as they engage in a reflexive conversation that explores ways of undertaking decolonising practices in higher education. The chapter begins with a critical view of how colonial institutions of higher education are and how these colonial structures are experienced by the author. Then, the chapter explores some of the ways in which the author has led university reform towards decolonisation.

Decolonising knowledge transmission

The inclusion of the research process as a topic in and of itself is to explicitly expose the contradictions of academic discourse and knowledge production.[1]

Ever since I was invited to write this chapter I've been wrestling with my choices on how to represent the story of my work as an administrator working towards decolonising higher education. I began my career as a storyteller when I was still an undergraduate student. At that time, I began sharing stories at a local First Nations Heritage Centre, and later told stories in local schools as a way of modelling Indigenous pedagogy. Based on this earlier practice I've chosen to honour storytelling traditions in this chapter as a means of reflecting my Indigenous context. My purpose in writing this chapter is to offer the reader options that might inform their own decision making towards decolonising higher education. This work is not prescriptive but engages the reader in 'dialogic participation'[2] whereby the reader is asked to 'take what you will from what you read'.

For me, privileging storytelling here is a decolonising act. This choice to decolonise knowledge transmission troubles dominant ideas about what scholarship should look like, especially as articulated in the discourse norms of higher education administration. I remember during my thesis defence one of my committee members raised the question – 'Can we tell stories in educational administration?' The committee, all white males, engaged in a vigorous debate for several minutes, and I sat back and watched the discussion unfold … I realised how far they had yet to come in relation to thinking differently about knowledge and knowledge production in our field. Today, like during my thesis defence, I do not/did not apologise for troubling the norms: decolonisation begins with naming colonial structures then moving to reframe, remake and reform them. I understand that like Coyote in traditional narratives, the best role that I can play in university transformation is to serve as that outsider voice working within the organisation; at once a participant and observer to the reforms. I choose to accept my role as 'Coyote' in higher education knowing full well that my job will be primarily to expose inequity and pose decolonial possibilities for restructuring.

I would position storytelling in the realm of qualitative research. I would also position it alongside Narrative Inquiry[3] and Self-Study research traditions. Both of these traditions turn the research gaze inward; a reflexive practice of telling the story then engaging in a critical examination of 'how you have come to know what you know'. Yet, as an Indigenous methodology, storytelling engages the reader/listener in another way – storytelling is relational. The storytelling process often begins with the offering of a gift of tobacco to the storyteller (local cultural protocol norms) and the acceptance of the gift of learning from the listener. Storytelling in Indigenous paradigms[4] evokes deeply spiritual, emotional, mental and physical responses in the listener; the storyteller must be mindful of this impact if they are to ensure that the purpose for storytelling is achieved. With this in mind, I would like to state that my intention for engaging you in this way is to offer you the opportunity to gain cultural competence towards another way of knowing. In this way, you may grow more resilient towards the sorts of decolonising reforms that I speak to later in the chapter.

This chapter is not a prescription for institutional reform; it simply offers a case study of my experience in leading change towards decolonisation. As you read, you will see the presentation of two narratives: the first, the scholarly voice of the author (normal font), and then the second narrative forms an interaction between Coyote (in italics) and the author as they explore barriers and possibilities towards decolonising higher education. This conversational method is congruent with what Kovach (2009) calls an Indigenous research paradigm.

Colonial distractions

This chapter is written from a place of impatience and frustration. I have been working in higher education for sixteen years, as a professor and university administrator; before that I was a student in higher education for ten years and I've had enough (hands in the air, foot stomping!). I'm tired of being the go-to person on my campus for all things Indigenous. I'm tired of explaining why Indigenous content matters in higher education. I'm tired of the arguments over (light) inclusion and diversity vs (deep) decolonisation. I'm over teaching (white) students that they have an identity and it is white and privileged! I'm done!

Whew! I really needed to get that off my chest. As far as careers go, working as a faculty member can be pretty good (most of the time). But lately, I've been thinking that the pace of change isn't coming fast enough for my liking. You see, I'm an Indigenous scholar. For many years, I was the only Indigenous scholar in my faculty and one of only three on my campus. At this point in my presentation or lectures, there is always someone who is brave enough to ask – 'What does Indigenous mean?' (sigh) and so I should probably offer an explanation ... there is a knock at my front door, and a Coyote walks in wearing a cardigan sweater, a scarf over her hair, a pair of glasses ... She is carrying an umbrella. She nods at me to continue ...

I use the word 'Indigenous' to mean a more *global* or *international* reference to the original peoples of the land. The UN Declaration of the Rights of Indigenous Peoples states:

Indigenous communities, peoples and nations ... having a historical continuity with pre-invasion and pre-colonial societies that developed on their territories, consider themselves distinct from other sectors of the societies now prevailing in those territories, or parts of them. They form at present non-dominant sectors of society and are determined to preserve, develop and transmit to future generations their ancestral territories, and their ethnic identity, as the basis of their continued existence as peoples, in accordance with their own cultural patterns, social institutions and legal systems.[5]

When speaking about 'Aboriginal' people, I signal that the context is Canadian as under the Constitution Act (1982), Aboriginal people are understood to be *First Nations, Metis* and *Inuit* peoples. It is an inclusive term that speaks generally to all three recognised groups. That leads me to the term 'First Nation', which I use to refer to the group of people who were once referred to as Indian. When I use the term 'Indian', I mean those people deemed to be an *Indian* as defined by the Indian Act (1985). When I refer to 'settler' people, I mean members of the dominant group, in the case of Canada – that means 'white' people. When I am referring to settler folks, I am not referring to recent immigrants and refugees. ('*Hmmm, you sure use a lot of words there. Can't you just use one term and stick to it?*' Coyote removes her glasses to clean them on her cardigan). 'By for a visit are you?' I ask. 'I'm writing a chapter for a book.' ('*Don't mind me*' she says and settles into my armchair).

Ok, so what was I saying, oh yeah, I was saying, that there was only three of us on campus. Well, being one of only three Indigenous people on campus comes with certain responsibilities – you are asked to speak for all Aboriginal people ... you are asked to sit on every Indigenous students graduate committee and every white students committee if they write about Indigenous themes; you are asked to represent on institutional committees; be a cultural broker so colleagues can learn how to teach differently, relate differently, conduct research and service differently ... connect them to local elders and traditional knowledge keepers and demonstrate how to ask elders to work with them or teach them, and then there are the invitations to speak on Indigenous themes right across campus, oh, and to co-write the grant applications ... AND, you are supposed to still prepare for your own classes, mentor your own graduate students and conduct your own research, finish those publications and sit on department and university committees – whew! I'm kinda worn out! (Sigh). So, where was I going?

Oh yeah, this chapter. This chapter is designed to bring a tricksters lens to Canadian higher education. In this case, I channel my old friend Coyote – *Meschachakanis*. (Coyote leans forward to see my computer screen, she smiles her wicked little smile.) She and I go way back to when I was a teacher candidate. My Children's Literature professor asked our class to prepare to tell a story to our classmates. I was a single mom with a busy toddler and homework up to here … and as I remembered one of the Blackfoot stories of coyote that ol' girl kinda took me over. During my performance my classmates sat transfixed, and afterwards my professor took me aside and remarked, 'I think you have something there.' Thus began my storytelling life; I did weekly shows for three years at a local heritage park, in schools and across the provincial campground system. Me and Coyote we sort of became one being … but that's how she works. She is you and me, and everyone. She has the ability to shape-shift. She is a mischievous character, though a wise teacher through her tomfoolery. She may seem greedy, but she is also innocent in her ways. She's a fast talking, fast walking, lazy, wise woman: she's a contradiction, *partly truth and partly fiction* – oops! (Sorry, I had a Kris Kristofferson flashback to *The Prophet*). Thomas King says, 'Boy, that Coyote is one silly Coyote.'[6] King writes, 'Tricky one, that coyote. Walks in circles, I guess'[7] and 'You got to watch that one … full of bad business.'[8] As an Indigenous scholar I often feel a little off myself … perhaps my mind too is walking in circles. There is two-eyed seeing when you can observe the colonial constructions around you and you can see the decolonial possibilities offered by Indigenous ways of knowing. There are two ways of thinking – those that are colonial and those that speak against it. In my Master's thesis[9] and an earlier book chapter,[10] Coyote played an important role by addressing the tensions between dominant norms and Indigenous sensibility; I utilise that trope once again, here in this chapter. (Coyote has lost her glasses in the cushions of my chair, she has settled back into the chair with a blanket thrown over herself for warmth.)

The chapter embraces the storytelling traditions I've grown old with. The structure of this chapter is meant to subvert dominant Western traditional norms of scholarship. The trickster story presented here is a purposeful disruption. I am guided by Sium and Ritskes who state, 'Stories in Indigenous epistemologies are disruptive, sustaining, knowledge producing, and theory-in-action. Stories are decolonisation theory in its most natural form.'[11] The stories are often recursive: talking back to earlier components and (re)presenting them. The narratives weave together the experience as one who 'lives out decolonization'[12] with the critical reflective (inner) voice of Coyote to say those things that for me seem too dangerous in the academy. To continue to subvert dominant norms, I also speak in Cree where appropriate; and I choose to privilege Indigenous scholars.

So my colonised mind is self-correcting here 'get on with it – write the chapter, the people are expecting a *scholarly* piece of work'. Ok, the aim of this chapter is to explain what decolonising experience in higher education requires for educators and administrators alike, especially those who are members of the dominant group. I will begin the chapter by explaining my positionality as an Indigenous scholar, then I will provide four scenarios ('*Tell them why the number four is important ...*' Coyote is poking at my shins; I give her a look to silence her) ... that speak to common contradictory challenges and responses that are required for individuals who are engaged in the work of Indigenising and decolonising the academy.

My story towards understanding decolonising responsibilities

Tansi. Pesakastew iskwew nitisiyhkason. My name is Dr Shauneen Pete, I am from Little Pine First Nation (SK). I am an associate professor in the Faculty of Education at the University of Regina. My area of specialisation is Aboriginal Education. I have worked as a professor and university administrator for 16 years. I've served most recently as the Executive Lead: Indigenisation. In that role I animated the Indigenisation strategic plan. ('*You sure use big words, what's that mean?*' She asks as she sits down to scratch.) I clear my throat and continue. The Indigenisation strategic plan had five key priorities, including *administration and leadership, student supports, community engagement, Indigenous research* and *academic Indigenisation*. The Indigenisation strategic plan was imagined by the members of the President's Indigenous Advisory Circle (IAC). The IAC reported directly to the President and was made up of volunteer staff and faculty of Indigenous ancestry.

For the members of IAC, Indigenisation re-centred Indigenous ways of knowing, pedagogies and scholarship, as well as students and faculty, in our academic pursuits in higher education. In our view, Indigenisation was a shared responsibility and was designed to benefit all learners. As we began to work on our strategic priorities we came to recognise that this work was hampered by the pervasive ignorance of the university. To effectively address the ignorance we would have to reform the university through processes of decolonisation. (Coyote had fallen asleep, and her foot lay across my keyboard. When I moved it over to be able to hit the period – she stirred and said, '*De-what?*'.)

Decolonisation, Coyote. She is sitting up now and looking through my reading glasses which she has put on her nose. She is wearing my best scarf. '*You better start from the beginning*', she asserts. I begin to explain.

My understanding of colonialism and thus decolonisation is informed by several Indigenous peoples including my father, Jacob Pete; Life Speaker, Noel Starblanket; the late Isadore Pelletier; the late Alma Goodfeather and the late Laura Wasacase. My understanding is also informed by Indigenous scholars.[13] I understand that colonialism is by definition – violent. It is undertaken through the use of force to remove peoples from their traditional lands. In the case of Canada and First Nations peoples, the colonisation of *Turtle Island*[14] ('*Oh, I like it when you call her that*' Coyote claps her hands together) was undertaken through the violent extermination of the Beothuk; through the systematic removal of children from their families through both the residential school system and the child welfare system; and through forced assimilation as articulated through the Indian Act. Colonialism, says Green, 'involved the creation of institutional and administrative apparatuses to serve imperial needs ...',[15] in this case, the Indian Act and the Constitution Act (1982). Green states, the 'political realities of colonialism have been shaped by state-specific policies, practice and political and economic structures'.[16] Violence is not only the manner in which lands and resources are originally acquired, but also how power over these lands and resources is maintained. (Coyote is blinking wide-eyed, she is tsk tsking and cleaning her teeth.) When stated in this way, readers can begin to understand that colonisation is not simply a historical event, but an ongoing system of oppression and advantage. A system designed to privilege the settler state at the expense of the Indigenous peoples.

Coyote thrusts a paw into my face. '*Whoa there missy! You are talking awfully politically – it makes my hair stand on end!*'

Colonisation is political Coyote. It's about the violent confiscation of lands from Indigenous peoples and the assertion that lands and resources now belong to the dominant group – it's by definition violent and therefore highly political. (She turns her back to me and crosses her arms.) To make matters worse, Green states, 'Colonialism lies at the base of Indigenous dehumanisation and oppression.' She (Green) continues,

'Settler states have used armed force, colonial bureaucratic institutions and racialized policing to dominate Indigenous peoples'[17] and that knowledge, as I understand it, has been silenced in higher education; therefore many people, colleagues included, understand very little about the ongoing system of colonisation. This pervasive ignorance has to be addressed in formal education. Only through a process of confronting *epistemic ignorance* (Kuokkanen, 2008) and *Cognitive Imperialism* (Battiste, 2013) can we alter the knowledge base for all higher education institutions. I believe that only through both Indigenising the curriculum and decolonising the academy can we possibly achieve reconciliation. (*'Ok, there it is again – decolonisation, what does that mean? Where did reconciliation come in?' Coyote is standing over my shoulder, watching the words appear on my screen as I type them.*)

Laenui states:

> True decolonization is more than simply replacing Indigenous or previously colonized people into the positions held by colonizers. Decolonization includes the revaluation of political, social, economic and judicial structures themselves, and the development, if appropriate, of new structures which can hold and house the values and aspirations of the colonized people.[18]

Those aspirations include not only a giving back of the land,[19] but the re-establishment of connection between the land and Indigenous peoples[20] for the fulfilment of the right to self-determination and sovereignty,[21] and to facilitate the 'everyday practices of resurgence ...' that serve to 'reclaim, restore and regenerate'[22] relationships to homelands, cultures and communities.

Coyote takes a moment to offer a smudge.[23] *'That's heavy ... that's so much bigger than the discussions of cultural inclusion that I often hear when I am on campus ...'.* I know, I hear the same thing. Neoliberal discourses of 'inclusion' are comfortable for members of the dominant group because it allows them to retain a belief in 'settler innocence', a narrative that often begins with 'that all happened a long time ago ...' and continues with 'but I wasn't involved, so why do I have to pay for the injustices of the past?' These 'moves to innocence ... problematically attempt to reconcile settler guilt'[24] and shifts the onus of responsibility onto the backs of Indigenous peoples: but this isn't *my* work (alone).

I want my non-Indigenous colleagues to take greater responsibility for exposing settler-colonialism because it is – ultimately – their story.

But I've come to understand that many Canadians have been structurally denied the opportunity to learn about Indigenous peoples (and also a deeper history of colonialism). As a result, the dominant narratives in formal schooling are what Battiste (2013) refers to as *Cognitive Imperialism* – an insistence on English as the dominant language of formal schooling as well as a knowledge system that is rooted in Eurocentrism. We inherit a system of knowledges that reinforce colonial dominance. This appears in the structures of university departments and colleges, and in the content/objectives of individual courses. Cognitive Imperialism results in what Kuokkanen refers to as *epistemic ignorance*, or the inability ('... *or unwillingness*', Coyote chirps) of faculty to teach what they don't know. I assert that it is no longer acceptable or possible to relegate an exploration of Indigenous experience only to Departments of Indigenous Studies/Native Studies (though as a site of Indigenous knowledge production, these departments are essential). I believe that all faculties and departments must begin decolonising their curricula in order to facilitate learners developing an understanding of and responsibility for reconciliation (Coyote stares at me. She has donned my winter cap, and my red high-heeled shoes and has started to eat my lunch. One eyebrow raised she asks, '*And what does that mean?*').

I turn towards her to explain. We are on an unequal footing in Canada: Indigenous peoples intimately understand the nature of colonialism and its effects; members of the dominant group tend to know very little (Coyote, chuckles, '*yes, yes ... I remember how I laughed when the former Prime Minister, Harper was his name, he stated that there was no history of colonisation in Canada*'). As a result, when Indigenous peoples assert recognition of their sovereignty they are often viewed as a threat to nationalism, when in my mind they are simply a threat to national ignorance. This unequal footing means that reconciliation, as presented in the Truth and Reconciliation Final Report, is impossible. White folks and new Canadians must demonstrate the effort needed to address their own deficits in their understanding of the truth of our shared past and present. Their demonstration of denial, dismissal and violent rejection of the truth on their part is no way to begin to walk forward together on a path to reconciliation.

As educators in higher education I want my colleagues to engage in deeper exploration of both colonialism and decolonisation in their own teaching practice. I never intended for the discussion of colonialism and decolonisation in this chapter to offer a deep investigation, for you can seek that out by following the story threads that have been offered, by going back and reading for yourself some of these Indigenous scholars. In that way, you can gain for yourself a better understanding of (de) colonisation as content and process in ways that may inform curricular reform. Curricular reform must expose the violence of colonialism, the limitations of discourses of inclusion and diversity; and facilitate an exploration of the possibilities for self-determination and sovereignty as sources of reconciling relationships between settlers and Indigenous peoples. (Coyote is standing over me, with my coffee in her paw ... *'Hold up there sister, when I go around campus I hear people talking about bringing elders in to teach something ... or having their students write a paper on an Indigenous theme – but, that's them having other people do the work for them and you want **them** to change how **they** teach don't you?'.*) I nod my head.

As stated earlier, in my role as Executive Lead: Indigenisation my focus was establishing a shared understanding for Indigenisation (and decolonisation) as well as working towards a shared responsibility for both. In my experience in leading this work I have confronted several limiting narratives, these are explored in the remainder of the next sections.

Limiting narrative 1: But I don't teach any Indigenous peoples

At a recent decolonising teacher education conference, I was asked by a participant, 'I don't have any Indigenous peoples in my school, why would I decolonise our programme?' My response was (and remains), decolonisation is not only designed for Indigenous peoples but has transformative potential for all people whose lives have been impacted by the limitations of white dominance. Decolonising curriculum and course design has the potential to shift how all learners understand the notion of land, nationhood, rights and treaties. Imagine, if you will, how a treaty-based understanding of land would shift our thinking about resource development, revenue sharing and sovereignty. How would that newly formed perspective shift everyday thinking about land ownership, land protection and resources?

(*'Tell them about Colton Bushie'*, Coyote shouts. *'Tell them about that young man that was shot...'*)

Last year a young Indigenous man was shot at close range while inside a parked vehicle. The white farmer who shot the youth believed that he posed a threat to his property even though the youth was sitting in the backseat of the vehicle. The youth and his friends had driven into the farmyard seeking help for a flat tire. The case has not been heard by the courts yet, but in the days following the shooting a barrage of social media posts and media comments exposed the racial hostility that exists among white farmers directed specifically towards Indigenous peoples who, in their words, *are a threat to settler farmlands*. The persistence of the colonial narrative of the hostile Indian still plays out today … troubling curricula about land, land ownership and ties to treaty making which facilitated settlement in the first place would allow for a very different perspective on Indigenous/settler relationships. This work does not require Indigenous peoples to be present – this is about exposing white dominance and working to correct it.

Limiting narrative 2: Decolonisation is not my work

In the absence of understanding about Indigenous content too often colleagues claim that they can't/won't take up this work because they don't know how, or they rely on Indigenous peoples to address the knowledge gap for them; this results in the utilisation of Indigenous faculty as cultural knowledge brokers. In the absence of Indigenous colleagues, I have played this role myself for many years. I've spoken in over a hundred classes and rarely has there been a reciprocal offer to lighten my workload. Sure there has been an occasional offer of a coffee or gift card for the local book store, but these responsibilities serve as a distraction from other activities: primarily, work that supports Indigenous learners and communities. By refusing to provide these services, there is a very real risk that faculty simply won't address the content and learners will once again be denied the opportunity to learn. (*'Tell them about how you opened up a file folder in your in-box of your email that is titled cultural broker'*, Coyote is laughing as she puts her lipstick on, getting it on her tooth. *'Tell them you have a category in your portfolio that has that heading'*, she is chuckling and applying mascara from my purse.) It's true, I now report annually on the numbers of requests that I receive from faculty and students alike, within and outside of my faculty and university. By reporting on these requests I want to communicate to my peers and my employer that as Indigenous faculty we often serve in ways that other faculty are not expected to; we bring added value that I insist on being considered in tenure/promotion review processes.

When I question faculty about why they want me to do this work for them, they often reply, 'You are so good at it …' or 'You have the experience ...' and when I press them further, then I come to understand that their lack of understanding actually makes them feel fearful of saying the wrong thing, or being perceived as racist. That settler 'move to innocence' that Tuck and Yang address has a real effect on the distribution of work in our faculty. Now that I've been here for ten years, and have served as the cultural broker for all that time, I am no longer willing to allow my colleagues to shirk the responsibility for this work. This is not *my* work alone. I need my colleagues to address their own learning needs and I need them to engage deeply in the process of curricular decolonisation. (Coyote smiles sweetly, *'And you need the reader to engage deeply too.'*)

Limiting narrative 3: YOU are going to do some work

I began my graduate work in a white, male-dominated department with little access to diverse voices (women, minority or Indigenous scholarship). I learned about the colonial structures of education through my own volition. It was double-work to learn in this way because I still had to understand the dominant discourses of my field of study, and I took it upon myself to read beyond my area into feminist theory, anti-oppression, anti-racism, whiteness studies, as well as exploring the experiences of minoritised educators and administrators. Learning what is not taught requires effort but that is one way to move past the limitations of the colonial, patriarchal, Eurocentric constructions of higher education.

You can't simply fall back on expecting minoritised students to fill in curricular gaps for you (and all your students). Their job is to learn: not teach. If you want them to teach, then you need to compensate them for their contributions. Otherwise they carry a burden of responsibility that is unequally applied in the classroom and they are even more marginalised and can face victimisation when the knowledge and experience they share is resented by classmates (and sometimes by instructors too).

I would suggest that departments and faculties undertake an equity audit to identify how often faculty are drawing from the scholarship of women, people of colour and Indigenous scholars. This audit would also include a survey of Indigenous scholarship in your subject area. Use this data as a jumping off point to begin to address curricular gaps.

Decolonising your teaching is going to mean you must do some work, and there is a body of scholarship that can guide you. I've already referenced Dr Marie Battiste's work, and the writing of Dr Rauna Kuokkanen (they are my go-to authors). But I would also suggest an examination of Tuck and Yang; Corntassel; Grande; Cote-Meek;[25] Green; and the earlier text edited by Mihesuah and Wilson. These scholars offer readers a starting point for exploring how to re-centre a critique of colonialism and its effects; and the possibilities that decolonisation offers.

We have the great privilege to work in institutions of higher learning. We can choose to invite decolonial and Indigenous scholars, writers and public intellectuals to offer public lectures and workshops on our campus in order to address the collective capacity for our faculty to engage in decolonial work. I would suggest that educators begin to inventory the number of people of colour generally that have been featured in annual lectures and speaker series. If people of colour are under-represented, then organisers have an obligation to ensure that equity is achieved. I would suggest that university administrators seek out the advice and recommendations of Indigenous scholars on who to invite that would help support institutional reform efforts.

I suggest that faculty learn about and practise anti-oppressive pedagogy. Again, there is a growing body of scholarship that speaks to how to structure courses, how to engage learners, what to expect in classes, and how to anticipate/respond racist responses by students.

Limiting narrative 4: Teaching about racism is oppressive

I've been teaching members of the dominant group for 16 years. I have often witnessed what Di'Angelo calls, 'white fragility'.[26] Upon hearing (often for the first time) about the systems of domination, violence, institutionalised racism and hegemonic systems which offer white privilege, learners express feelings of deep anger, guilt and shame. Sometimes, they interpret these feelings as evidence that *they* are being oppressed by their instructor (often a person of colour). They misinterpret their discomfort as *racism*, when what they are experiencing is cognitive dissonance as a result of the purposeful exposure of dominant views of whiteness and the disruption of the *luxury of ignorance* and the *assumptions of rightness*.[27] Like Howard, I have come to understand that these feelings are the price of the luxury of ignorance and a legacy of privilege.

Scholars recognise that participants in courses which expose white dominance often *insulate* (Di'Angelo, 2011) themselves through the assertion of *innocence* (Tuck and Yang, 2012). As instructors, it's important to anticipate resistance to the content. When learners insulate themselves they often (a) argue against their membership within whiteness, (b) downplay their individual white identity, (c) distance themselves from the event or incident, in the case of residential schooling they proclaim 'that all happened a long time ago' and 'I'm not responsible for what happened back then' and 'why can't you people just get over it'. They also deflect by telling you of a time when a visible minority person bullied them. Tuck and Yang inform us that participants will engage in 'settler moves to innocence' that include the assertion that since they have an Indigenous relative/friend/child/partner they couldn't be responsible for white dominance. This strategy is an 'attempt to deflect a settler identity'.[28] Educators must anticipate these strategies and be prepared to provoke a deeper exploration of the impact of this resistance towards undermining the goals of reconciliation.

Too often, colleagues and learners alike shut down when these (unfamiliar) feelings overwhelm, but I want them to push through them. I want them to build their resiliency for the ambiguity of a decolonial curriculum (Coyote – *'it's not like you had a choice to sit and pout ... you moved through it'*). I would love them to engage in more obvious dialogue with their colleagues about their positionality in relation to the field of study. I'd love them to take up research on how to engage learners in this type of curriculum and pedagogy. I want them to explore the politics of teaching in this way. *('There you go again, acting all political. But I get it – colonisation was a politically violent act; and the maintenance of the colonial structures too is political therefore decolonisation must be a political act.'* She peers at me from her seat at the window. She sighs, *'Don't you ever get tired?')*

I do get tired; I am tired.

Limiting narrative 5: Can't we call it 'inclusion' and be done with it?

During a presentation at my university where I introduced the Indigenous Advisory Circles definition of Indigenisation, a colleague proclaimed, 'You'd be more effective if you weren't so political'. I responded that Indigenisation and decolonisation were political. I stated that this was not a simple matter of being 'respectful of difference' but that what we were working towards was the reformation of the academy (Coyote is rocking back and forth, she is holding her belly as she guffaws!)

Let me recap the earlier discussion of colonisation and decolonisation to make explicit what decolonised academic programmes would entail. They would require an honest examination of the violence of colonisation and how this is maintained today through systems of oppression (the Indian Act), and institutions like Indigenous and Northern Affairs. They would include what Laenui calls 'the dreaming' – the facilitation of learning opportunities which encourage a cultural resurgence (Corntassel, 2012), and a reimagining of governing, judicial, educational and community structures designed to empower Indigenous peoples. I would add to this that, alongside the reformation of Indigenous institutions, there must be a reformation of programmes directed towards non-Indigenous peoples so that they can leave behind their cognitive and experiential deficits. Once these are under way then we can begin to realise the possibilities of reconciled relationships. But in order to achieve this end, it will cost us all something.

As I've said before, this is not my work alone; the longer I do this work the more I am convinced that this is white work. I want my white colleagues (Coyote – *'Don't they get mad at you for calling them that?'*) uh, uhm, I want members of the dominant group to ask themselves this question – what measure of my privilege am I willing to give up in order to create equity for another?

Coyote: *'You are asking a lot of your colleagues, and I can see that you have grown weary in your leadership role. You should take a break ... (I had a 6-month administrative leave following the end of my term) it's time for you to regroup and let them do their work. I understand you want them to conduct an equity audit in their faculty; conduct a survey of Indigenous scholars in their field; plan for events featuring Indigenous and decolonial scholars and speakers; and you want them to take up the work of changing policies and procedures ... do you think these changes will be enough?'*

Author: I can only hope so. They have to begin somewhere. That's your assignment – walk around with it ... get busy ... and then tell your stories of institutional reform. We need a new narrative in higher education in Canada: one with the potential to lead us towards reconciliation.

Coyote and I sit quietly for a moment. She is dangling my red shoe off one hind foot. She is looking at me through my reading glasses perched on her nose, she sighs, and smiles her toothy grin. *'Are you ready for some cultural resurgence?'* I throw my head back and laugh, and laugh. 'I sure am, let's go.'

Bibliography

Battiste, M. (2013) *Decolonizing Education: Nourishing the Learning Spirit.* Saskatoon: Purich Publishing.

Cobo, J.M. (1986) Study of the Problem of Discrimination against Indigenous Populations. UN Doc. E/CN.4/Sub.2/1986/7 and Add. 1-4, available at: www.un.org/development/desa/indigenouspeoples/publications/martinez-cobo-study.html

Corntassel, J. (2012) 'Re-envisioning Resurgence: Indigenous Pathways to Decolonization and Sustainable Self-determination', *Decolonization: Indigeneity, Education & Society* 1(1): 86–101.

Cote-Meeks, S. (2014) *Colonized Classrooms: Racism, Trauma and Resistance in Post-Secondary Education.* Halifax: Fernwood Publishing.

Di'Angelo, R. (2011) 'White Fragility', *International Journal of Critical Pedagogy* 3(3): 54–70.

Green, J. (2014) *Indivisible: Indigenous Human Rights.* Halifax: Fernwood Publishing.

Howard, G. (2006) *We Can't Teach What We Don't Know: White Teachers in Multiracial Classrooms*, 2nd edn. New York: Teachers College Press.

Kovach, M.E. (2009) *Indigenous Methodologies: Characteristics, Conversations, and Contexts.* Toronto: University of Toronto Press.

Kuokkanen, R. (2008) 'What is Hospitality in the Academy? Epistemic Ignorance and the (Im)Possible Gift', *Review of Education, Pedagogy, and Cultural Studies*, 30(1): 60–82.

Laenui, Poka (Burgess, Hayden F.) (2000) 'Processes of Decolonization', in Marie Battiste (ed.) Reclaiming Indigenous Voice and Vision. Vancouver, BC: UBC Press, pp. 150–60.

Laenui, P. (2006) 'Processes of Decolonization', 30 May, available at: www.sjsu.edu/people/marcos.pizarro/maestros/Laenui.pdf

Sium, A. and Ritskes, E. (2013) 'Speaking Truth to Power: Indigenous Story-telling as an Act of Living Resistance', *Decolonization: Indigeneity, Education & Society* 2(1): I–X.

Tomaselli, K.G., Dyll, L. and Francis, M. (2008) '"SELF" AND "OTHER": Auto-reflexive and Indigenous Ethnography', in N. Denzin, Y. Lincoln and L. Smith (eds) *Handbook of Critical and Indigenous Methodologies*. Thousand Oaks, CA: Sage, pp. 347–72.

Tuck, E. and Yang, K.W. (2012) 'Decolonization Is Not a Metaphor', *Decolonization: Indigeneity, Education & Society* 1(1): 1–40.

United Nations (2008) United Nations Declaration on the Rights of Indigenous Peoples, March, available at: http://www.un.org/esa/socdev/unpfii/documents/DRIPS_en.pdf

Notes

All urls last accessed February–March 2018.

1. Tomaselli, K.G., Dyll, L. and Francis, M. (2008) '"Self" and "Other": Auto-reflexive and Indigenous Ethnography', in N. Denzin, Y. Lincoln and L. Smith

(eds) *Handbook of Critical and Indigenous Methodologies*. Thousand Oaks, CA: Sage, pp. 347–72 at p. 352.

2. Kovach, M. (2010) *Indigenous Methodologies*. Toronto: University of Toronto Press.
3. Clandinin, D.J. and Connelly, F.M. (2000) *Narrative Inquiry*. Jossey Bass.
4. Kovach 2010 op. cit.
5. Cobo, J.M. (1986) Study of the Problem of Discrimination against Indigenous Populations. UN Doc. E/CN.4/Sub.2/1986/7 and Add. 1-4, available at: www.un.org/development/desa/indigenouspeoples/publications/martinez-cobo-study.html
6. King, T. (1995) *One Good Story, That One*. Toronto: HarperCollins.
7. Ibid. p. 9.
8. Ibid. p. 69.
9. Willett, 1998.
10. Pete-Willett, 2001.
11. Sium, A. and Ritskes, E. (2013) 'Speaking Truth to Power: Indigenous Storytelling as an Act of Living Resistance', *Decolonization: Indigeneity, Education & Society* 2(1): I–X at p. II.
12. Ibid. p. III.
13. Battiste, M. (2013) *Decolonizing Education: Nourishing the Learning Spirit*. Saskatoon: Purich Publishing Ltd; Corntassel, J. (2012) 'Re-envisioning Resurgence: Indigenous Pathways to Decolonization and Sustainable Self-determination', *Decolonization: Indigeneity, Education & Society* 1(1): 86–101; Green, J. (2014) *Indivisible: Indigenous Human Rights*. Halifax: Fernwood Publishing; Tuck, E. and Yang, K.W. (2012) 'Decolonization Is Not a Metaphor', *Decolonization: Indigeneity, Education & Society* 1(1): 1–40.
14. Turtle Island – I am referring to Canada.
15. Green 2014 op. cit. p. 2.
16. Ibid. p. 3.
17. Ibid. p. 13.
18. Laenui, P. (2006) 'Processes of Decolonization', available at: www.sjsu.edu/people/marcos.pizarro/maestros/Laenui.pdf, p. 4; Laenui, Poka (Burgess, Hayden F.) (2000) 'Processes of Decolonization', in M. Battiste (ed.) *Reclaiming Indigenous Voice and Vision*. Vancouver, BC: UBC Press, pp. 150–60.
19. Tuck and Yang 2012 op. cit.
20. Corntassel 2012 op. cit. p. 89.
21. Green 2014 op. cit.; Laenui 2000 op. cit.
22. Corntassel 2012 op. cit. p. 89.
23. A smudge is a prayer.
24. Tuck and Yang 2012 op. cit. p. 3.
25. Cote-Meeks, S. (2014) *Colonized Classrooms: Racism, Trauma and Resistance in Post-Secondary Education*. Halifax: Fernwood Publishing.
26. Di'Angelo, R. (2011) 'White Fragility', *International Journal of Critical Pedagogy* 3(3): 54–70.
27. Howard, G. (2006) *We Can't Teach What We Don't Know: White Teachers in Multiracial Classrooms*, 2nd edn. New York: Teachers College Press.
28. Tuck and Yang 2012 op. cit. p. 11.

11

Decolonising Education:
A Pedagogic Intervention

Carol Azumah Dennis

In this chapter I explore what it might mean to decolonise education. My exploration starts, however, with a reflexive examination of the position from which to speak about this subject. In most instances, I prefer to speak from rather than about a preferred stance, inviting the reader to offer me the respectful anonymity preserved for the unmarked scholar. However, with decolonisation it soon becomes clear that my attempt to occupy this space is not an active yearning. It is a defiant refusal of refusal. I am, on reflection, more at home when associated with the undercommons. And it is from this position that I speak directly about decolonising education. From this workable position, my discussion draws on three broad decolonising approaches.

I first explore decolonising education through the idea of a curriculum centred on multiplicity. Once the unmarked scholar is placed within a geopolitical context, the curriculum that emerges is one in which the disciplinary founding fathers [*sic*] of contemporary philosophy and social sciences are put in their place. They are firmly located within a context rather then allowed to speak from a place which is just there, that place which is no place. I then explore decolonising education as a continuity between the pedagogical and the political, weaving threads of resistance, opposition and insurgency to accomplish its purpose. It does more than update pre-existing categories of thought and engages instead in guerrilla acts of 'epistemic disobedience'. It thinks alongside, from and within knowledges that have been rendered invisible. Free from the fetters of Cartesian duality, a decolonised education invites the pedagogue to think otherwise. My final decolonising turn is mindful that the struggle for global social justice is inextricably linked to the struggle for global epistemic justice. An acceptance of different and diverse forms of knowledge leads towards an ecology of knowledges in which the limits and values of knowledges are ascribed according to the notion of 'knowledge-as-intervention-in-reality' rather than 'knowledge-as-a-representation-of-reality'. I conclude by summarising ten distinct actions implied by decolonising education.

Decolonising education: a starting point

Who talks about what is often challenged based on what that person is.[1]

In this chapter I explore what it might mean to decolonise education. My quest is stimulated by a visceral act of student protest at the University of Cape Town (UCT) in South Africa. In March 2015, a student Chumani Maxwele threw human faeces at a statue of the British imperialist Cecil Rhodes, which had since 1934 adorned the university campus. The university's initial response was to have Maxwele arrested. However, swift and supportive action by students and staff who coalesced around him compelled the university management to instead negotiate with a rapidly growing student protest movement,[2] a movement which has since become known internationally as #RhodesMustFall. Within a matter of weeks, the situation had changed. Maxwele was not charged and the UCT senate ultimately voted in favour of dismantling the statue.

What was inaugurated as a protest centred on colonial iconography, spoke to and from issues that were always so much more than aesthetics. The movement that erupted in support of Maxwele sought to create a space within which 'free alternative versions of blackness otherwise denied' by higher education might be allowed to flourish.[3] As Mbembe explains, the economy of symbols has a force.[4] They are able to create or induce states of humiliation. In its public celebration of Cecil Rhodes, UCT were actively celebrating a brutish, genocidal regime whose legacy lingers. The statue signals to some who inhabit its space: *You do not belong here. This is not your home. You are a stranger.*

My purpose in this chapter is to explore the implications of this international movement to decolonise education (Pillay, 2016).[5] But before I can ponder what possible actions are implied by this desire, I must first identify a space from which I might speak. If #RhodesMustFall is my arbitrary starting point for this discussion, I am surely positioned as a 'not knower'.[6] A South African student's call to decolonise higher education does not immediately connect to my experience as an academic working for a university in the south of England. There are few moments when I am confronted by the institution's unbridled fervour for Europe's colonial past.

Invading the space of the unmarked scholar

My preferred approach to writing about decolonising education is to assume the stance of the unmarked scholar. In this chapter, I wrestle with the unmarked scholar's ambiguous stance, a stance which is both desirable and discomforting. The unmarked scholar requires no introduction. He does not need to explain his appearance in the text and he requires no further markers of qualification. What the unmarked scholar says is more important than who he is. He speaks from that place which is *just there*, that place which is no place. But, my attempts to assume this position are thwarted. If such a position were ever possible, it has already been filled by some other body. I can try to write as the unmarked scholar, but I am restless, accusatory, sometimes emotional and I am aware that I occupy the wrong body. I am immediately recognised as not from that place of disembodied neutrality. I am aligned to this or that struggle and my being there is strange. I am a stranger and my presence has a meaning that precedes me.[7]

The space of the unmarked scholar is a Cartesian *Weltanschauung*; it is a space predicated on a fundamental difference between the human and the non-human as the foundation upon which the mental is different to the physical. Claiming philosophy as a uniquely human phenomenon, a discrete set of problems are posited as distinctly human, that is, independent of the particularities of culture, society and history. This human status is not open to *all humans*. It is denied to females and those racialised as black. Charles Mills offers an elaboration of this thinking.[8] Spaces are normed as either civil or wild, a division that represents a racialised and gendered dichotomising hierarchy. Black (and female) bodies are represented as coming from uncivilised spaces, as savages, 'whose being is so penetrated by wildness that the door to civilisation, and to philosophy and politics, is barred to him'.[9] Whiteness is associated with spirit and mind, the flight from the body. It is imbued with the capacity to occupy an unmarked space: a space which is *just there*. It requires no introduction, no explanation and no further markers of qualification. Black and female bodies are associated with nature, and therefore not fully human. Indeed, definitions of human are constructed as negations of what women and blackness symbolise.[10] Occupying the space of the unmarked scholar, the space which is *just there*, is beyond their ontological status.

Perhaps then I should name myself more clearly: I am a diasporan.[11] This grammatical phrasing playfully echoes a tribal identity. I could say, 'I am a diasporan' in the same way and in answer to the same question as others might say 'I am a Fanti' or 'I am a Yoruba'. In this I signal a past both mythologised and reclaimed; a past that refuses erasure. But my unbelonging, my status as stranger, has not disappeared. When I write *from* a position, I assume a right to be *just there*. This is preferable to writing *about* my positioning which implies an acceptance that I have no right to be *just there*. It implies my scholarly self requires an explanation of its presence, a qualificatory marker of some sort. It requires that I make my invisibility visible.

I would like to adopt a disembodied authorial voice; a voice that speaks for us all. Yet it is not just naming or not naming which is at stake when writing about decolonisation. This is a subject the unmarked scholar cannot write about. (The unmarked scholar is oblivious to this limitation.) When scholarship turns to the subject of decolonisation, it becomes embroiled in an embodied struggle. It becomes an intervention, a performative, reflexive socio-political writing act.[12] To talk of decolonising higher education is to bring into question the foundations upon which the unmarked scholar stands. It implies that epistemic traditions other than her own can no longer be disregarded. It implies that colonialism is other than a historical phase which, thanks to the beneficence of the former colonisers, ended before or by the 1960s. For the unmarked scholar, colonisation is an inconsequential matter of historical record. For him, the important discussions about the relationship between Europe and Africa, Europeans and Latin America, England and the Caribbean, India and all the rest revolves around other 'isations': internationalisation or globalisation.

To write about decolonisation in the guise of the unmarked scholar requires that I mask my emotion, that I mask my being human. Affectivity has no place in academic discourse. Emotions are banished or bracketed, as an epistemic pollutant that betrays the status of transcendental signifiers – method, truth, validity, objectivity and knowledge. Yet, if emotions are removed from the epistemic encounter, is it possible for the unmarked scholar to say she has *really understood* the visceral ways in which history is sometimes experienced.[13] The unmarked

scholar transcends cultural heritage and political struggle.[14] Decolonisation requires she speaks directly to (or from) those struggles. Even
if I accept the invitation to move beyond the politics of anger towards
what Hattam and Zembylas refer to as a 'post-indignation critical
pedagogy',[15] the emotional entanglements linger. Is it possible to launder,
bracket or banish emotional landscapes that one does not acknowledge as existing? To decolonise means to analyse the historical legacy
of empire, its genocidal brutalities and the racial hierarchies that are
among its legacies.[16] It is at this point that the transgressive eruption of
emotion is at its most potent. It is not that the psychological impact of
colonialism is insurmountable; it is that, once concretised in the form of
social and political structures, sentiments' impact remains long after the
heat of emotion has been drained. The unmarked scholar replicates the
systematic amnesia that defines Europe's engagement with its colonial
past. Guilt and pride define this emotional landscape which ultimately
coalesces into a postcolonial melancholy. Paul Gilroy defines this melancholia with the help of Freudian motifs.[17] He suggests that European
nations have been unable to get past their loss of empire and their erstwhile
global pre-eminence, and that this inability folds into itself to generate a
pathological tension in their contemporary global encounters.[18] Unable
to acknowledge Europe's loss of empire, the European is unable to mourn
its loss and as such remains in a repetitive ritualised dramatisation of the
event. Thus, the moment of their global ascendancy is fixed and allowed
to resonate indefinitely. Gilroy argues that this chronic ritualisation is
calcified as victimhood. In the imagination of the former coloniser Great
Britain is the primary victim of colonial history. After all, if 'the problem
with empire is not that Britain was once in charge but that it is no longer
so',[19] Britain's resentment at having been cast aside by its former colony
is justified. The desire to decolonise, and the rage that prompts and fuels
the movement, cannot be fathomed. The colonised have usurped the
space of victimhood that the coloniser, the unmarked scholar, holds as
her own.

If the unmarked scholar assumes the entire space of universal human,
she is unable to recognise the significance of difference, particularity and
specificity. But to dissolve the particularities of race, culture, gender and
other embodiments is to dissolve the experience of being human. It is
at this moment that the stance of the unmarked scholar becomes less
desirable. This hollowing out of what it means to be human produces a
yearning for a more thoroughly grounded, a more fulsomely embodied

understanding of decolonisation. Writing about (and not just from) the position of the *marked scholar* is unavoidable for a meaningful engagement with the world.

In a text which explores the corporeal place of the (usually denied) body Puwar asks, 'what happens when women racialized as minorities take up privileged positions which have not been reserved for them and for which they are not the somatic norm.'[20] In part this is what my discussion has been attempting to address. Can I, a diasporan, assume the stance of the unmarked scholar – a privileged position for which I am not the somatic norm? This encounter, this misplaced occupation, causes disruption, necessitates negotiation and invites my complicity. Some bodies, female bodies, bodies racialised as black, bodies with disabilities, queer bodies make up the constitutive boundary that defines the universal space of the unmarked scholar. Such bodies are out of place and denied the right to speak for us all. Such bodies are marked as trespassers[21] and do not belong, nor do they have the right to belong. They are – as Puwar's analysis so evocatively shows – *space invaders.*[22]

The desire then to write as the unmarked scholar, is the desire to write from a stance of privileged neutrality. But it is also a refusal to accept the multiple binds which require that I declare or deny identities or allegiances – female academic, an academic racialised as black, or a female academic with disabilities, queer academic. It is also perhaps a desire to hide behind the anonymity of a white-male-as-norm ideology, even though it is a space which has been marked as one to which not all bodies can belong. My desire for the authority that emanates from the position implicates me in the very structures and practices I aim to dismantle. I am implicated in and therefore compelled to confront what I am desperate to avoid.

This perhaps is my first move towards decolonising education, a reflexive exploration in which I question the geopolitics of knowledge which universalises European thought while subalternising and invisibilising all other epistemes. It is a move which requires the deconstruction of not only external oppressive structures, but also my own complicit internalisation of and participation in those structures. I am a long way from an idealised position hinted at by Deleuze and Guattari:

To reach, not the point where one no longer says I, but the point where it is no longer of any importance whether one says I.[23]

Amid this discomfort and contradiction, Moten and Harney[24] offer a more dignified stance from which to speak. My conscious unbelonging is accompanied by a willingness to 'sneak into the university and steal what [I] can. To abuse its hospitality, to spite its mission, to join its refugee colony, its gypsy encampment, to be in but not of the university'. This is the space of the undercommons. It is a space of self-organisation developed by the despised, the discounted, the dispossessed and the unbelonging. From this stance, I can write and speak without seeking approval or recognition and get along very well without the authorisation of the university. My purpose then, in positioning myself and speaking about, to and from within the undercommons is to utilise the space – the language, the time, the authorial voice – provided by the university, not as desirable goals in themselves but as accoutrements that allow me to accomplish something. The diasporan wishing to decolonise education does not assert a fixed identity or space, she instead participates in an epistemic project that develops in exodus, in the maroons, the hidden crevices and alcoves of the university, in its constantly moving, shape-shifting spaces.[25] It is from this site of knowledge production that I seek to decolonise education.

A decolonised education engages with a distinct set of ideas and principles

A pedagogy centred on multiplicity

In a short piece exploring the decolonisation of philosophy, ~~Coleman~~[26] argues that there is an unrecognised pedagogic relation between who gets to produce knowledge and what gets produced as knowledge. He outlines how the Critical Philosophy of Race was produced as knowledge within his own teaching, specifically through a module entitled, 'The philosophy of anti-slavery'. His approach to decolonising is premised on several curricular strategies, two of which I highlight here. First, he argues for placing texts in their context, that is, making explicit the relationship between text and context. His second suggestion is putting the philosophical canon, the disciplinary founding fathers [sic], in their place, that is, not a privileged place of neutrality which assumes a universal forefront and placing persons racialised as black to the fore.

The unmarked scholar is radically undermined once their scholarly contribution is appropriately named, dated and given a geopolitical location. The particularities and peculiarities of *that place which is no place*, the place from which they speak is exposed. Once the founding disciplinary fathers [*sic*] of contemporary disciplines such as philosophy, sociology, anthropology and so forth are located in time and space, in specific cultures, prevailing discourses, embodiments and histories their capacity to assume a universal voice is dismantled.

This allows contemporary scholars to acknowledge the embodiments which lurk undeclared in the guise of the generic anthropoid. The decolonising pedagogic project is here framed as one that centres multiplicity. I hesitate in centring blackness as I want to acknowledge variation within a broad theme. The turn towards hybridity, nomadology, brisure and indeterminacy exceeds a single centring. To centre otherness is to accept that no single voice speaks for us all. In his critique of postcolonial discourse as a symptom of the colonial imagination, Acheraïou[27] calls for a discursive move away from the 'hegemonic core of the diaspora' towards the migrant masses of the West and the peripheries of the South. A decolonising pedagogy centred on multiplicity is one that accepts the 'cacophony of voices', where the risk of disintegration is preferable to selective silencing. What this centres is not blackness as such. Nor is it the *non-whiteness* implied by fragmented, alienating third-space hybridity. Instead what it centres are identities defined in their own terms, an otherness premised on political, ideological, epistemological multiplicity.

There is a slight anxiety here, an anxiety that has been well rehearsed in the field of language, literacy and linguistics. It is a dilemma posed when critiquing the status of non-standard forms of English is interpreted as an invitation to reject the teaching of standard English completely instead of an invitation to reject teaching *the supremacy of standard English*.[28] To lead a module in educational philosophy in which, to soften ~~Coleman~~'s words, the disciplinary founding fathers of philosophy and social sciences make no appearance, would be to do students a disservice. It would deny them access to the cultural capital stored in those texts. Part of what a curriculum does is provide bodies of knowledge which equip students to participate culturally in particular spaces, providing them with a 'feel for the game'. People are differentiated (in part at least) by the extent to which they are insiders, that is, the extent to which their communicated sense of who they are is adjusted to the demands of the situation that surrounds them. The decolonising curriculum allows students to gain a 'critical' feel for the game. Thus, we teach the English language in its standard forms but not the supremacy of those standard forms. To teach a curriculum centred on otherwise, is to teach standard forms critically. In other words, it is to teach them but to 'put them in their place'.[29] It is to resist decolonising the curriculum as a superficial cultural and spatial turn and instead reframe it in historicised, contextualised and diachronic terms.

An Ubuntu pedagogy

A brief note about context might help frame my discussion at this point: In 2016 the British government held a referendum on whether the UK should remain part of the European Union (EU) or leave. In a move that sent shock waves across Britain and European capitals, those wishing to leave the EU won the vote by a margin of less than 2 percent.[30] However, some regions of the UK voted leave by an overwhelming majority of 68 percent. The issues surrounding this vote are complicated and it is not my intention to consider them here. I wish to establish a point about context. Imbued with a deep postcolonial melancholia, the case built to persuade the leave vote drew upon residual memories of imperialism and the loss of empire to shape an image of Britain's future, a future in which old colonial ties of domination would be rekindled. One slogan associated with the campaign for the UK to withdraw was, 'I want my country back'.[31] This rallying cry betrays sentiments of resistance, loss and yearning: resistance to 'state multiculturalism';[32] loss of pride, privilege and former colonial glory; and a deep yearning for 'Great' Britain. This 'Great' Britain is not a place. It is a past. It is a yearning for the past greatness of the old days when white Christian Britain sat at the top of the table. In this account, empire is viewed as benevolent, paternalistic and civilising. This view of empire has been facilitated by a collective amnesia. I do not present this context as a precursor to suggesting a decolonised education is one that seeks to present a less sanitised account of British colonial history, though this would be a legitimate perspective. I map this context to make clear that, in some instances, a decolonising education is one that might arouse opposition, incredulity and even outright hostility. It interrupts the perceived order of things.

A decolonising education understands pedagogy from within the frame of socio-political struggle, viewing that struggle in pedagogical terms.[33] This is at odds with a view of decolonising education as something straightforward and accomplished without opposition or contestation. A decolonising approach to education is not a matter of pedagogic technique.

> Political action on the side of the oppressed must be pedagogical action in the authentic sense of the word, and, therefore action with the oppressed.[34]

The pedagogic and the political are a continuity. Like critical pedagogy, a decolonising education is one that exceeds the confines of the school, college or university to intervene in the reinvention of the world. A decolonising education is an activist one that makes use of the language, time and authorial voice provided by the university to accomplish its purposes. It is not a discipline but a practice of weaving the threads of resistance, opposition and insurgency to prefiguratively build a different world. The identified continuity is opportunistic and short lived. Decolonisation may be framed in terms allied to critical theory, but critical theory cannot fully account for the colonial experience. Mignolo asks: 'What should "critical theory" aim to be when the *damnés de la terre* are brought into the picture?'[35] In other words, to incorporate race, gender and nature into the conceptual and political frame of critical theory would require its substantive transformation, such that it might well become another project altogether. To decolonise is to develop a new cartography; to engage in 'epistemic disobedience'.[36] This implies working from different spatial sites of struggle. The point that Mignolo makes here is significant for what a decolonising education might mean.

Decolonising education emerged from the moment of modernity/coloniality as its counterpart. Its genealogy is located within the dense history of planetary decolonial thinking: in the Americas, in indigenous and Afro-Caribbean thinking, in Asia and in Africa. A decolonised education is one that emerges in sharp relief against and despite coloniality. As such it is a pedagogy premised on otherwise: 'Other ways of being, thinking, knowing, sensing, feeling, doing and living.'[37] A decolonised pedagogy thinks alongside, from and within knowledges that have been rendered invisible. It is at this point that my instinct is to code switch, to create an (auto) ethnographic multivocal performance text[38] in which distinct decolonising and cacophonous critical voices might struggle and be heard. But the decolonising project is also a pragmatic one, able to generate concrete suggestions amenable to a bullet point brevity.

A decolonising curriculum is free from the fetters of Cartesian duality.[39] It works within a different cartography. For example, the concept of Ubuntu brought into the academy as a living standard of judgement[40] leads potentially to a radically transformed curriculum. As a clear manifestation of African cosmology, Ubuntu is an active force which celebrates the oneness of mind and body; the oneness of humans and the more-than-human world. Subjectivity is not reduced to the individual but is instead an ecological construct. The Ubuntu 'I' is embedded, embodied, extended and enacted,[41] an extension that works comfortably with a decolonising curriculum which refuses the arrogance of Cartesian cogito. A curriculum that centres around Ubuntu does not and cannot prescribe this or that way of doing. Instead it signifies a mutuality of movement between us and our worlds. In openness and creativity, the solidarity between self and others is an instantiation of the relationship between humans and the more-than-human world. Emphasising 'dialogue, respect and commitment to co-building a future, drawing on our collective resources rather than falling prey to competitive self-interest'.[42] An Ubuntu curriculum is based on the 4Rs of *relational accountability* – a recognition of the fact that all parts of the curriculum are connected in a co-relation of accountability to humans and non-humans; *respectful representation* – a recognition that curriculum must create space for the voices and knowledges of indigenous people; *reciprocal appropriation* – a recognition that the benefits of knowledge are shared by both the universities and communities; and *rights and regulation* a recognition of ethical profiles which accord ownership of knowledge to the indigenous communities if and when they have generated it.[43]

The trouble, not with Ubuntu, but with the decorative use of such concepts is that they are mellifluous but easily exoticised. Ubuntu itself is such an all-encompassing way of being, it represents a fundamental challenge to the hegemony and universality of capitalism and a Western civilisatory logic. The conflict that ensues is perhaps part of the process of knowledge construction that inaugurates students into the world of critical thinking.

A pedagogy of co-presence

The struggle for global social justice is inseparable from the struggle for global cognitive justice.[44]

A decolonising education disentangles itself from all power which is not constituted by free decisions made by free people. It rejects the academic and pedagogic posture, premised on colonialism, that assumes that the mainstream (that which is Western, colonial or Eurocentric) is global and universal and others – indigenous, local knowledges are a deviation.[45] The implications of this point are carefully illustrated by the sociologist Santos who demonstrates 'abyssal thinking' as one of the legacies of epistemological dominance.[46] 'Abyssal thinking' is a system of visible and invisible distinctions established through a logic that defines social reality as either on 'this side of the abyssal line' or on 'the other side of the abyssal line'. This division is such that the other side of the line vanishes as reality and becomes non-existent in any relevant or comprehensible way. Fundamental to abyssal thinking is the impossibility of the co-presence of the two sides of the line. This side of the line prevails by exhausting the field of relevant reality. Beyond the line is non-existence, invisibility, non-dialectical absence.[47] He exemplifies abyssal thinking by reference to truth and falsity, which is projected as universal. Arguing that this hierarchical binary is premised on the invisibility of ways of knowing that are in excess of acceptability parameters established by the abyssal mode of operation that typifies modern knowledge.

Viewed from this side of the line there is no real knowledge on the other side. The truth/falsity hierarchy does not hold. On the other side of the abyssal line there is no knowledge. There are beliefs, opinions, intuitions, subjective understandings – but nothing that is recognisable as knowledge. The substance on the other side is of value only as objects or raw materials for scientific, knowledge-generating activity. Santos refers to this trashing of the epistemologies on the other side of the abyssal line as 'epistemicide'.[48] He goes on to equate the struggle for social justice with a struggle for cognitive justice, which is actually a struggle for co-presence, premised on epistemological resistance. This ultimately leads towards a sociology of emergences. The sociology of emergences is predicated upon the symbolic amplification of inchoate and fragmented signs, clues and latent tendencies which point towards new constellations of meaning, new and transformative understandings of the world. It also involves an acceptance of diverse forms of knowledge of matter, society, life and spirit, along with diverse concepts of what counts as knowledge and the criteria used to validate it. What this becomes is an ecology of knowledges in which the limits and values of knowledges are ascribed according to the notion of 'knowledge-as-intervention-in-reality' and not 'knowledge-as-a-representation-of-reality'.[49] Thus, a decolonising project is highly actionable.

Implication for pedagogic action: decolonising education

By way of conclusion, the chapter offers ten defining pedagogic approaches to decolonising education.

(1) Establish a space within which it is possible to speak about decolonisation. This may require a rejection of the most readily and easily available spaces, necessitating the deliberate cultivation of an undercommons, or an otherwise space.

(2) Recognise and reflexively explore your own implicatedness within the structures you critique. It is possible that this might not feel empowering.

(3) Interrogate the existing cultural interpretive monopoly of European knowledges, assumptions and methodologies.

(4) Identify those too frequently unexplored ways of being that are of most interest to you; imagine the shape of a curriculum driven by them.

(5) Acknowledge the curriculum in its breadth, as including not only the specific content taught but also the way it is taught and the enactment of particular sorts of pedagogic relationships.

(6) Refuse a single authoritative voice, perspective or approach. Remain within indeterminacy, accepting all conclusions as tentative, all settlements as temporary – including this suggestion. This may be uncomfortable.

(7) Place the disciplinary founding fathers of philosophy and social sciences in their place: contextualise them and their ideas as emergent from a specific time and place rather than universal.

(8) Locate unheard, silenced or trivialised voices relevant to your discipline – exemplify and amplify them, placing them alongside orthodox voices in an implicit motion of critique.

(9) Explore and identify the political implications of specific pedagogic approaches. These may not be the ultimate drivers of your pedagogy but they are its inescapable by-products.

(10) Extricate your curriculum from all power which is not constituted by free decisions made by free people and use the resources of imagination, organising, opposition and resistance in pursuance of that end, pausing only when it is accomplished.[50]

Bibliography

Acheraïou, A. (2011) *Questioning Hybridity, Postcolonialism and Globalization*. Houndmills: Palgrave Macmillan.

Ahmed, S. (2000) *Strange Encounters – Embodied Others in Post-Coloniality*. Abingdon: Routledge.

Ashe, S. (2016) 'UKIP, Brexit and Postcolonial Melancholy', *Discover Society* 33(1 June), available at: http://discoversociety.org/2016/06/01/ukip-brexit-and-postcolonial-melancholy/

Battiste, M. (2004) 'Bringing Aboriginal Education into Contemporary Education: Narratives of Cognitive Imperialism Reconciling with Decolonization', in J. Collard and C. Reynolds (eds) *Leadership, Gender and Culture: Male and Female Perspectives*. Maidenhead: Open University Press, pp. 142–8.

Carr, P.R. and Thésée, G. (2012) 'Discursive Epistemologies by, for and about the De-colonizing Project', in A.A. Abdi (ed.) *Decolonizing Philosophies of Education*. Rotterdam: Sense Publishers, pp. 15–28.

Charles, E. (2007) *How Can I Bring Ubuntu as a Living Standard of Judgment into the Academy? Moving beyond Decolonization through Societal Reidentification and Guiltless Recognition*. Unpublished PhD thesis, University of Bath.

Chaturvedi, R. (2015) 'The Rise of a Post-colonial University – Africa is a Country', available at: http://africasacountry.com/2015/04/the-rise-of-a-post-colonial-university/

Cho, L. (2007) 'The Turn to Diaspora', *TOPIA: Canadian Journal of Cultural Studies* 17: 11–30.

Coleman, N.A.T. (n.d.) 'Decolonizing My Discipline by Teaching Research on "Race"', available at: https://www.academia.edu/6651199/Decolonising_my_discipline_by_teaching_research_on_race

Conquergood, D. (1998) 'Beyond the Text: Toward a Performative Cultural Politics', in S.J. Dailey (ed.) *The Future of Performance Studies: Visions and Revisions*. Annadale, VA: National Communication Association, pp. 25–36.

Deleuze, G. and P.F. Guattari (1987) *A Thousand Plateaus: Capitalism and Schizophrenia*. London: Continuum.

Denzin, N.K. (2003) *Performance Ethnography: Critical Pedagogy and the Politics of Culture*. London: Sage.

Dworkin, D. (2009) 'Paul Gilroy and the Cultural Politics of Decline', *Rethinking History* 13(4): 521–39.

Freire, P. (1970) *Pedagogy of the Oppressed*. New York: Herder and Herder.

Gilroy, P. (1991) 'It Ain't Where You're From, It's Where You're At …', *Third Text* 5(13): 3–16.

—— (2006) *Postcolonial Melancholia*. New York: Columbia University Press.

—— (2012) '"My Britain Is Fuck All" Zombie Multiculturalism and the Race Politics of Citizenship', *Identities: Global Studies in Culture and Power* 19(4): 380–97.

Grande, S. (2008) 'Red Pedagogy: The Un-methodology', in: N.K. Denzin, Y.S. Lincoln and L.T. Smith (eds) *Handbook of Critical and Indigenous Methodologies*. Thousand Oaks, CA: Sage, pp. 233–54.

Harris, R., Leung, C. and Rampton, B. (2002) 'Globalization, Diaspora and Language Education in England', in Black, D. and Cameron, D. (eds) *Globalization and Language Teaching*. Abingdon: Routledge, pp. 29–46.

Hattam, R. and Zembylas, M. (2010) 'What's Anger Got to Do With It? Towards a Post-indignation Pedagogy for Communities in Conflict', *Social Identities* 16(1): 23–40.

Hobolt, S. (2016) 'The Brexit Vote: A Divided Nation, a Divided Continent', *Journal of European Public Policy* 23(9): 1259–77.

Johnson, B. (2002) 'Cancel the Guilt Trip: Africa Is a Mess, but It Is Simply Not Credible to Blame Colonialism', *Spectator* 288(9052): 14.

le Grange, L. (2016) 'Decolonizing the University Curriculum', *South African Journal of Higher Education* 30(2): 1–12.

Mbembe, A.J. (2016) 'Decolonizing the University: New Directions', *Arts and Humanities in Higher Education* 15(1): 29–45.

Mignolo, W.D. (2011) 'Epistemic Disobedience and the Decolonial Option: A Manifesto', *Transmodernity: Journal of Peripheral Cultural Production of the LusoHispanic World* 1(2): 4467.

Mills, C.W. (1999) 'The Racial Contract', *Ethics* 109.

Moten, F. and Harney, S. (2004) 'The University and the Undercommons: Seven Theses', *Social Text* 22(2): 101–15.

Penny, L. (2016) 'I Want My Country Back', *New Statesman*, 24 June, available at: www.newstatesman.com/politics/uk/2016/06/i-want-my-country-back

Pillay, S.R. (2016) 'Silence is Violence: (Critical) Psychology in an Era of Rhodes Must Fall and Fees Must Fall', *South African Journal of Psychology* 46(2): 155–9.

Puwar, N. (2004) *Space Invaders: Race, Gender and Bodies Out of Place*. Oxford: Berg.

Quijano, A. (2007) 'Coloniality and Modernity/Rationality', *Cultural Studies* 21(2): 168–78.

Roy, S. and Nilsen, A.G. (2016) 'Globalizing Sociology: An Introduction', *International Journal of Politics, Culture, and Society* 29(3): 225–32.

Samuel, M. and Vithal, R. (2011) 'Emergent Frameworks of Research Teaching and Learning in a Cohort-based Doctoral Programme', *Perspectives in Education* 29(1): 76–87.

Santos, B. de S. (2007) 'Beyond Abyssal Thinking: From Global Lines to Ecologies of Knowledges', *Review* 30(1): 45–89.

Sebambo, K. (2015) 'Azania House as a Symbol of the Black Imagination', *The Salon* 9, available at: http://jwtc.org.za/resources/docs/salon-volume-9/Khumo_Azania_House_Vol9_34.pdf

Shukaitis, S. (2009) 'Infrapolitics and the Nomadic Educational Machine', in R. Amster, A. DeLeon, L.A. Fernandez, A.J. Nocella II and D. Shannon (eds) *Contemporary Anarchist Studies: An Introductory Anthology of Anarchy in the Academy*. New York: Routledge, pp. 166–74.

Shultz, L. (2013) 'Decolonizing Social Justice Education: From Policy Knowledge to Citizenship Action', in A.A. Abdi (ed.) *Decolonizing Philosophies of Education*. Rotterdam: Sense Publications, pp. 29–42.

Walsh, C.E. (2015) 'Decolonial Pedagogies Walking and Asking. Notes to Paulo Freire from AbyaYala', *International Journal of Lifelong Education* 34(1): 9–21.

West, C. (2007) 'Philosophy and the Afro-American Experience', in T. Lott and J.P. Pittman (eds) *A Companion to African-American Philosophy*. Malden, MA: Blackwell, pp. 7–32.

Notes

All urls last accessed 21 March 2018.

1. Carr, P.R. and Thésée, G. (2012) 'Discursive Epistemologies by, for and about the De-colonizing Project', in A.A. Abdi (ed.) *Decolonizing Philosophies of Education*. Rotterdam: Sense Publishers, pp. 15–28.

2. Roy, S. and Nilsen, A.G. (2016) 'Globalizing Sociology: An Introduction', *International Journal of Politics, Culture, and Society* 29(3): 225–32.

3. Sebambo, K. (2015) 'Azania House as a Symbol of the Black Imagination', *The Salon* 9, available at: http://jwtc.org.za/resources/docs/salon-volume-9/Khumo_Azania_House_Vol9_34.pdf

4. Mbembe, A.J. (2016) 'Decolonizing the University: New Directions', *Arts and Humanities in Higher Education* 15(1): 29–45.

5. Pillay, S.R. (2016) 'Silence Is Violence: (Critical) Psychology in an Era of Rhodes Must Fall and Fees Must Fall', *South African Journal of Psychology* 46(2): 155–9.

6. Shultz, L. (2013) 'Decolonizing Social Justice Education: From Policy Knowledge to Citizenship Action', in A.A. Abdi (ed.) *Decolonizing Philosophies of Education*. Rotterdam: Sense Publications, pp. 29–42.

7. Ahmed, S. (2000) *Strange Encounters: Embodied Others in Post-coloniality*. London: Routledge.

8. Mills, C.W. (1997) *The Racial Contract*. Ithaca, NY: Cornell University Press.

9. Ibid. p. 42.

10. Puwar, N. (2004) *Space Invaders: Race, Gender and Bodies Out of Place*. Oxford: Berg.

11. Cho, L. (2007) 'The Turn to Diaspora', *TOPIA: Canadian Journal of Cultural Studies* 17(spring): 11–30; Gilroy, P. (1991) 'It Ain't Where You're From, It's Where You're At ...', *Third Text* 5(13): 3–16.

12. Conquergood, D. (1998) 'Beyond the Text: Toward a Performative Cultural Politics', in S.J. Dailey (ed.) *The Future of Performance Studies: Visions and Revisions*. Annadale, VA: National Communication Association, pp. 25–36.

13. Chaturvedi, R. (2015) 'The Rise of a Post-colonial University – Africa is a Country', available at: http://africasacountry.com/2015/04/the-rise-of-a-post-colonial-university/

14. West, C. (2007) 'Philosophy and the Afro-American Experience', in T. Lott and J.P. Pittman (eds) *A Companion to African-American Philosophy*. Malden, MA: Blackwell, pp. 7–32.

15. Hattam, R. and Zembylas, M. (2010) 'What's Anger Got to Do With It? Towards a Post-indignation Pedagogy for Communities in Conflict', *Social Identities* 16(1): 23–40.

16. Dworkin, D. (2009) 'Paul Gilroy and the Cultural Politics of Decline', *Rethinking History* 13(4): 521–39.
17. Gilroy, P. (2006) *Postcolonial Melancholia*. New York: Columbia University Press.
18. Ashe, S. (2016) 'UKIP, Brexit and Postcolonial Melancholy', *Discover Society*, available at: http://discoversociety.org/2016/06/01/ukip-brexit-and-postcolonial-melancholy/
19. Johnson, B. (2016) 'Africa Is a Mess, but We Can't Blame Colonialism', *The Spectator* 288(9052): 14.
20. Puwar 2004 op. cit. p. 1.
21. Ibid.
22. Ibid.
23. Deleuze, G. and Guattari, P.F. (1987) *A Thousand Plateaus: Capitalism and Schizophrenia*, trans. Brian Massumi. London: Continuum.
24. Moten, F. and Harney, S. (2004) 'The University and the Undercommons: Seven Theses', *Social Text* 22(2): 101–15, at 101, available at: https://muse.jhu.edu/article/55785/summary
25. Shukaitis, S. (2009) 'Infrapolitics and the Nomadic Educational Machine', in R. Amster, A. DeLeon, L.A. Fernandez, A.J. Nocella II and D. Shannon (eds) *Contemporary Anarchist Studies: An Introductory Anthology of Anarchy in the Academy*. New York: Routledge, pp. 166–74.
26. Coleman, N. (n.d.) 'Decolonizing My Discipline by Teaching Research on "Race"', available at: www.academia.edu/6651199/Decolonising_my_discipline_by_teaching_research_on_race
27. Acheraïou, A. (2011) *Questioning Hybridity, Postcolonialism and Globalization*. Basingstoke: Palgrave Macmillan.
28. Harris, R., Leung, C. and Rampton, B. (2002) 'Globalization, Diaspora and Language Education in England', in D. Black and D. Cameron (eds) *Globalization and Language*, pp. 29–46.
29. Coleman n.d. op. cit.
30. Hobolt, S. (2016) 'The Brexit Vote: A Divided Nation, a Divided Continent', *Journal of European Public Policy* 23(9): 1259–77.
31. Penny, L. (2016) 'I Want My Country Back', *New Statesman*, 24 June, available at: www.newstatesman.com/politics/uk/2016/06/i-want-my-country-back
32. Gilroy, P. (2012) '"My Britain Is Fuck All": Zombie Multiculturalism and the Race Politics of Citizenship', *Identities: Global Studies in Culture and Power* 19(4): 380–97.
33. Grande, S. (2008) 'Red pedagogy: The Un-methodology', in N.K. Denzin, Y.S. Lincoln and L. Smith (eds) *Handbook of Critical and Indigenous Methodologies*. Thousand Oaks, CA: Sage, pp. 233–54.
34. Freire, P. (1970) *Pedgaogy of the Oppressed*. New York: Herder and Herder, p. 53.
35. Mignolo, W.D. (2011) 'Epistemic Disobedience and the Decolonial Option: A Manifesto', *Transmodernity: Journal of Peripheral Cultural Production of the LusoHispanic World* 1(2): 44–67, at p. 44.
36. Ibid.

37. Walsh, C.E. (2015) 'Decolonial Pedagogies Walking and Asking: Notes to Paulo Freire from AbyaYala', *International Journal of Lifelong Education* 34(1): 9–21 at p. 12.
38. Denzin, N.K. (2003) *Performance Ethnography: Critical Pedagogy and the Politics of Culture.* London: Sage.
39. le Grange, L. (2016) 'Decolonizing the University Curriculum', *South African Journal of Higher Education* 30(2): 1–12.
40. Charles, E. (2007) *How Can I Bring Ubuntu as a Living Standard of Judgment into the Academy? Moving beyond Decolonization through Societal Reidentification and Guiltless Recognition.* Unpublished PhD thesis, University of Bath.
41. Ibid.
42. Samuel, M. and Vithal, R. (2011) 'Emergent Frameworks of Research Teaching and Learning in a Cohort-based Doctoral Programme', *Perspectives in Education* 29(1): 76–87, at p. 84.
43. Ibid.
44. Santos, B. de S. (2007) 'Beyond Abyssal Thinking: From Global Lines to Ecologies of Knowledges', *Review* 30(1): 11.
45. Battiste, M. (2004) 'Bringing Aboriginal Education into Contemporary Education: Narratives of Cognitive Imperialism Reconciling with Decolonization', in J. Collard and C. Reynolds (eds) *Leadership, Gender and Culture: Male and Female Perspectives.* Maidenhead: Open University Press, pp. 142–8.
46. Santos 2007 op. cit.
47. Ibid.
48. Ibid.
49. Ibid.
50. Quijano, A. (2007) 'Coloniality and Modernity/Rationality', *Cultural Studies* 21(2): 168–78.

Internationalisation and Interdisciplinarity: Sharing across Boundaries?

Angela Last

Recently, movements such as 'Why is My Curriculum White?' and 'Rhodes Must Fall' have drawn attention to the university as a space of racial exclusion – both of students and scholars of colour or other 'minorities', but also of non-white intellectual histories. While some activists argue that the whole university system is beyond any possibility for racial equality, due to the compartmentalisations it perpetuates and its focus on professionalisation over social transformation,[1] others have attempted to undertake a 'decolonisation' of the curriculum and of recruitment and teaching practices, with numerous workshops, committees and consultations being dedicated to the effort. At the same time, university managements themselves have become invested in diversifying the curriculum, albeit with a focus on expanding the market towards overseas and ethnic minority students. This drive towards diversification is tied to a wider project of internationalisation that is, in turn, tied to competition in the global market. It is the same kind of market that, in parallel, generates the demand for international research collaboration. Using the examples of two roles that I, as a white UK academic, currently occupy, I would like to bring these contrasting types of internationalisation into critical conversation and draw out potential implications.

Editing in a global world

One of the areas where the tensions around internationalisation play out is editing, in this case the process of selecting and advising on contributions to themed, multi-author books or journal volumes. Editing is always a difficult process where personalities, aims and cultural differences have to be negotiated. At present, an increasing amount of debate has surrounded the geopolitical divisions of publishing, reflected in conferences such as the British Library's 'The Academic Book in the South' and critiques of racism in the REF (Research Excellence Framework), the UK's university audit that determines funding distribution.[2] Such discussions have highlighted the uneven valuation of international contributions and its impact on reinforcing publishing hierarchies. For instance, academics who seek to challenge global North–South publishing divisions by publishing in the global South have to expect lower REF scores or an additional amount of justification for the significance of their work.[3] This, in turn, affects their job security. The same seems true for US academics who compromise their chance for tenure when publishing outside the global North.[4] Yet such geopolitical academic divisions also impact in subtler ways. One does not have to publish in or on the global South to find oneself a participant in issues surrounding international publishing.

After finishing my PhD, I was invited to be co-editor of a handbook on methods by a large, mainstream educational publisher. For the publisher, it was important to turn this publication from an admittedly Eurocentric experimental collection on interdisciplinary methods into an 'international handbook', which ended up altering not only my relationship with the book, but also the politics of soliciting entries. Over recent years, I have had to ask myself: what does participation in 'international publishing' mean? During the conversations leading up to the contract, it became clear that 'international' particularly meant 'Asia', as this geographical area is a growing market for academic publishing. Not only do many students come to the UK from China, Malaysia and other Asian countries – currently there are around 90,000 from China alone[5] – but British universities also have about 45 external campuses, most of which are located in Asia and the Middle East.[6] Since what counts as 'international' is economically determined, it increasingly also means 'Africa', due to growing educational markets such as Nigeria (Nigeria sends about the same number of students as India; there were around 16,000 in the UK in 2015/16, according to UKCISA, the UK Council for International Student Affairs.[7]

Although 'British' and 'American', as a brand, still have appeal as a provider of quality education – and this package includes identifiable Eurocentric syllabuses – the publishers sense that it is increasingly important to appeal to foreign students, educators and aspirations differently, for instance by featuring local authors with whom people in these key markets can identify. On the one hand, including a greater geographical and ethnic diversity of authors could be seen as a positive development, since such diversification is likely to contribute to greater global dialogue among researchers, and also to a potential dismantling of publishing and knowledge hierarchies. Not only might new perspectives be added, but researchers themselves might be forced to learn how to communicate across academic cultures. On the other hand, the background for such a kind of knowledge exchange does make a difference: why do I decide to get in touch with a colleague from another country, and what sorts of conditions are attached to such a collaboration?

In the case of the methods handbook, for example, the relatively standard production conditions became problematic to me as an editor when soliciting international contributions from the global South. Apart from asking for many hours of unpaid labour for a book that most people, let alone libraries, in the world will not be able to afford – handbooks tend to be priced a lot higher than 'ordinary' books, usually in three-figure amounts – I had to be sensitive to differences in authors' working conditions across the world. While attending a seminar by Senegalese academic Felwine Sarr in the UK, I was again alerted to the conflicted attitudes of intellectuals in formerly colonised countries who are torn between the seduction of assimilation into Western academia, and the desire not to further feed this same system with free raw materials. Sarr, for example, laments the ongoing problem that many of his students did not wish to read Black 'African authors', as they consider them inferior to white Western authors.[8] Tanzanian publisher Walter Bgoya reports similar issues, such as the attraction of flashy US- and European-produced books, and the tragic student and government support for the idea that only European languages should be used for academic work and even school education.[9] If Sarr or Bgoya then chose to publish their work in a European book or journal, this might positively affect the acceptance of this work by their students. At the same time, such a strategy perpetuates the sort of colonial structures and imaginaries that Sarr and others in his position strive to fight in their work and teaching practices. Since colonialism and its ongoing structures constitute a two-way relation, this does not only affect authors in formerly colonised countries – it affects the coloniser as well in terms of responsibility if we do not want to perpetuate cultural imperialism.

Similar problems have been debated by other authors who live under ongoing conditions of colonialism. At present, topics such as indigenous rights and decolonisation are 'really hot' in publishing terms, as several white editors from North American university presses have told me, because of the demand from academics, students and the general public. Academics who work on these topics tend to be cautious about the negative aspects of Western knowledge production, namely '*appropriation, exploitation* and even *surveillance*', as authors such as Richa Nagar,[10] Linda Tuhiwai Smith[11] and many other Black, indigenous and authors of colour phrase it. There is the concern that a flurry of (white) academic activity around decolonisation will not result in progressive politics and greater space (both in terms of representation and land restitution), but in an eliding of responsibility on the part of the coloniser. As Tuck and Yang put it: 'The metaphorisation of decolonisation makes possible a set of evasions, or "settler moves to innocence", that problematically attempt to reconcile settler guilt and complicity, and rescue settler futurity'.[12]

The coloniser participates in the knowledge production on decolonisation, but usually refuses to concede privileges. Entire workshops and conferences on decolonisation are led and conducted by white academics *for* those wishing to decolonise. In my own discipline, UK Geography, the 2017 Royal Geographical Society with the Institute of British Geographers' (RGS-IBG) Annual Conference is entitled 'Decolonizing Geographical Knowledges', to the consternation of many of the few geographers of colour.[13] Not only is the event taking place at an institution that is still largely dependent on the money of British colonial families and extractive economies, and still proudly displaying its colonial history, it is also led by a white Russell Group academic with almost exclusively white keynotes. Academics who have to put up with ongoing conditions of racism/colonialism again become the objects or problem, not the leaders on this issue. Again, this conflict does not just extend to events and publications on decolonisation, but to all events and publications, since they are part of global knowledge making and therefore entwined with global relations, funding, rankings and imaginaries. As a white editor, even (or especially?) of a methods handbook, I have to ask myself: how can I negotiate such conflicts without aggravating the problem? And, more generally, how can knowledge and 'knowledge production' be shared in a world that is not shared on equal terms?

The challenges of curriculum diversification

For my second example, I draw upon my membership in the Race, Culture and Equality Working Group of the RGS-IBG (RACE). In this group, we research a number of issues relating to race and racial discrimination, one of these being the diversification of the curriculum at British universities. Our work mirrors that of many similar academic groups who seek to illustrate and counteract the continued 'whitewashing' of European knowledge. By 'whitewashing', we mean the strategic non-recognition of contributions to Western knowledge production by non-Euro-American or non-white intellectuals. Not only is it important to study and counteract the racist structures of European knowledge,[14] it is equally crucial to support colleagues and students who are still negatively affected by these structures. In this context, we recently talked to Robbie Shilliam from the Colonial/Postcolonial/Decolonial Working Group of the British International Studies Association (CPD-BISA). As well as uncovering and highlighting Black intellectual histories, Shilliam works with higher education statistics. One example is his much-cited blog post 'Black Academia in Britain'.[15] According to current statistics, as Shilliam argues, white students are gradually becoming a minority on campuses, partly because ethnic minorities are being aggressively recruited as the white middle-class market is saturated. At the same time, the statistics show that white students, on average, are receiving better grades. This is put down to a number of factors, including how knowledge is represented at universities, white socialising structures and 'unconscious bias'.

Because of the aim to recruit more fee-paying students, especially from overseas, universities tend to be uncomfortable about publishing such trends and statistics. Because of the students' new consumer relationship to the university, however, there is an increasing pressure to undertake and circulate such research. Many students are already aware of the factors that lead to their alienation from the university system – and thus to worse evaluations. In the UK, as mentioned in the introduction to this chapter, this has resulted not only in protests over tuition fees and contact time with staff, but also in initiatives such as 'Why is My Curriculum White?' or 'Rhodes Must Fall' (inspired by the South African campaign of the same name). Such movements can be read as an indicator that there is a growing critical mass for a challenge to the current standards of European knowledge production and its embeddedness in ongoing colonial structures.

Depressingly, it is often fellow academics, or other educators and intellectuals, who criticise such campaigns. This became evident during the debates prompted by the complete erasure of women from music and political theory A-level curricula in the UK. Calls for diversification or decolonisation of the curriculum equally have a history of resistance from academics. Hannah Arendt's tirade against 'soul courses' – her adoption of Bayard Rustin's description of African literature or Swahili language courses – comes to mind.[16] In the opinion of their critics, such demands for decolonisation 'disfigure' European intellectual history, a history that has consequently privileged and educated elite white men and rendered alternative knowledge production non-existent. According to this logic, women and anyone who is not of exclusive white upper-/middle-class European descent simply did not have the access to the same educational possibilities and could thus not create any material that was of equal or tolerable standard. For this reason, such works cannot possibly appear at schools or institutions of higher education. Further, it is making the history of European knowledge unnecessarily complicated – many educators feel too overstretched, underqualified and under-resourced to undertake such a decolonial revision of knowledge in their area.

In such cases, an unexpected ally offers itself to the decolonial activist: the internationalisation strategies of university managements. At my own institution at the time of writing,[17] the University of Glasgow, the first sentence of their internationalisation strategy, following De Wits and Knight,[18] reads as follows: '"Internationalization" is considered to be the process of integrating an international or intercultural dimension in to our teaching, research and service functions'.[19] In this strategy document, we also find the main aim, namely '[t]o enhance the student experience at Glasgow by offering a culturally diverse learning environment that prepares students for global employment and citizenship and an experience built upon a wide range of world class support services, from point of enquiry to post graduation'.[20]

Although such aims and intentions can be interpreted in many different ways, they can operate to the benefit of decolonial education activists who, theoretically or practically, can draw upon such documents as soon as they hit an obstacle in their immediate environment. Armed with the power of official policy, they can wield management-speak about economic and career advantages, creating enlightening images about future diverse student bodies and ensuing equality awards: 'our curriculum change will generate your rewards'. Being guilty of selling curriculum diversification and other previously controversial strategies to a variety of university gatekeepers, I am aware of how problematic such manoeuvres are when measured against decolonial critique. Advocates of internationalisation often embed the process in a European intellectual tradition, as exemplified by the aforementioned Knight and De Wit,[21] who trace the justification and benefits of internationalisation back to the European Middle Ages. These histories celebrate not only the creation of an international European/Christian elite through replicated Latin curricula, but also, further down the line, the imposition of European higher education models on the colonies and colonial elites.[22]

Against such a background, it is important to realise that, while various forms of diversification may result in temporary institutional improvements, their location in the very ideology that continues to create inequalities in the first place is likely to lead to cosmetic rather than structural changes. As Robin D.G. Kelley (2016) put it in his article on Black students and scholars in the US university system:

> granting the university so much authority over our reading choices, and emphasising a respect for difference over a critique of power, comes at a cost. Students not only come to see the curriculum as an oppressor that delimits their interrogation of the world, but they also come to see racism largely in personal terms.

This is true for academics (and even administrators) as well. For Kelley, this is additionally reflected in the calls for improved mental health services, mentoring and other remedial actions that are aimed at helping minorities fit with the present system: once again, not the system, but the obstinate individual are at fault. This problem of individualisation has even been recognised by institutions such as the Equality Challenge Unit that, in their recommendations for Athena Swan applications (a UK scheme for supporting the retention of women in academia, particularly science), warn against 'changing the women, not the processes'.[23] There is a constant danger of reproducing existing structures, even through well-intentioned and well-informed activism.

Sharing across boundaries?

Decolonial (and feminist/queer) activists have had to deal with questions of hierarchies within and outside of knowledge production for a long time. In her book *Muddying the Waters*, which focuses on academic North–South relations, geographer Richa Nagar works through these tensions between market demands (and here the question 'which market?' might be interesting to think with) and ethical demands.

Speaking from the position of a feminist scholar from the global South who works at an academic institution in the global North, she is aware of both the scepticism towards (white) feminism on the part of decolonial scholars and the potential of a critique of what bell hooks has called the 'imperialist white supremacist capitalist patriarchy'[24] from a feminist position. Her questions aimed at feminists are also relevant for academics following a queer or decolonial approach:

> First, how can feminists use fieldwork to produce knowledges across multiple divides (of power, geopolitical, and institutional locations, and axes of difference) without re-inscribing the interests of the privileged? Second, how can the production of knowledges be tied explicitly to a politics of social change favouring less privileged communities and places?[25]

Many such experiments that are concerned with alternative approaches to existing hierarchies are met with predictable commentary, such as this piece of advice that Nagar received: 'Why don't you develop this study [of Tanzanian Asians] as a comparative analysis of South Asians in Hong Kong and Tanzania so that you can diffuse the race and class politics while gaining access to an international market for your book?'[26] Such compromises are also often expected when it comes to applications for research project funding, where many academics are self-censoring or using problematic terms to have renewed successes with obtaining money, on the basis of which their own value is currently measured. While one still has a measure of control over one's authorship and funding as an individual researcher, this is getting more complicated in shared knowledge production within international and interdisciplinary projects.

On the one hand, such shared creations represent the ideal of much decolonial (and feminist) research, where collective knowledge production is frequently found preferable to individualised knowledge production.[27] The individual is understood as concealing a variety of influences that have contributed to the singular output: it is a product of the isolating and compartmentalising power of capitalism and Western philosophy (subjectivity) that specifically excludes oppressed populations.[28] Instead, a greater acceptance for joint authors or collectives prevails, including the acknowledgement of other persons and texts as co-constituting the author (the British geographer Ian Cook, for instance, chooses to publish as Ian Cook et al. to emphasise the intersubjective and intertexual constitution of authorship). Shared knowledge production hypothetically enables the formation of such a collective, or of an even more valued agonistic collective.[29]

On the other hand, many international (and local) research projects are driven by agendas or practices that stand in complete opposition to decolonial ideals. The practice of internationalisation and interdisciplinarity involves competition over funding and university status, the predominant allocation of funding (and thus research direction) by Western institutions, a narrow economic conception of 'innovation' and the search for singular 'star academics' to head grants. In addition, academics of colour in the UK and US have complained that they are excluded from networks and more often overlooked in terms of funding.[30] This situation invites a questioning of academic structures, from examining criteria for success – what gets valued as achievements, both in research and in teaching? – to more fundamental challenges such as: For what purpose do universities exist? Why do we do research?

Such questions are crucial, not only because they give us clarity with regard to how we relate to the academy, but also because they show us more immediate alternative paths in terms of how we could work and share with our research collaborators, participants and audiences. Growing efforts by research councils to integrate concerns over power relations in research have led to additional selection criteria. These have included screening by ethics committees, balanced influence on the research process, involvement of female and Black academics, and plans for continuity of research impact. Despite such criteria, many strategically assembled projects only fulfil 'fairness criteria' on paper, due to ongoing colonial knowledge relations: what use are such criteria, if institutional structures around academics in (and emanating from) the global North – based on geopolitical, economic and individual competition – do not allow for a more sensitive or equitable way of working?

Against such doubts about inequality within and beyond academia, many academics and university managers suggest that 'the boundaries between resource countries and target countries of internationalization have started to become blurred'.[31] According to this view, the increased ambiguity through a universal embracing of internationalisation (of the curriculum, of institutional exchange, of increasing reach) will eventually lead to a shrinking of distances and other problems of global inequality, supported by recent moves such as open access publishing.

If this is the case, the question that remains is to what kind of solutions this is leading, given that they are brought about by the dominance of a Western capitalist/cultural imperialist model that is effectively imposed on global partners in order to make them 'more equal'. Under such conditions, is it possible to be an ethical (white) researcher in the global North at all?

One possibility is to continue those experiments that have always been part of anti-colonial and anti-capitalist movements and their critique of hierarchies. This encompasses practical things ranging from writing experiments to the contestation of university policies. The geographer Melissa Wright[32] poses the challenge to researchers 'of generating knowledge that supports the growth of progressive political subjects, before they fall away from fear, or exhaustion, or violence'. Such a demand comes unreasonably at a time where many academics in supposed positions of power complain about fear and exhaustion themselves, due to increasing job insecurity and corporatised research conditions in the neoliberal academy. Triggers manifest in the form of individual publication and financial targets, and increasing demands to put together large transregional and interdisciplinary projects. Under such conditions, shared knowledge production does not become a manifold creative challenge but turns into an individual or joint survival strategy. Ironically, this leads to the question: who rescues whom? The researcher the colleague or client from a less privileged country – or is it the other way round?

Practical implications for research

For many researchers in the global North, especially white researchers, the above analysis may sound too harsh as a bar for criteria in shared knowledge production. Such considerations, it has been argued, would counterproductively paralyse the more sensitive researchers and make way for those who are not fazed by such power inequalities. In many cases, people shy away from attempting decolonial practices, because their complexity and potential for failure can become overwhelming: no matter what one does, there is likely to be criticism. The various researchers who have, however, made attempts to change practices have negotiated these tensions differently. As a first step, one could look towards the many questions that have been raised in this context about the combined importance and impossibility of maintaining purity in activism. Here, phrases such as 'the ends justify the means' are often pitted against Audre Lorde's[33] observation that 'the master's tools will never dismantle the master's house'. The decision as to where one stands in this debate is not an easy one: wherever white researchers, or researchers who use the tools of the global North, turn, they remain the problem, although they feel that they are also its victims. In addition, the demand to take and renegotiate one's position keeps returning.

At the same time, there are benefits. Dialogue with others in the same situation can provide support and new avenues for experimentation regarding the practical implementation of ideas. At the very least, one can make an effort to create aims and criteria with one's collaborators or intellectual exchange partners for how one could intervene to improve local research and teaching conditions. Based on the decolonial work and other institutional critiques that I have come across during my recent research, I would like to draw together the three strategies as prompts for such actions.

Caring across disciplines

I think that a critical first step is to care about wider geographical power relations within collaboration. As academics such as Chanda Prescod-Weinstein[34] complain, academia 'weeds out the carers'. Researchers are supposed just to focus on knowledge production, not its context. This is why caring is perhaps quite a significant demand. Especially in interdisciplinary collaboration, one can quite easily get wrapped up in the immediate encounter: new paradigms, concepts, vocabulary, methods demand a lot of attention. Indeed, in many publications on interdisciplinarity, power relations are solely framed within inequalities between disciplines, for instance, the financial power of the natural sciences versus the lack of resources in the humanities. While such relations, too, are important, interdisciplinarity, as a concept and practice, offers opportunities to think beyond disciplines, to think about common systemic issues. What kinds of problems run across all or more than one discipline? How are different disciplines placed in terms of addressing those problems? How might different discourses that run across disciplines be utilised?

The decolonisation discourse is a good example in terms of how different disciplines and discourses have pursued different strategies. Anthropology has often been the discipline that has been the most associated with decoloniality because it had to endure the closest scrutiny of its association with colonialism. Although there continue to be disagreements on the success of efforts to 'decolonise' the discipline, a lot of provocative theoretical work has come out of Anthropology, especially from indigenous scholars addressing past and present colonial practices.[35]

The natural sciences, on the other hand, are usually the least associated with efforts to 'decolonise', partly because of their own self-perception as a neutral discipline. Although this neutrality has been critiqued by scientists such as Prescod-Weinstein,[36] who points to the dominance of a specific European white male perspective and the perpetuation of an impression that everyone else is new to science, and by a whole discourse of science and technology studies, many scientists argue that they undertake 'decolonisation' simply in a different way: by pushing for things such as open access publishing, open data, open labs and hackspaces, scholarship programmes or researcher exchanges. Projects such as Tekla-Labs and D-Labs, for example, focus on building science communities in the global South that do not have to rely on buying in Western equipment and expertise. The argument is that enabling access to resources, such as the latest articles and technology, will contribute to tackling global knowledge inequalities at least as much as changing the way knowledge is taught or produced at Western universities.

At present, there is some tentative movement and turbulent debate between the natural and social sciences, and the humanities, in terms of strategies. While the open access model, with all its opportunities and problems, has been increasingly adopted across disciplinary divisions – in the UK, all research councils support the model – other disciplinary contributions to creating or maintaining inequality have received less attention, despite numerous conferences and publications on the subject. Bottom-up proposals such as 'Science Must Fall' – a critique of Western knowledge production and its ongoing role in the oppression of other knowledge systems and valuations – have been distorted and met with incomprehension and ridicule.[37] Realising that there are different strategies, but also asymmetries, might help build interdisciplinary conversations without denying the ability of each discipline to participate in addressing inequalities, while being aware that the success of certain strategies might be used to argue that one has already done enough. In such a situation, the question becomes: how can institutions and scholars in the global North do more?

For Prescod-Weinstein, the move to increase diversity in the academy needs to go beyond a simple 'colouring' of the academy under internationalisation programmes, and instead 'needs to become a "reclamation project": an anti-colonial project that seeks to reorient science, and knowledge in general, towards more benevolent goals that benefit all of humanity.'[38] This seems quite a stake. Some critics say that in order to be a totally equitable system, the university has to be redesigned from the ground up, since it participates in the creation of elites and is increasingly inaccessible (e.g. through fees, tests). At the same time, people still operate within the current system, and, for this long-term aim to be achieved, more than just a few of these people first need to know why 'decolonisation' is an aspiration. It seems important to demonstrate how caring across disciplines, and other borders can work, for instance, by showing how methods (other than the obligatory research methods and their ethical approval) and other research practices, and teaching can be made accessible through open discussion, open syllabuses and increased demands for space to allow 'care' in the academy.

(Re)valuing

The notion of care also extends to questioning established hierarchies of value within research. As Helen Verran[39] has pointed out, 'measures and values are now the pervasive instrument choreographing performance of interventions over wealth creation' in the kind of society we are living in. Through her comparison of two consecutively funded programmes for river rehabilitation in Australia, Verran suggests that a shift in governance has occurred through the introduction of market values, which, I would argue, have also been introduced in the university setting where 'knowledge production' implies the creation of a marketable product. While Verran critiques the ensuing shift in the attribution of value, and the anticipated lack of enduring projects, she also wonders about other implications of the new forms of re-evaluation, which now have come to admit that knowledges cannot be neutral.[40]

In the context of research collaborations, there is also a lot of discussion of value. Project aspects such as grant preparation, fieldwork or dissemination are all associated with varying degrees of status. It may be insightful to reflect on what is valued by whom and why. In many cases, the same process or role is valued very differently not only by management and faculty, but also by individual researchers, especially when they come from different disciplines. With regard to publishing hierarchies, for instance, postcolonial science studies scholar Uli Beisel asks:

> Who gets to be first author? The person who did the most work? Who has brought in the most money? Who has brought in the most empirical material? Who has contributed the conceptual framing? With any of these options, power and privilege play out very differently, with very different effects.[41]

Indeed, there are many ugly cases of scholars in less privileged positions being employed to write grants, access communities, conduct the entire fieldwork and/or to write the first article drafts, only to get made redundant before project outputs are prepared for publication. While no amount of awareness raising may be able to prevent such situations, it may still help to have strategies in place to address possibilities of re-evaluation under the current value system.

In their book on interdisciplinary research with social scientists and neuroscientists, Felicity Callard and Des Fitzgerald note how dynamics around status and value can become amplified through interdisciplinarity.[42] When the emphasis is placed on negotiating disciplines, other factors such as race, gender or class can end up becoming sidelined. However, when it comes to the distribution of roles, these factors tend to creep back in, especially in the distribution of low- and high-status work. In response, Callard and Fitzgerald offer a checklist of questions that are aimed at making valuation transparent. Among the topics are administrative or 'housework', conceptualisation versus data collection, public engagement work, publishing outlets (high ranking/low ranking; open access/standard publishing model; online/print; and author hierarchies).[43] Such lists can become a useful component of project design, especially when hierarchies are not as pre-established as in most disciplinary projects. Again, additional administrative clout such as equality charters can be brought into the discussion as a means of holding people accountable. In practice, success depends very much on individuals as well as on structures, but even if such attempts at questioning value are unreliable, they at least constitute one available tool.

At the same time, the re-valuations that may happen need to be translated into the current value system. This is where another tool comes in handy: theory. Power relations around theory have been critiqued from a postcolonial perspective, also relating to research projects[44] where academics from the global North tend to overemphasise and often also guard theory as their territory. At the same time, theory helps us understand the system we are dealing with, but it can also be mobilised to create new kinds of value in a way that the system may have to acknowledge. The concept of intersectionality, for instance, until recently mainly debated and utilised in Black feminist activist spaces, is now formally on the agenda of the UK's Athena Swan, a national initiative to retain women in academic science. While it is frightening when a radical concept is problematically institutionalised (another coloniser 'move to innocence'?), such transitions also offer hope for other sorts of shifts, perhaps also in attention to the geopolitical implications of method.

The most important aspect of re-valuing, however, must be to question existing hierarchies of knowledge and practice. Why are certain tasks attributed more value than others? How does that fit within colonial, patriarchal or capitalist logic? Or, in the words of Audra Simpson, 'where will this get us?'[45] Following Verran, debates around decolonisation of the academy must go beyond simply celebrating that the current value system can be critiqued, while the same problems continue to be reproduced in the supposedly more 'enlightened' mode. We need to question concepts and practices such as 'theory' (what practices constitute theorising?),[46] 'syllabus' (what other knowledge sources are there other than academic texts?), 'teaching' (as a uni-directional practice – who teaches whom in the class room?) 'marking/grading' (isn't this in contradiction to furthering critical thinking?) and Western education as a whole (e.g. see Robbie Shiliam on Western knowledge production/education versus 'deep relating'),[47] because we need to know what we are doing and why, before we impose it on others. While we may not be able to change practices during our career, we can at least embed these queries into our work.

Refusing

The question of 'where does this get us?' also relates, as Audra Simpson illustrates, to refusal. Much academic 'diversity' and ethics talk focuses on sharing, negotiating and other forms of communicative togetherness. But what about instances where no negotiation, no sharing is possible? Or desirable? Refusal is not only relevant to oppressed people, but increasingly as a more widely needed strategy of resistance to quasi-colonial/capitalist knowledge production. At present, many academics in the global North feel themselves to be in a position where their critique of the present system is demonised as a lack of openness or imagination, and, perversely, as an unwelcome adherence to the 'old system'. But does a dismissal of 'old-fashioned' critique have to be equated with acceptance and compromise in the face of a 'new' system that clearly is equally, if not more problematic? Does a researcher not have a duty, for instance, to protect the people they are researching/researching with from being turned into a 'knowledge product'? Can refusal be an appropriate response, and not just for those being researched, but for the researchers themselves?

In her blog post on 'fragility', Sara Ahmed describes such points of no return:

> Relationships can break, we know this. Have you ever been with someone, someone who you are trying to love, trying not to give up on, and they say something that you find unbearable? You can hear glass shatter; that point when you realize what you had is something that cannot be reassembled.[48]

Using a series of other examples, Ahmed continues to illustrate the horror caused by refusal. As a challenge to the prevailing paradigm, she states that 'we can share a refusal'. This statement is provocative, because it not only elevates an apparent lack of ambition as something to aspire to, but also recasts it as a basis for community. Refusal, too, presents something generative – this is something not only compromise can do. Perhaps, despite its apparent violence, refusal can even allow for greater sensitivity and complexity than compromise. 'I refuse to produce certain types of books under the current conditions.' 'I refuse to be the lead author or project leader.' 'I refuse to be satisfied with yoga classes and unconscious bias training as solutions to institutional inequality.' 'I refuse to accept Prevent duty[49] as a new normality.' Perhaps, despite its apparent gesture of closing down possibilities, the shock of refusal has a greater ability to provoke shifts and reconsiderations. Perhaps, as Ahmed makes quite explicit, refusal, despite its gesture of cutting ties, can raise an 'army' – be a call to arms. As Audra Simpson affirms, refusals are not barriers to communication, but 'speak volumes, because they tell us when to stop'. They can constitute a vital indicator of what relations are acceptable.

In the currently lauded space of the 'inter' – internationalisation, interdisciplinarity, interactive learning environments – refusal is a drastic measure. It is often mistaken as a product of arrogance and even, in a move to re-appropriate decolonial goals, as a stubborn persistence in isolating Western subjectivity. But even renowned advocates of cultural hybridity and relation, such as Edouard Glissant, insist that refusal or 'opacity' (in the face of the constant demand for transparency) should be a legitimate action, especially if it is the West setting the condition of non-refusal.[50] We have to ask if 'old impositions' are merely being put into new words.[51] As Ahmed insists, we should not have to aspire to wholeness, to covering up what is broken or missing through 'making up'.[52] Not everything should be negotiable, especially as constant discomfort will stretch beyond the space of a project, both into the lives of the researchers and those they would involve in the project. Perhaps, when one is attacked for refusal, one can take the aforementioned step of strategic re-evaluation: 'I'm not critiquing – I'm refusing! Refusal is opportunity! Refusal is possibility! Refusal is care!' If care-ful refusal can be asserted as method in the academia of the global North, a whole new level of interrelations could come into being, one that recognises that much more is at stake than just another project, article or lecture.

Bibliography

Ahmed, S. (2014) 'Fragility', feministkilljoys, available at: https://feministkilljoys. com/2014/06/14/fragility/

Arendt, H. (1969) *On Violence*. Orlando, FL: A Harvest Book/Harcourt Inc.

Bgoya, W. (2016) 'Academic Publishing in Africa', in *The Academic Book in the South*. London: British Library, available at: www.youtube.com/ watch?v=KibTWqMShvA

Bhopal, K. and Jackson, J. (2013) *The Experiences of Black and Minority Ethnic Academics: Multiple Identities and Career Progression*. Southampton: EPSRC.

Brandenburg, U. and DeWit, H. (2012) 'Higher Education Is Losing Sight of What Internationalization Is All About', *Guardian Higher Education Blog*, available at: www.theguardian.com/higher-education-network/blog/2012/apr/ 02/internationalisation-labeling-learning-outcomes

Callard F. and Fitzgerald D. (2015) *Rethinking Interdisciplinarity across the Social Sciences and Neurosciences*. Houndmills, Basingstoke: Palgrave Macmillan.

Check Hayden, E. (2015) 'Racial Bias Continues to Haunt NIH Grants', *Nature* 527: 286–87, available at: www.nature.com/news/racial-bias-continues-to-haunt-nih-grants-1.18807

Crowe, T. (2016) 'Science Decolonizers "Reprehensible", Says Top UCT Scientist after Watching THIS Video', BizNews, available at: www.biznews.com/mailbox/2016/10/18/science-decolonizers-reprehensible-uct/

Da Silva, D.F. (2007) *Towards a Global Idea of Race*. Minneapolis: University of Minnesota Press.

Degirmen, E. (2016) 'How about Decolonization "Debates" Fall Down, Instead?', MancUnion, available at: http://mancunion.com/2016/10/24/decolonisation-debates-fall-instead/

Equality Challenge Unit (2015) *Academic Flight: How to Encourage Black and Minority Ethnic Academics to Stay in UK Higher Education*. London: Equality Challenge Unit, available at: www.ecu.ac.uk/wp-content/uploads/2015/03/ECU_Academic-flight-from-UK-education_RR.pdf

Esson, J., Noxolo, P., Baxter, R., Daley, P. and Byron, M. (2017) 'The 2017 RGS-IBG Chair's Theme: Decolonizing Geographical Knowledges, or Reproducing Coloniality?', *AREA* 49(3): 384–8.

Gilligan, R.E. (2016) 'Going for Bronze, Silver and Gold – Athena SWAN Departmental Applications', Royal Geographical Society Athena Swan Workshop, London, available at: www.rgs.org/NR/rdonlyres/EA0DD8C4-E9EF-4976-AE16-CEE7D96EE208/0/RuthGilliganECU11March2016RoyalGeographicalSociety.pdf

Glissant, E. (2010) *Poetics of Relation*. Ann Arbor: University of Michigan Press.

hooks, b. (2004) *We Real Cool – Black Men and Masculinity*. New York: Routledge.

Jones, S. (2013) 'The "Star" Academics Are So Often White and Male', *Guardian Higher Education*, available at: www.theguardian.com/education/2013/apr/22/university-jobs-not-being-advertised

Kelley, R.D.G. (2016) 'Black Study, Black Struggle', *Boston Review*, available at: http://bostonreview.net/forum/robin-d-g-kelley-black-study-black-struggle

Knight, J. and De Wit, H. (1995) 'Strategies for Internationalization of Higher Education: Historical and Conceptual Perspectives', in H. De Wit (ed.) *Strategies for Internationalization of Higher Education: A Comparative Study of Australia, Canada, Europe and the United States of America*. Amsterdam: European Association for International Education, pp. 5–33.

Lane, J.E. and Kinser, K. (2017) 'C-BERT Branch Campus Listing', Cross-Border Education Research Team, Albany, NY, available at: http://cbert.org/branchcampuses.php

Lorde, A. (1984) *Sister Outsider: Essays and Speeches*. Berkeley, CA: Crossing Press, pp. 110–14.

Matthews, D. (2015) 'Black and Asian Scholars "Less Likely" to Have Been Submitted to the REF – HEFCE Study Finds Large Differences in Submission Rates by Ethnicity and Gender', *Times Higher Education*, available at: www.timeshighereducation.com/news/black-and-asian-scholars-less-likely-have-been-submitted-ref

McGranahan, C. and Rizwi, U.Z. (2016) *Decolonizing Anthropology* (Intro, part 1 of a 20-part series). Savage Minds, 19 April, available at: https://savageminds.org/2016/04/19/decolonizing-anthropology/

Miller, N.K. (1986) *The Poetics of Gender*. New York: Columbia University Press.

Minh-ha, T.T. (1989) *Woman, Native, Other: Writing Postcoloniality and Feminism*. Bloomington and Indianapolis: Indiana University Press.

Moten, F. and Heaney, S. (2013) *The Undercommons: Fugitive Planning and Black Study.* Minor Compositions.

Mouffe, C. (2013) *Agonistics: Thinking the World Politically.* London: Verso.

Murray, P.R. (2016) 'New Directions', in *The Academic Book in the South.* London: British Library, available at: www.youtube.com/watch?v=KibTWqMShvA

Nagar, R. (2014) *Muddying the Waters: Coauthoring Feminisms across Scholarship and Activism.* Urbana: University of Illinois Press.

Nolan, A. (2010) 'University of Glasgow Internationalization Strategy (Executive Summary)', University of Glasgow, available at: www.gla.ac.uk/media/ media_206903_en.pdf

Prescod-Weinstein, C. (2008) *Getting Physicists to Invest in Caring, Not Killing: Who Takes Responsibility?* Is Greater Than. Available at: http:// warningsignmedia.com/igt/2008/01/getting-physicists-to-invest-in-caring-not-killing-who-takes-responsibility/ [Accessed: 20 July 2017]

Prescod-Weinstein, C. (2015) 'Intersectionality as a Blueprint for Postcolonial Scientific Community Building', *Medium*, available at: https://medium. com/@chanda/intersectionality-as-a-blueprint-for-postcolonial-scientific-community-building-7e795d09225a#.6ijse2h1r

Prescod-Weinstein, C. (2017) 'What Does It Mean to Decolonize Science?', Critical Pedagogies Group Annual Lecture, London, Birkbeck College, available at: www.bbk.ac.uk/learning-and-teaching/supporting-teaching/ critical-pedagogies-group/annual-lecture

Race, Culture & Equality Working Group of the Royal Geographical Society with Institute of British Geographers (RACE) (2016) 'Comments on the Research Excellence Framework (REF). Race in Geography', available at: https:// raceingeographydotorg.files.wordpress.com/2016/03/race_ref_comments_ final.pdf

Sarr, F. (2015) 'Thinking Africa: A New Radical Perspective', Presentation at Africa Research Group, Queen Mary, University of London, 13 March.

Shilliam, R. (2014) 'Black Academia in Britain: The Disorder of Things', available at: http://thedisorderofthings.com/2014/07/28/black-academia-in-britain/

Shilliam, R. (2015) *The Black Pacific: Anti-Colonial Struggles and Oceanic Connections.* London: Bloomsbury.

Simpson, A. (2007) 'On Ethnographic Refusal: Indigeneity, "Voice" and Colonial Citizenship', *Junctures* 9, available at: http://junctures.org/index.php/ junctures/article/view/66/60

Smith, L.T. (2012) *Decolonizing Methodologies.* London: Zed Books.

Tate, S.A. (2014) 'Why Isn't My Professor Black?', Panel contribution, University College London, 10 March, available at: www.dtmh.ucl.ac.uk/videos/isnt-professor-black-shirley-ann-tate/

Todd, Z. (2016) An Indigenous feminist's take on the ontological turn: 'Ontology' is just another word for colonialism. *Journal of Historical Sociology*, 29(1), pp. 4-22.

Tuck, E. and Yang, K.W. (2012) 'Decolonization Is Not a Metaphor', *Decolonization* 1(1): 1-40.

UK Council for International Student Affairs (UKCISA) (2017) 'International Student Statistics: UK Higher Education', available at: https://institutions.ukcisa. org.uk/Info-for-universities-colleges--schools/Policy-research--statistics/

Research--statistics/International-students-in-UK-HE/#Top-Ten-non-EU-sending-countries

Verran, H. (2011) 'The Changing Lives of Measures and Values: From Centre Stage in the Fading "Disciplinary" Society to Pervasive Background Instrument in the Emergent "Control" Society', *Sociological Review* 59(s2): 60–72.

Wright, M. (2013) 'Feminism, Urban Knowledge and the Killing of Politics', in L. Peake and M. Rieker (eds) *Rethinking Feminist Interventions into the Urban*. London: Routledge, pp. 41–52.

Notes

All urls last accessed November 2015 – November 2017.

1. Andrews, K. (2017) 'It's a Dangerous Fiction that One Exam Will Decolonise Oxford's History Degrees', *The Guardian*, 30 May, available at: www.theguardian.com/commentisfree/2017/may/30/oxford-decolonise-british-history-degrees-rhodes-must-fall; Kelley, R.D.G. (2016) 'Black Study, Black Struggle', *Boston Review*, 7 March, available at: http://bostonreview.net/forum/robin-d-g-kelley-black-study-black-struggle; Moten, F. and Heaney, S. (2013) *The Undercommons: Fugitive Planning and Black Study*. Minor Compositions.

2. Bhopal, K. and Jackson, J. (2013) *The Experiences of Black and Minority Ethnic Academics: Multiple Identities and Career Progression*. Southampton: EPSRC; Equality Challenge Unit (2015) *Academic Flight: How to Encourage Black and Minority Ethnic Academics to Stay in UK Higher Education*, available at www.ecu.ac.uk/wp-content/uploads/2015/03/ECU_Academic-flight-from-UK-education_RR.pdf; Race, Culture and Equality Working Group of the Royal Geographical Society with Institute of British Geographers (RACE) (2016) *Comments on the Research Excellence Framework (REF)*. Race in Geography, available at: https://raceingeography dotorg.files.wordpress.com/2016/03/race_ref_comments_final.pdf

3. Bhopal and Jackson 2013 op. cit. p. 9.

4. Bgoya, W. (2016) 'Academic Publishing in Africa', in: *The Academic Book in the South*. London: British Library, available at www.youtube.com/watch?v=KibTWqMShvA

5. UK Council for International Student Affairs (UKCISA) (2017) 'International Student Statistics: UK Higher Education', available at: https://institutions.ukcisa.org.uk/Info-for-universities-colleges--schools/Policy-research--statistics/Research--statistics/International-students-in-UK-HE/#Top-Ten-non-EU-sending-countries

6. Lane, J.E. and Kinser, K. (2017) 'C-BERT Branch Campus Listing', Cross-Border Education Research Team, Albany, NY, available at: http://cbert.org/branchcampuses.php

7. UKCISA 2017, op. cit.

8. Sarr, F. (2015) 'Thinking Africa: A New Radical Perspective', Presentation at the Africa Research Group, Queen Mary, University of London, 13 March 2015.

9. Bgoya 2016 op. cit.
10. Nagar, R. (2014) *Muddying the Waters: Coauthoring Feminisms across Scholarship and Activism*. Urbana, IL: University of Illinois Press, p. 84.
11. Smith, L. T. (2012) *Decolonizing Methodologies*. London: Zed Books.
12. Tuck, E. and Yang, K.W. (2012) 'Decolonization Is Not a Metaphor', *Decolonization* 1(1): 1–40.
13. Esson, J., Noxolo, P., Baxter, R., Daley, P. and Byron, M. (2017) 'The 2017 RGS-IBG Chair's Theme: Decolonizing Geographical Knowledges, or Reproducing Coloniality?', *AREA* 49(3): 384–8.
14. Da Silva, D.F. (2007) *Towards a Global Idea of Race*. Minneapolis: University of Minnesota Press.
15. Shilliam, R. (2014) 'Black Academia in Britain: The Disorder of Things', available at: http://thedisorderofthings.com/2014/07/28/black-academia-in-britain/
16. Arendt, H. (1969) *On Violence*. Orlando, FL: A Harvest Book/Harcourt Inc.
17. Chapter history: the original draft of this chapter was completed in autumn 2015 for an ethnology workshop/publication entitled 'Geteilte Forschung' (Divided/Shared Knowledge – the ambiguity of the German word *'teilen'* seems very apt) at the Goethe University of Frankfurt, Germany. A second draft of this chapter was written for *The International Handbook of Interdisciplinary Methods* (ed. Celia Lury, Rachel Fensham, Sybille Lammes, Angela Last, Mike Michael, Emma Uprichard).
18. Knight, J. and De Wit, H. (1995) 'Strategies for Internationalization of Higher Education: Historical and Conceptual Perspectives', in H. De Wit (ed.) *Strategies for Internationalization of Higher Education: A Comparative Study of Australia, Canada, Europe and the United States of America*. Amsterdam: European Association for International Education, pp. 5–33.
19. Nolan, A. (2010) 'University of Glasgow Internationalization Strategy (Executive Summary)', University of Glasgow, available at: www.gla.ac.uk/media/media_206903_en.pdf
20. Nolan (2010) op. cit.
21. Knight and De Wit op. cit. 1995.
22. Ibid. p. 7.
23. Gilligan, R.E. (2016) 'Going for Bronze, Silver and Gold – Athena SWAN Departmental Applications', Royal Geographical Society Athena Swan Workshop, London, available at: www.rgs.org/NR/rdonlyres/EA0DD8C4-E9EF-4976-AE16-CEE7D96EE208/0/RuthGilliganECU11March2016RoyalGeographicalSociety.pdf
24. hooks, b. (2004) *We Real Cool – Black Men and Masculinity*. New York: Routledge.
25. Nagar 2014 op. cit.
26. Ibid. p. 50.
27. Miller, N.K. (1986) *The Poetics of Gender*. New York: Columbia University Press, p. 105.
28. Minh-ha, T.T. (1989) *Woman, Native, Other: Writing Postcoloniality and Feminism*. Bloomington and Indianapolis: Indiana University Press, p. 6.
29. Mouffe, C. (2013) *Agonistics: Thinking the World Politically*. London: Verso.

30. Check Hayden, E. (2015) 'Racial Bias Continues to Haunt NIH Grants', *Nature* 527: 286–87, available at: www.nature.com/news/racial-bias-continues-to-haunt-nih-grants-1.18807; Jones, S. (2013) 'The "Star" Academics Are So Often White and Male', *Guardian Higher Education*, 22 April, available at: www.theguardian.com/education/2013/apr/22/university-jobs-not-being-advertised; Matthews, D. (2015) 'Black and Asian Scholars "Less Likely" to Have Been Submitted to the REF – HEFCE Study Finds Large Differences in Submission Rates by Ethnicity and Gender', *Times Higher Education*, available at www.timeshighereducation.com/news/black-and-asian-scholars-less-likely-have-been-submitted-ref; Tate, S.A. (2014) 'Why Isn't My Professor Black?', (panel contribution), University College London, 10 March, available at: www.dtmh.ucl.ac.uk/videos/isnt-professor-black-shirley-ann-tate/

31. Brandenburg, U. and DeWit, H. (2012) 'Higher Education Is Losing Sight of What Internationalization Is All About', *Guardian Higher Education Blog*, available at: www.theguardian.com/higher-education-network/blog/2012/apr/02/internationalisation-labeling-learning-outcomes

32. Wright, M. (2013) 'Feminism, Urban Knowledge and the Killing of Politics', in L. Peake and M. Rieker (eds) *Rethinking Feminist Interventions into the Urban*. London: Routledge, pp. 41–52.

33. Lorde, A. (1984) *Sister Outsider: Essays and Speeches*. Berkeley, CA: Crossing Press, pp. 110–14.

34. Prescod-Weinstein, C. (2008) 'Getting Physicists to Invest in Caring, Not Killing: Who Takes Responsibility?', *>Is Greater Than*, 30 January, available at: http://warningsignmedia.com/igt/2008/01/getting-physicists-to-invest-in-caring-not-killing-who-takes-responsibility/

35. For recent examples see McGranahan, C. and Rizwi, U.Z. (2016) *Decolonizing Anthropology* (Intro, part 1 of a 20-part series). Savage Minds, 19 April, available at: https://savageminds.org/2016/04/19/decolonizing-anthropology/; Simpson, A. (2007) 'On Ethnographic Refusal: Indigeneity, "Voice" and Colonial Citizenship', *Junctures* 9, available at: http://junctures.org/index.php/junctures/article/view/66/60; Todd, Z. (2016) 'An Indigenous Feminist's Take on the Ontological Turn: "Ontology" Is Just Another Word for Colonialism', *Journal of Historical Sociology* 29(1): 4–22.

36. Prescod-Weinstein, C. (2015) 'Intersectionality as a Blueprint for Postcolonial Scientific Community Building', *Medium*, available at https://medium.com/@chanda/intersectionality-as-a-blueprint-for-postcolonial-scientific-community-building-7e795d09225a#.6ijse2h1r

37. Crowe, T. (2016) 'Science decolonizers "reprehensible", says top UCT scientist after watching THIS video', BizNews, available at: www.biznews.com/mailbox/2016/10/18/science-decolonizers-reprehensible-uct/; Degirmen, E. (2016) 'How about decolonisation "debates" fall down, instead?', *MancUnion*, available at: http://mancunion.com/2016/10/24/decolonisation-debates-fall-instead/

38. Prescod-Weinstein, C. (2017) 'What Does It Mean to Decolonize Science?', Critical Pedagogies Group Annual Lecture 2017, London, Birkbeck College, available at: www.bbk.ac.uk/learning-and-teaching/supporting-teaching/critical-pedagogies-group/annual-lecture

39. Verran, H. (2011) 'The Changing Lives of Measures and Values: From Centre Stage in the Fading "Disciplinary" Society to Pervasive Background Instrument in the Emergent "Control" Society', *Sociological Review* 59(s2): 60–72 at p. 63.
40. Verran 2011 op. cit.
41. Personal communication, 24 November 2015.
42. Callard F. and Fitzgerald D. (2015) *Rethinking Interdisciplinarity across the Social Sciences and Neurosciences.* Houndmills, Basingstoke: Palgrave Macmillan.
43. Ibid. pp. 110–11.
44. Murray, P.R. (2016) 'New Directions', in *The Academic Book in the South.* London: British Library, available at www.youtube.com/watch?v=Kib TWqMShvA
45. Simpson, A. (2007) 'On Ethnographic Refusal: Indigeneity, "Voice" and Colonial Citizenship', *Junctures* 9, available at: http://junctures.org/index. php/junctures/article/view/66/60
46. The question of what constitutes theory is, for instance, asked by the Global Social Theory project (e.g. Gurminder K. Bhambra), see: http://global socialtheory.org/
47. Shilliam, R. (2015) *The Black Pacific: Anti-Colonial Struggles and Oceanic Connections.* London: Bloomsbury.
48. Ahmed, S. (2014) 'Fragility', feministkilljoys, available at: https://feminist killjoys.com/2014/06/14/fragility/
49. Prevent duty is a UK 'violent extremism' prevention programme, primarily involving the monitoring of Muslim students.
50. Glissant, E. (2010) *Poetics of Relation.* Ann Arbor: University of Michigan Press.
51. Ibid. p. 191.
52. Ahmed 2014 op. cit.

13

Understanding Eurocentrism as a Structural Problem of Undone Science

William Jamal Richardson

One sense in which we can conceptualise the idea of 'decolonising the university' is in the decolonisation of the curricula of instruction that are employed in the classrooms and seminars of said university. As a basic unit of the university itself, the classroom is, I argue, one of the key places that the colonial nature of universities, especially in metropoles and settler-colonies, manifests itself. Works such as *The Death of White Sociology*[1] and *White Logic, White Methods*[2] have highlighted how the 'imperial unconscious' of these curricula shapes how undergraduates, graduate students and academics understand and study the world.[3] This is one of the reasons why curricula have become a popular target of marginalised students and academics seeking to decolonise the university.

The task of decolonising the curriculum, at least in the social sciences, has taken the form of epistemological critiques of who produces knowledge and what knowledge those people produce. Decoloniality, postcolonialism and other bodies of scholarship have all dissected the ways in which the ideas of the Enlightenment have structured how we think about the modern, the human and legitimate knowledge of the social world.[4] Although challenging Eurocentric epistemologies in text is an important component of decolonising knowledge systems, less attention is given to how structural and physical factors of the colonial world help create and maintain the same epistemology that scholars are currently struggling to decolonise. Using the framework of undone science, I argue that the struggle to decolonise university knowledge systems is intimately intertwined with addressing forms of physical and economic colonial violence. These forms of violence, including genocide, interpersonal racism in academia and global structures of academic knowledge transmission, serve to ensure that the configurations of people, resources and space that allow for new decolonial knowledges to emerge never come to exist. Considering these forces, I argue that to effect real decolonisation of our knowledge systems, we have to consider how marginalised communities and decolonial scholars need not only to intervene in epistemic debates but also to intervene politically in the physical spaces in which these debates often take place.

What is undone science?

Most discussions of knowledge production and epistemic cultures focus on describing or analysing questions of how particular pieces of knowledge are produced, used and disseminated among scientific actors and the communities and societies they inhabit. What is not often talked about is all the other possible research projects, proposals, papers and agendas that are not completed or taken up by these same actors. Frickel et al. defined this non-produced knowledge as 'undone science', which can be defined as 'areas of research identified by social movements and other civil society organizations as having potentially broad social benefit that are left unfunded, incomplete, or generally ignored'.[5] I would add to Frickel et al's definition, for the purpose of this chapter, that the 'identifiers' can also be other scholars, or members of other communities who encounter scientific institutions. Undone science is understood to be a systematic occurrence that is embedded within relationships of power and influence within and around academia. For every scientific project or research paper that is supported and funded there is another project or paper that is not being funded or given attention by scholars and those that support them, that is, support and funding is a zero-sum game. The concept of undone science also highlights the importance of agenda setting as an overtly political process that determines what science is done and what science is undone. This framework puts an emphasis on how actors both within and outside academia influence which agendas, among a number of alternatives, are taken up or marginalised.

The concept of undone science allows scholars to speak about marginalisation outside of a narrative of simply higher quality projects winning out over lower quality projects and instead focus on the power relationships that determine what quality is and what scientific pursuits are important or not important. These qualities make the concept of undone science valuable to discussions of Eurocentrism in the social sciences. Eurocentrism in the social sciences is not only about how the focus of academic work tends to be on European societal phenomena, but also about how this focus on European social life leave the social life and thought of other communities and nations understudied, unattended to or, worse, actively suppressed.

Eurocentrism and undone science

Eurocentric critiques have been levied at mainstream sociology and other social sciences primarily by scholars of colour and those coming from the global South.[6] The most prominent perspective in this space is postcolonial sociology, which argues that sociology is a product of the intersection of science and European imperialism. As mentioned above, one example of this critique is Julian Go's descriptions of the 'imperial unconscious' of sociology that underpins the epistemology of mainstream sociology. Raewyn Connell alternatively describes the field as 'metropolitan sociology'.[7] A similar critique of sociology comes from Black sociology. Black sociology, as both a political movement within sociology and a theoretical perspective driven by Black scholars during the Civil Rights/Black Power era developed a conceptualisation of sociology based on its relationship to the American racial system. Black sociological writings argued that American sociology is really a 'White sociology' that constitutes the scientific reflection of American racism. This description of American sociology also understood the field as an institution within itself which held an ideology, stratification structure and culture, as well as an epistemology.[8] Similar descriptions of social science as a white/European space in general come from scholars within the North American indigenous community and other places in the global South.[9]

Postcolonial and Black sociology echo the logic of scholars working in the new political sociology of science (NPSS) perspective that one can't understand the production of knowledge and science independent of its relationship to societal interests and structures of power.[10] What makes these discussions of Eurocentrism interesting is the way in which they extend arguments about 'the relationships embedding scientific knowledge systems within and across economic, legal, political, and civil society institutions' to argue that these scientific perspectives are constructors of whole societies, namely modern Euroamerican society. The history of the social sciences reflects this in the birth of national sociological spaces reflecting the angst and interests of the dominant powers of those societies. European sociology, for instance, was primarily concerned with the birth and growing pains of 'modernity' and how it was different from their previous 'primitive' state. American sociology on the other hand, especially if you include W.E.B. Du Bois as part of the first wave of American scholars, was primarily concerned with inequality and (racial) difference.[11] The national/civilisation-level relationship between Eurocentric scientific enterprise and the societies that produced and are produced by them changes somewhat how we understand a thing such as undone science, as I will go into below.

Undone science as a concept takes on new importance when coupled with these analyses of Eurocentrism. Edward Said argued that Enlightenment thought, which laid the basis for the creation of the social sciences, constructed Europeans as the dialectical opposite of 'Orientals', whereby Europeans produce logic and science while all others produce myths and superstition.[12] This racist conception of European's relationship to the world both justified colonialism and, within academia, determined what people and whose societies were allowed to produce legitimate scientific knowledge. Orientalism and other colonial logics reject whole societies and the possible scientific agendas they may possess as superstition or folk knowledge. This categorical writing off of colonised peoples and their societies as knowledge producers ensures that, at least within Western-defined academic spaces, certain ideas always remain unthought. This move by Western academe to 'unthink' colonised people as knowledge producers is related to what Knorr-Cetina calls 'negative knowledge', which is unknown knowledge that is deemed insignificant and/or dangerous to actors.[13] Constructing colonised people as non-knowledge producers creates a geography of negative knowledge whereby knowledge that comes from or is influenced by that geography is always already inferior to European-derived knowledge.

An example of undone science and negative knowledge is mainstream sociological accounts of the rise of modernity. Gurminder Bhambra argues that European modernity, and its scientific avatar sociology, are grounded in an understanding of European society as separate and unique among all other societies.[14] She defines Eurocentrism as 'the belief, implicit or otherwise, in the world historical significance of events believed to have developed endogenously within the cultural-geographical sphere of Europe'.[15] What's important here is the agenda-setting power of the idea of modernity as a uniquely European phenomenon. Karl Marx, for instance, developed his stages of history from a European perspective that ignored the historical developments of other societies, while arguing that these same stages were universal in nature.[16] When he did address non-European societies and their historical development, as he did Asia, he created a category called the 'Asiatic mode of production' that set Asia apart from 'normal' trajectories of class conflict.[17] The agenda-setting power of the European modernity literature and Marxist historical materialism produced conditions in which research on Third World class conflict seemed both useless and/or a threat to orthodox Marxism, an example of negative knowledge.[18] Examples such as Marxist theory show us epistemically how Eurocentrism established itself within the social sciences over time by systematically privileging one research agenda and perspective over all others.

Although scholarship has broadly done an exemplary job exposing the epistemic trajectories that produce Eurocentrism, NPSS opens the door to tracing the physical and structural forces that also contribute to the production of Eurocentrism. This turn towards a not strictly epistemic understanding of how science is conducted is one of the major contributions of science and technology studies as an interdisciplinary field. What it shares with the above-mentioned literature on Eurocentrism is an understanding of science as a social activity that is not strictly driven by logic and methods, but also by the interactions of scientists with each other and with the public. If we can identify Eurocentrism as a structural problem within sociology and the social sciences in general, there should be individuals, groups and institutions that perpetuate the logic across space and time.

To illustrate my point about Eurocentrism as a structural problem I've chose three phenomena that serve to shape intellectual agendas in the university that ultimately become the curricula that students are taught from. These phenomena include generalised colonial violence, racial discrimination in academia, and structures of global knowledge transmission. These phenomena exist outside the bounds of what we call the epistemic, but I argue have profound impacts on it all the same. An important dimension to consider is how it is often institutions and individuals within the university itself who are creating policies, initiatives and decisions that drive all three of these phenomena.

Generalised colonial violence

Implied in discussions of Eurocentrism is its historical relationship to European colonialism. As argued above, much of the grounding that allowed for Marx's historical materialism and Eurocentric modernity narratives to thrive was the idea that people in the global South had nothing to contribute empirically or intellectually to understanding human social development. This idea of non-European inferiority contributed to justifying colonial invasion and violence. Colonial enterprise, which includes the killing of colonised peoples, destruction of records and texts, and imposition of metropolitan culture ensured that much of the already existing knowledge structures, cultures and intellectual agendas of colonised people were outright destroyed, leaving European epistemologies unchallenged. We can consider the hypothetical for example of what kinds of knowledge systems would have developed in colonised societies/nations had they not been invaded and controlled by European empires. These hypothetical knowledge systems represent the undone science that no longer exists or will exist because the civilisations it hails from have either been pushed onto new 'development' trajectories or, worse, have been eradicated by genocidal violence, something I will be going into next.

The clearest examples of how generalised violence encouraged and ensured the supremacy of Eurocentrism is settler-colonialism in the Western hemisphere. Settler-colonialism can be best defined by its difference from classical colonialism. Where classical or resource colonialism seeks to simply extract resources and/or labour from the dominated nation or people, settler-colonialism is typified by the establishment of a permanent presence that usually involves displacing or eradicating the dominated population. Patrick Wolfe, in his theorisation of settler-colonial logics, coined the idea of the logic of elimination.[19] Wolfe argues that in any settler-colonial society there exists a contradiction whereby the settler seeks to claim sovereignty over the space while dealing with the fact that the original inhabitants of the land still exist, challenging their sovereignty. The logic of elimination is the manifestation of the need to rectify this contradiction by eradicating the indigenous population from the land in various ways. Wolfe states 'elimination is an organizing principle of settler-colonial society rather than a one-off (and superseded) occurrence.'[20] The general idea is that any process that leads to the invisibility or disappearance of indigenous peoples is a positive for the settler regime.

When we consider undone science in the context of settler-colonialism, it is easy to see how indigenous knowledge agendas become marginalised. The direct genocide of the vast majority of the indigenous peoples in North and South America over 500 years destroyed much of the knowledge, scientific or otherwise, held by their communities. Today, one of the manifestations of this genocide is the dying out of indigenous languages worldwide as the survivors of genocide fail to maintain numbers that allow for the transmission of language from one generation to the next.[21] Another means by which indigenous people were prevented from maintaining their knowledge base, scientific or otherwise, was residential schools. In both Canada and the United States residential schools were established that took indigenous children from their families to be taught how to think and act like white Americans/ Canadians.[22] These residential schools, aside from having obscenely high mortality rates that further reduced the indigenous populations also ensured that those who survived wouldn't engage in any of their traditional culture or lifeways. The combined physical and cultural genocide of indigenous peoples means that there were few individuals to carry indigenous intellectual agendas and, among those individuals, cultural genocide via assimilationist policies may have stripped them of the potential to produce indigenous knowledges. Similar arguments can be made of African Americans with regard to the impact of chattel slavery on knowledge transmission from one generation to the next.[23]

Racism within academia

Since the advent of desegregation in the United States many more scholars of colour have entered the academy as students and scholars. With the inclusion of more people of colour the assumption is that the academic and intellectual agendas ought to reflect the increasing diversity of people in the institution. Unfortunately, as I will discuss below, academia embodies the same kinds of prejudices towards people of colour that exist in broader American society. Interpersonal and institutional racism within academia ensures that scholars of colour don't survive within academia, and don't have the social power to set research agendas or directly challenge their more privileged peers. As with generalised colonial violence, the agenda-setting power of racism in academia is contingent on understanding that eliminating people from institutions also eliminates the intellectual agendas and knowledges embodied within those same people. People of colour in academia must contend with white peers who were socialised into similar racial logics and ideologies to those that led to the colonial violence mentioned above. This socialisation encourages behaviour that makes scholars of colour, particularly women of colour, feel unwelcomed, unappreciated and marginalised.

One of the base mechanisms of racial exclusion within academia is via hiring. Lauren Rivera's concept of cultural matching is a concept that embodies much of what happens on the job market and in other kinds of evaluations of scholars of colour. Cultural matching refers to the ideas that evaluators often increase their opinion of interviewees when they share hobbies, institutional memberships or cultural habits.[24] Scholars of colour, especially those who come from low-income communities, often lack the same kinds of networks and relationships that their white and middle-class counterparts may have. The result is that people of colour in any professional setting are less advocated for than their white counterparts and therefore less likely to get hired.

Another mechanism of marginalisation is the culture of silence and politeness within academia. Scholars of colour are often scared of challenging their white counterparts on racist or exclusionary activity because of a norm of collegiality that exists within many academic spaces. As Christine Stanley observed when trying to recruit scholars of colour to discuss biases in journal review processes:

> As a result, there are many faculty members of color who remain fearful about publicly sharing their narratives concerning their academic lives on university campuses. Many declined to participate in this study for several reasons. Some said that their narratives were too painful to share, while others expressed that they could be targeted because they were among a few or the only ones in their departments. Still others in the junior faculty ranks declined because they felt that their untenured status would be at risk. A continued sanction on silence and politeness, with the result that the master narrative norms are not troubled, obscures open and frank dialogue about diversity issues and, in particular, about racism in the editorial-review process.[25]

This silencing of scholars of colour due to fear of marginalisation is a theme that is nearly universal within narratives of marginalisation.[26] As Stanley noted, this silence enables other forms of marginalisation to go unnamed and unchallenged.

Lastly, we can look at graduate training as another place where scholars of colour are marginalised with two major results: their assimilation into mainstream (i.e. Eurocentric) patterns of behaviour and scholarship or being filtered out of academia all together for refusing to assimilate. Relationship with faculty and other students are a primary mechanism by which graduate students are shaped. One scholar, describing their political science education, noted that fellow students would question her with 'How is your work political?'[27] Alternatively, we can see how African women graduate students are denied professional courtesy as advanced graduate students and faculty alike.[28] These two examples are indicative of situations where scholars of colour are forced to alter their behaviour or research agendas to fit into the mainstream culture of their departments or disciplines, or see themselves in a position where they may be pushed out or denied tenure and other accolades.

What we see through this mechanism is how routine racism (and misogyny) within academia can lead to the marginalisation of scholars of colour. What is important to note here is that, as students and scholars are pushed to the margins or pushed out, the knowledge that they have or intend to produce is marginalised along with them. When considering undone science, we can easily see how racism within academia would ensure that one does not have the power or influence to change the trajectory of fields, departments, or committees.

Structures of global knowledge transmission

The last major mechanism that prevents marginalised people from shaping academic agenda and research trajectories is the relationship between scholars of colour, especially those in the global South, and academic institutions and norms in the global North. This mechanism is primarily driven by the inertia of the legacy of Eurocentrism in the social sciences manifesting itself in academia today. Scholars studying these dynamics are primarily concerned with the ways in which former colonial powers influence the research and structure of academic spaces in the global South.

The central framework that discusses this North–South academic relationship is work on what is called academic dependency or, alternatively, intellectual imperialism. Academic dependency is the dependence of academic spaces in the global South on the resources of global northern institutions for academic and financial support, while intellectual imperialism is defined as the colonisation of the intellectual life of a colonised people by European social thought.[29] Scholars in this space saw academic dependency as a kind of neocolonial form of intellectual imperialism. The most fleshed out of these theories is seen in the work of Syed Farid Alatas. In his work on academic dependency he identified mechanisms that impacted the way research in the global South was conducted.[30] He identifies four major ways in which the global South is dependent on the global North academically: (1) dependence on ideas and the media of ideas; (2) dependence on the technology of education; (3) dependence on aid for research as well as teaching; (4) dependence on investment in education.

Dependence on ideas and media of ideas is a reference to both the domination of already existing Eurocentric ideas within the social sciences and the domination of journal publication outlets by global North nations and academics. In sociology, for example, the top two journals, the *American Journal of Sociology* and the *American Sociological Review* are both United States-based journals, one of which is owned by the American Sociological Association. Alatas argues that the dominance of these outlets and the ideas they contain creates a situation where Western scholars have well-established publishers and distributors while the global South largely imports foreign journals from these publishers instead of having their own publishing houses and journals. Due to the realities of publishing in academic journals, the expectations of the type of language used as well as the style of writing and selection of article topics, are shaped in the global South on the model of those in the global North.

The next three forms of dependence are all more explicitly tied to the realities of global economic inequalities. In all three cases we see a situation where the ability to do scientific work and educate those who can engage in scientific work is hinged upon the support of institutions and governments of the global North. Particularly when it comes to education, many parts of the world inherited the education systems set up by their former colonial masters. In addition, many scholars in the global South go to European or American universities to get advanced training, taking that training and the ideas back to their home nations. Because the money and resources for these educational and scientific endeavours come from the global North, academics in the global North are able to determine what does and doesn't get funding, who gets an education and what knowledge looks like on a global scale. Scholars in the global South who reject this agenda-setting process are likely to be cut off from networks of scholarship and funding thus ensuring that their work is marginalised.

We see a number of scholars in the global South take up versions of academic dependency theory to critique the development of scientific institutions within their societies or conceptualise how to develop sociological spaces outside these relationships of dependency. Solvay Gerke and Hans-Dieter Evers, for example, looked at how different Southeast Asian nations conceptualised what constituted 'local knowledge', and how that impacted their institutional development over time.[31] Akinsola Akiwowo in his research explored how indigenisation could make space for new forms of sociological thought in Africa and elsewhere in the global South.[32] Kang Jun, in focusing on Korean political science, showed how the United States occupation influenced the development of their political science scholarship in a way that marginalises indigenous Korean concepts and experiences.[33] These efforts and others highlight how hard it is for intellectual production in the global South to happen outside of the influence of Western academic and political institutions, but it is a problem that scholars in those regions are actively challenging.

Resisting structural Eurocentrism in the university

As argued earlier in this chapter, the three phenomena I identified that structurally perpetuate Eurocentrism have in common the fact that universities themselves, as institutions, help to create and perpetuate these phenomena. The task of decolonising the university curriculum then requires us, as scholars, activists and marginalised people, to struggle both within the university and outside, acknowledging that the line between the campus and the community is a thin one at best. I will end this article with some recommendations for points where these mechanisms of marginalisation can be disrupted and reversed.

The core mechanism by which we can begin to disrupt these processes of structural Eurocentrism is by ensuring that colonised and marginalised people don't die. It's not often that social scientists talk about death outside of it being a research finding or observation, but it indeed stalks our struggle as scholars to challenge Eurocentric institutions. Eurocentric institutions, including the university, were all midwifed into existence by the actual physical deaths of colonised peoples. My academic institution, Northwestern University, was funded into existence with blood money obtained via the genocide of indigenous women and children.[34] The

University of Chicago on the other hand was founded on land gifted by a slaveowner who was famous for regularly working his slaves to death.[35] Decolonisation means prioritising the survival of colonised peoples above other interests. As scholars and activists, our work can influence policy and social movements that promote the survival of colonised people, ensuring they survive, physically and socially, to possibly join the academy or, if we want to be truly radical, perhaps subvert it all together.

Another place where we can begin to disrupt structural Eurocentrism is in academic institutions such as departments, committees, disciplinary organisations and the like. These institutions provide actors with the power to hire, fire, fund, defund, promote and marginalise scholars and research agendas, and serve as the primary levers of power within academia. Scholars interested in decolonisation need to consider the politics of these institutions in the sense that by controlling or making oneself independent of these institutions we can open space for new knowledge agendas to emerge and have the means to protect and nurture them. These moves may include campaigns for electing officers to national academic organisations or simple informal institutions such as group chats or message boards on social media platforms that provide grounds for collective action and coordination. For scholars in the global South and those colonised through settler-colonies, I would add the necessity for developing independent institutions where possible that don't rely on funding or validation from mainstream academic spaces. Although an incredibly hard objective to pull off, this independence will help to re-establish intellectual sovereignty, which then allows colonised communities to interact with European-derived academic spaces as independent and autonomous entities vs marginalised others.

All the above-mentioned ways of subverting structural Eurocentrism require academics to theorise and organise themselves as explicit political actors vs. thinkers whose work may contribute to one or another political movement or debate. The importance of this distinction is connected to Stanley's work, mentioned when discussing racism in academia.[36] Much of the silence Stanley noted is connected to respectability norms that are dominant in Western academe. By respectability norms, otherwise known as professionalism, I mean the ways in which academics are influenced to engage in disagreement and dissension in certain prescribed ways that often allow already dominant and abusive behaviours to continue largely unabated.[37] Engaging in scholar-activist behaviours, especially those that are geared towards decolonial ends, requires us to release ourselves from many of these respectability norms. By doing this we will be able to engage in more substantive action for change within the academy, the university, and in the wider communities the former two impact. Although anti-respectability carries with it the risk of marginalisation, the creation of support systems and institutions among decolonial scholars, students and activists can help protect actors from some forms of marginalisation.

To conclude I would like to reiterate the original conceit of this chapter, which is the idea that to decolonise the university we must target the curriculum which itself is impacted by the long history of Eurocentrism and colonialism. This work is a reminder that what is at stake in struggles to destroy racist monuments, include marginalised people in class syllabuses, or create safe spaces for marginalised peoples is not simply making it easier for marginalised people to get through university. What is really at stake is the protection or undoing of the colonial world itself, within which the university is a core component. Part of these movements is to think beyond the rules, norms and concepts of this existing social order. My hope is that this essay does some of the work of questioning some of the conceptual binds that prevent us from challenging Eurocentrism, university curricula and, ultimately, our modern colonial order itself.

Bibliography

Abdo-Zubi, N. (1996) *Sociological Thought: Beyond Eurocentric Theory*. Ontario: Canadian Scholars' Press.

Akiwowo, A. (1988) 'Universalism and Indigenization in Sociological Theory: Introduction', *International Sociology: Journal of the International Sociological Association* 3(2): 155–60.

Akiwowo, A. (1989) 'Building National Sociological Tradition in an African Subregion', in N. Genov (ed.) *National Traditions in Sociology*. London: Sage, pp. 151–66.

Akiwowo, A. (1999) 'Indigenous Sociologies: Extending the Scope of the Argument', *International Sociology: Journal of the International Sociological Association* 14(2): 115–38.

Alatas, S.F. (2003) 'Academic Dependency and the Global Division of Labour in the Social Sciences', *Current Sociology/La Sociologie contemporaine* 51(6): 599–613.

Alatas, S.H. (2000) 'Intellectual Imperialism: Definition, Traits, and Problems', *Southeast Asian Journal of Social Science* 28(1): 23–45.

Alfred, T. and Corntassel, J. (2005) 'Being Indigenous: Resurgences against Contemporary Colonialism', *Government and Opposition* 40(4): 597–614.

Alkalimat (Gerald McWorter), A.-L.H.I. (1969) 'The Ideology of Black Social Science', *The Black Scholar* 1(2): 28–35.

Beoku-Betts, J.A. (2004) 'African Women Pursuing Graduate Studies in the Sciences: Racism, Gender Bias, and Third World Marginality', *NWSA Journal: A Publication of the National Women's Studies Association* 16(1): 116–35.

Bhambra, G.K. (2007) *Rethinking Modernity: Postcolonialism and the Sociological Imagination*. Basingstoke: Palgrave Macmillan.

Bhambra, G.K. (2011) 'Historical Sociology, Modernity, and Postcolonial Critique', *American Historical Review* 116(3): 653–62.

Bhambra, G.K., Shilliam, R. and Orrells, D. (2014) 'Contesting Imperial Epistemologies: Introduction', *Journal of Historical Sociology* 27(3): 293–301.

Boyer, J.W. (2015) *The University of Chicago: A History*. Chicago: University of Chicago Press.

Brown, R.N. (2007) 'Persephone's Triumph', *Qualitative Inquiry: QI* 13(5): 650–9.

Castellano, M.B., Archibald, L. and DeGagné, M. (2008) 'From Truth to Reconciliation', available at: http://speakingmytruth.ca/downloads/AHFvol1/AHF_TRC_vol1.pdf

Cetina, K.K. (2009) *Epistemic Cultures: How the Sciences Make Knowledge*. Boston, MA: Harvard University Press.

Connell, R. (2007) *Southern Theory: The Global Dynamics of Knowledge in Social Science*. Sydney: Allen and Unwin.

Dei, G.J.S. (2000) 'Rethinking the Role of Indigenous Knowledges in the Academy', *International Journal of Inclusive Education* 4(2): 111–32.

Fogel, J.A. (1988) 'The Debates over the Asiatic Mode of Production in Soviet Russia, China, and Japan', *American Historical Review* 93(1): 56–79.

Frickel, S. et al. (2010) 'Undone Science: Charting Social Movement and Civil Society Challenges to Research Agenda Setting', *Science, Technology & Human Values* 35(4): 444–73.

Gerke, S. and Evers, H.-D. (2006) 'Globalizing Local Knowledge: Social Science Research on Southeast Asia, 1970–2000', *Sojourn: Journal of Social Issues in Southeast Asia* 21(1): 1–21.

Go, J. (2013) 'For a Postcolonial Sociology', *Theory and Society* 42(1): 25–55.

Hunter, M. (2002) 'Rethinking Epistemology, Methodology, and Racism: or, Is White Sociology Really Dead?', *Race and Society* 5(2): 119–38.

In, K.J. (2006) 'Academic Dependency: Western-centrism in Korean Political Science', *Korean Journal* 46(4): 115–35.

John Evans Study Committee (2014) *Report of the John Evans Study Committee*, Northwestern University, available at: www.northwestern.edu/provost/committees/equity-and-inclusion/study-committee-report.pdf.

Keskin, T. (2014) 'Sociology of Africa: A Non-Orientalist Approach to African, Africana, and Black Studies', *Critical Sociology* 40(2): 187–202.

Ladner, J.A. (1973) *The Death of White Sociology: Essays on Race and Culture*. Baltimore, MD: Black Classic Press.

Magubane, Z. (2016) 'American Sociology's Racial Ontology: Remembering Slavery, Deconstructing Modernity, and Charting the Future of Global Historical Sociology', *Cultural Sociology* 10(3): 369–84.

Maia, J.M. (2014) 'History of Sociology and the Quest for Intellectual Autonomy in the Global South: The Cases of Alberto Guerreiro Ramos and Syed Hussein Alatas', *Current Sociology/La Sociologie contemporaine* 62(7): 1097–115.

Manigault-Bryant, J.A. (2014) 'The "Image of Africa" in Africana Sociology', *Critical Sociology* 40(2): 203–15.

Marx, K. and Others (1972) *The Marx Engels Reader*, New York: Norton.

Morris, A. (2015) *The Scholar Denied: W.E.B. Du Bois and the Birth of Modern Sociology*. Oakland: University of California Press.

Muhs, G.G.Y. et al. (2012) *Presumed Incompetent: The Intersections of Race and Class for Women in Academia*. Boulder: University Press of Colorado.

Patterson, O. (1982) *Slavery and Social Death*. Boston, MA: Harvard University Press.

Quijano, A. and Ennis, M. (2000) 'Coloniality of Power, Eurocentrism, and Latin America', *Nepantla: Views from South* 1(3): 533–80.

Rivera, L.A. (2012) 'Hiring as Cultural Matching', *American Sociological Review* 77(6): 999–1022.

Said, E. (1978) *Orientalism*. New York: Vintage.

Scott, F. and Kelly, M. (2006) *The New Political Sociology of Science*. Madison: University of Wisconsin Press.

Sexton, J. (2016) 'The Vel of Slavery: Tracking the Figure of the Unsovereign', *Critical Sociology* 42(4–5): 583–97.

Stanley, C.A. (2007) 'When Counter Narratives Meet Master Narratives in the Journal Editorial-Review Process', *Educational Researcher* 36(1): 14–24.

Ward Randolph, A. and Weems, M.E. (2010) 'Speak Truth and Shame the Devil: An Ethnodrama in Response to Racism in the Academy', *Qualitative Inquiry: QI*, 16(5): 310–13.

Wolfe, P. (2006) 'Settler Colonialism and the Elimination of the Native', *Journal of Genocide Research* 8(4): 387–409.

Wright, E. and Calhoun, T.C. (2006) 'Jim Crow Sociology: Toward an Understanding of the Origin and Principles of Black Sociology via the Atlanta Sociological Laboratory', *Sociological Focus* 39(1): 1–18.

Zuberi, T. and Bonilla-Silva, E. (2008) *White Logic, White Methods: Racism and Methodology*. Plymouth: Rowman and Littlefield.

Notes

All urls last accessed 10 January 2017.

1. Ladner, J.A. (1973) *The Death of White Sociology: Essays on Race and Culture*. Baltimore, MD: Black Classic Press.
2. Zuberi, T. and Bonilla-Silva, E. (2008) *White Logic, White Methods: Racism and Methodology*, Rowman and Littlefield Publishers.
3. Go, J. (2013) 'For a Postcolonial Sociology', *Theory and Society* 42(1): 25–55.
4. Quijano, A. and Ennis, M. (2000) 'Coloniality of Power, Eurocentrism, and Latin America', *Nepantla: Views from South* 1(3): 533–80; Bhambra, G. (2007) *Rethinking Modernity: Postcolonialism and the Sociological Imagination*. Basingstoke: Palgrave Macmillan.

5. Frickel, S. et al. (2010) 'Undone Science: Charting Social Movement and Civil Society Challenges to Research Agenda Setting', *Science, Technology & Human Values* 35(4): 444–73.

6. Maia, J.M. (2014) 'History of Sociology and the Quest for Intellectual Autonomy in the Global South: The Cases of Alberto Guerreiro Ramos and Syed Hussein Alatas', *Current Sociology/La Sociologie contemporaine* 62(7): 1097–115.

7. Connell, R. (2007) *Southern Theory: The Global Dynamics of Knowledge in Social Science.* Sydney: Allen and Unwin.

8. Alkalimat (Gerald McWorter), A.-L.H.I. (1969) 'The Ideology of Black Social Science', *The Black Scholar* 1(2): 28–35; Hunter, M. (2002) 'Rethinking Epistemology, Methodology, and Racism: or, Is White Sociology Really Dead?', *Race and Society* 5(2): 119–38; Ladner 1973 op. cit.; Wright, E. and Calhoun, T.C. (2006) 'Jim Crow Sociology: Toward an Understanding of the Origin and Principles of Black Sociology via the Atlanta Sociological Laboratory', *Sociological Focus* 39(1): 1–18.

9. Akiwowo, A. (1999) 'Indigenous Sociologies: Extending the Scope of the Argument', *International Sociology: Journal of the International Sociological Association* 14(2): 115–38; Keskin, T. (2014) 'Sociology of Africa: A Non-Orientalist Approach to African, Africana, and Black studies', *Critical Sociology* 40(2): 187–202; Manigault-Bryant, J.A. (2014) 'The "Image of Africa" in Africana Sociology', *Critical Sociology* 40(2): 203–15; Dei, G.J.S. (2000) 'Rethinking the Role of Indigenous Knowledges in the Academy', *International Journal of Inclusive Education* 4(2): 111–32.

10. Scott, F. and Kelly, M. (2006) *The New Political Sociology of Science.* Madison, WI: University of Wisconsin Press.

11. Magubane, Z. (2016) 'American Sociology's Racial Ontology: Remembering Slavery, Deconstructing Modernity, and Charting the Future of Global Historical Sociology', *Cultural Sociology* 10(3): 369–84; Morris, A. (2015) *The Scholar Denied: W.E.B. Du Bois and the Birth of Modern Sociology.* Oakland: University of California Press.

12. Said, E. (1979) *Orientalism.* New York: Vintage.

13. Cetina, K.K. (2009) *Epistemic Cultures: How the Sciences Make Knowledge.* Cambridge, MA: Harvard University Press.

14. Bhambra, G.K. (2011) 'Historical Sociology, Modernity, and Postcolonial Critique', *American Historical Review* 116(3): 653–62.

15. Bhambra 2007 op. cit., p. 5.

16. Marx, K. and others (1972) *The Marx–Engels reader.* New York: Norton.

17. Fogel, J.A. (1988) 'The Debates over the Asiatic Mode of Production in Soviet Russia, China, and Japan', *American Historical Review* 93(1): 56–79.

18. Abdo-Zubi, N. (1996) *Sociological Thought: Beyond Eurocentric Theory.* Ontario: Canadian Scholars' Press; Bhambra, G.K., Shilliam, R. and Orrells, D. (2014) 'Contesting Imperial Epistemologies: Introduction', *Journal of Historical Sociology* 27(3): 293–301.

19. Wolfe, P. (2006) 'Settler Colonialism and the Elimination of the Native', *Journal of Genocide Research* 8(4): 387–409.

20. Ibid.

21. Alfred, T. and Corntassel, J. (2005) 'Being Indigenous: Resurgences against Contemporary Colonialism', *Government and Opposition* 40(4): 597–614.
22. Castellano, M.B., Archibald, L. and DeGagné, M. (2008) 'From Truth to Reconciliation', available at: http://speakingmytruth.ca/downloads/AHFvol1/AHF_TRC_vol1.pdf
23. Patterson, O. (1982) *Slavery and Social Death.* Cambridge, MA: Harvard University Press; Sexton, J. (2016) 'The Vel of Slavery: Tracking the Figure of the Unsovereign', *Critical Sociology* 42(4–5): 583–97.
24. Rivera, L.A. (2012) 'Hiring as Cultural Matching', *American Sociological Review* 77(6): 999–1022.
25. Stanley, C.A. (2007) 'When Counter Narratives Meet Master Narratives in the Journal Editorial-Review Process', *Educational Researcher* 36(1): 14–24.
26. Ward Randolph, A. and Weems, M.E. (2010) 'Speak Truth and Shame the Devil: An Ethnodrama in Response to Racism in the Academy', *Qualitative Inquiry: QI*, 16(5): 310–13.
27. Brown, R.N. (2007) Persephone's Triumph. *Qualitative Inquiry: QI*, 13(5): 650–59.
28. Beoku-Betts, J.A. (2004) 'African Women Pursuing Graduate Studies in the Sciences: Racism, Gender Bias, and Third World Marginality', *NWSA Journal: A Publication of the National Women's Studies Association* 16(1): 116–35.
29. Alatas, S.H. (2000) 'Intellectual Imperialism: Definition, Traits, and Problems', *Southeast Asian Journal of Social Science* 28(1): 23–45.
30. Alatas, S.F. (2003) 'Academic Dependency and the Global Division of Labour in the Social Sciences', *Current Sociology/La Sociologie contemporaine* 51(6): 599–613.
31. Gerke, S. and Evers, H.-D. (2006) 'Globalizing Local Knowledge: Social Science Research on Southeast Asia, 1970–2000', *Sojourn: Journal of Social Issues in Southeast Asia* 21(1): 1–21.
32. Akiwowo, A. (1989) 'Building National Sociological Tradition in an African Subregion', in N. Genov (ed.) *National Traditions in Sociology.* London: Sage, pp. 151–66; Akiwowo, A. (1988) 'Universalism and Indigenization in Sociological Theory: Introduction', *International Sociology: Journal of the International Sociological Association* 3(2): 155–60.
33. In, K.J. (2006) 'Academic Dependency: Western-centrism in Korean Political Science', *Korean Journal* 46(4): 115–35.
34. John Evans Study Committee (2014) *Report of the John Evans Study Committee*, Northwestern University, available at: www.northwestern.edu/provost/committees/equity-and-inclusion/study-committee-report.pdf. Last accessed 10/31/2017
35. Boyer, J.W. (2015) *The University of Chicago: A History.* Chicago: University of Chicago Press.
36. Stanley 2007 op. cit.
37. Muhs, G.G. et al. (2012) *Presumed Incompetent: The Intersections of Race and Class for Women in Academia.* Boulder: University Press of Colorado.

Notes on Contributors

Kehinde Andrews is Associate Professor of Sociology at Birmingham City University.

Kolar Aparna is a PhD candidate in the Department of Human Geography, Radboud Universiteit, and is associated with the Nijmegen Centre for Border Research (NCBR). She is author of 'Towards a Border Optics: Everyday Urban Border Mappings and Lived Spaces of the "US/Mexico border" in Tijuana (Tijuana/San Diego Border Regions)' in *Frontières et représentations sociales* and co-author of 'Lost Europe(s)' in the *Journal of Ethnography and Qualitative Research*.

Gurminder K. Bhambra is Professor of Postcolonial and Decolonial Studies in the School of Global Studies at the University of Sussex. She is author of *Rethinking Modernity* (Palgrave, 2007) and *Connected Sociologies* (Bloomsbury, 2014).

Carol Azumah Dennis is Senior Lecturer in Education, Leadership and Management at the Open University. Her latest publication is 'Further Education, Leadership and Ethical Action: Thinking with Hannah Arendt' in *Educational Management Administration & Leadership*.

Jeong Eun Annabel We is a doctoral candidate in the Program of Comparative Literature at Rutgers University (USA). Her work has appeared in *ACTA Koreana* and she is co-editing a special issue in *Bandung: Journal of the Global South* on 'Fanon, the Spirit of Bandung, and Decoloniality'.

Dalia Gebrial is a PhD student at the London School of Economics.

John Holmwood is Professor of Sociology in the School of Sociology and Social Policy at the University of Nottingham.

Rosalba Icaza is Senior Lecturer in Governance and International Political Economy at the International Institute of Social Studies, Erasmus University of Rotterdam. Her latest publication is 'Social Struggles and the Coloniality of Gender' in the *Routledge Handbook on Postcolonial Politics*.

Olivier Thomas Kramsch is Senior Lecturer in the Department of Human Geography, Radboud Universiteit, and is associated with the Nijmegen Centre for Border Research (NCBR). He is co-editor with Barbara Hooper of *Cross-border Governance in the European Union* (Routledge, 2004) and with Henk van Houtum and Wolfgang Zierhofer of *B/ordering Space* (Ashgate, 2005).

Angela Last is Lecturer in Human Geography at the University of Leicester. She writes the blog Mutable Matter.

Pat Lockley is an academic technologist who has spent over 10 years working for universities. He is now self-employed and runs Pgogy WebStuff.

Nelson Maldonado-Torres teaches in the Department of Latino and Caribbean Studies and in the Program in Comparative Literature at Rutgers University, New Brunswick. He is the author of *Against War: Views from the Underside of Modernity* (Duke University Press, 2008) and *La descolonización y el giro des-colonial* [Decolonization and the decolonial turn] (Universidad de la Tierra, 2011).

Kerem Nişancıoğlu is a Lecturer in International Relations at SOAS.

Shauneen Pete is from Little Pine First Nation in Treaty 6 Territory. She was a Professor in the Faculty of Education at the University of Regina and served as the Executive Lead: Indigenization and Interim President at First Nations University of Canada. Since writing the chapter, she and her partner have left Saskatchewan to open a restaurant in a thriving First Nation community.

William Jamal Richardson is a PhD student in Sociology at Northwestern University.

Robbie Shilliam is Professor of International Relations at Queen Mary University of London. He is most recently author of *Race and the Undeserving Poor: From Abolition to Brexit* (Agenda Publishing, 2018).

Rolando Vázquez is Associate Professor of Sociology at University College Roosevelt, affiliated to the Research Institute for Cultural Inquiry (ICON) and the Gender Studies Department of the University of Utrecht. With Walter Mignolo he has coordinated the Middelburg Decolonial Summer School and, in 2016, with Gloria Wekker et al., he wrote the report of the Diversity Commission of the University of Amsterdam.

Rafael Vizcaíno is a doctoral candidate in the Program in Comparative Literature at Rutgers University (USA). His work has been published in *Radical Philosophy Review, CLR James Journal,* and *Political Theology.*

Jasmine Wallace is a doctoral student in the Philosophy Department at Villanova University. Her work has appeared in the *Journal of Skeptical Philosophy* and *Southern Journal of Philosophy.*

Index